WORKBOOK FOR

The Musician's Guide
to Theory and Analysis

WORKBOOK FOR

The Musician's Guide to Theory and Analysis

Jane Piper Clendinning

Elizabeth West Marvin

W. W. NORTON & COMPANY
NEW YORK · LONDON

Manufacturing by Quebecor World, Eusey
Book design by Rubina Yeh
Production manager: JoAnn Simony
Music and page composition: Music by Design, A-R Editions

ISBN 0-393-97653-X (pbk.)

W. W. Norton & Company, Inc., 500 Fifth Avenue, New York, N. Y. 10110
        www.wwnorton.com
W. W. Norton & Company Ltd., Castle House, 75/76 Wells Street, London W1T 3QT

9 0

Contents

Part II   Linking Musical Elements in Time

Part III   The Phrase Model

Preface

The Musician's Guide to Theory and Analysis text and workbook—together with the coordinated anthology, aural skills text, and Web site—comprise perhaps the most comprehensive set of materials available today for learning music theory. This workbook provides you with writing, composition, and analysis exercises to help you master the concepts you need to know as a professional musician. Music theory is not a spectator sport! Like other aspects of music making, you will learn theory concepts best by applying them.

In each chapter of the text and workbook, we ask that you listen carefully to the pieces for analysis (works that we hope you will come to love as much as we do!). Scores for many of these pieces are found in the anthology and set of three CDs, which feature performances primarily by Eastman School of Music artists. When an exercise asks you to analyze a passage from one of these anthology pieces, consult the score in your anthology. We expect that you will use that most valuable of tools for the music analyst—your ears—by listening to the passage in question on the CDs. If the music is not familiar to you, it may help to listen several times, just to get to know the music first, before completing the exercises. Sound files for any musical example in the text or workbook "Analysis" sections not included on the CDs may be found on our Web site, along with flashcards of glossary definitions and "WebFacts" to challenge and interest you. The URL for the Web site is www.wwnorton.com/web/musictheory. Please visit it!

For written exercises, your skills will improve faster if you play through the completed exercises on the piano or other instrument or sing through them to check your writing. Many of the figured bass and writing exercises, when completed, will be finished pieces of music that you or classmates could perform.

Using This Workbook

The workbook is organized to make it as easy as possible for you to learn about music theory and analysis. Each chapter follows the same plan:

- **Basic Elements** provide practice in fundamental concepts with short exercises, such as chord spelling and two- or three-chord connections.

- **Writing Exercises** give you an opportunity to demonstrate your understanding of new concepts through harmonizing melodies, realizing figured basses, and writing short compositions. Most of these writing exercises are based on authentic passages from music literature, rather than author-constructed practice exercises.

- The **Analysis** portion of each chapter begins with brief excerpts, followed by longer examples or complete works. The longer analyses are often drawn from the works in the anthology, giving you the opportunity to revisit the core repertoire again and to hear these works on your CDs. Each analysis exercise asks questions related to important aspects of the passage; some ask you to answer questions in the form of a short analytical essay.

Using the Anthology and CD Set

In order to use *The Musician's Guide to Theory and Analysis* and its companion workbook, you need to buy the coordinated **Anthology** and CD set. The study of the works in the anthology is integral to the book's approach to learning music theory. Some of the works should be familiar to you, and other pieces will be new. While the anthology includes many "gems" of familiar repertoire, we also aim to stretch your ears by including representative works by women and African-American composers, varied performing ensembles and contrasting musical styles, and numerous diverse works written within the last century.

1.57 Wherever you see a headphone icon at the end of a caption, you know that this work is included in the anthology and on the CDs. The icon at left indicates that the piece is found on CD1, track 57. (In the "Analysis" sections, if no headphone icon appears, remember to listen to the passage instead on our Web site!) Most compositions on the CDs extend across several track numbers; this numbering system will help you find the right starting point with ease when we ask you to begin listening in the middle of a piece. Please take the time to listen to these works for musical analysis—it will increase your enjoyment of this text and workbook, make your analysis task easier and music theory more relevant to your performance studies, and broaden your knowledge of music literature.

Jane Piper Clendinning
Elizabeth West Marvin

Credits

PART I

Building a Musical Vocabulary: Basic Elements of Pitch and Rhythm

CHAPTER 1

Pitch and Pitch Class

Basic Elements

I. Using keyboard diagrams

A. On the keyboard diagram below, middle C (C4) is labeled for you. In the blanks, write in *two* possible letter names for each pitch marked by an arrow. Include the correct octave designation for each. Beneath the keyboard, list any octave-related pitches you have identified that belong to the same pitch class (for example, the pitches D3 and D4 belong to the same pitch class: D). The first one has been completed for you.

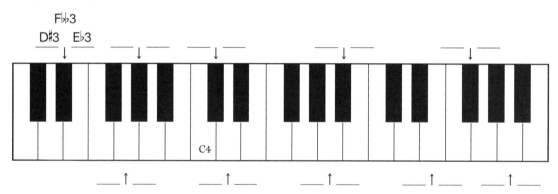

Pitch-class equivalent notes: _____

B. On the keyboard below, mark an X on any two adjacent pitches that match the pitch classes requested. (C4 is marked for you.) You may place your X *above* the black keys. Then beneath the keyboard, identify whether the pitches you marked will sound as a whole step (W) or half step (H). If the pitches do not form a whole or half step, mark (N) for neither. The first one has been completed for you.

(1) A♯–B
(2) B♭–C
(3) G♭–A
(4) D♭–C𝄪
(5) F–E
(6) F♯–A♭♭

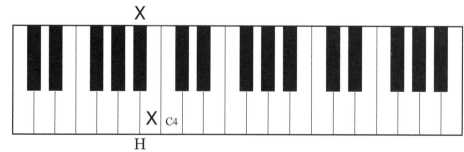

C. Start with the key marked X on each keyboard below, and move your finger along the following path of half and whole steps. Then mark the key where you end with an asterisk (*).

(1) Up W — down H — down W — down W — up H

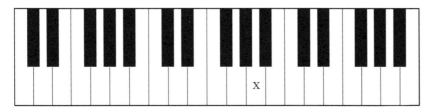

(2) Up W — up W — up W — down H — up W — up H

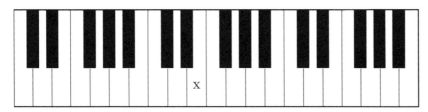

II. Staff notation

A. Write letter names and octave designations for the pitches written in the treble and bass clefs below.

(1) Treble clef:

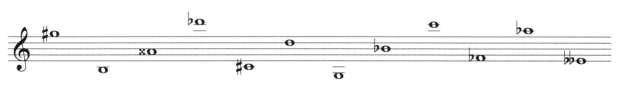

(2) Bass clef:

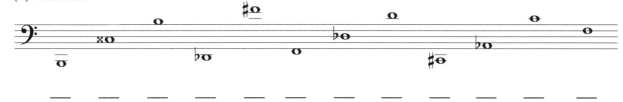

B. Rewrite the pitches below in the clef specified (do not change octaves!)

(1) For each of the five treble-clef pitches on the left, write the alto-clef equivalent on the right. Then label each pitch beneath the staff with the correct letter name and octave designation.

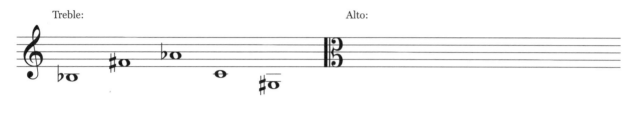

(2) For each of the five bass-clef pitches on the left, write the tenor-clef equivalent (do not change octaves!) on the right. Then label each pitch beneath the staff with the correct letter name and octave designation.

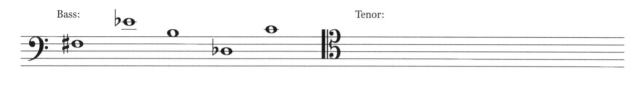

C. Practice writing whole and half steps, as indicated. Watch for changes in clef.

Write whole steps

(1) above the given note;

(2) below the given note.

Write half steps

(3) above the given note;

(4) below the given note.

Writing Exercises

I. Arranging

Arrangers frequently need to rewrite music in a register that is more comfortable for the singer or instrumentalist who will perform the line. Sometimes arrangers must recopy a melody into a new clef, to accommodate an instrument that reads in that particular clef, without changing the melody's sounding octave. Try your hand at arranging in the exercises below.

A. Rewrite these melodies from music literature, placing the pitches one octave higher or lower as specified, by using ledger lines. Do not change to a new clef.

(1) Henry Purcell, "Music for a While," mm. 23–24   **3.5** 🎧
Rewrite one octave higher.

(2) Andrew Lloyd Webber and Tim Rice, "Don't Cry for Me Argentina," mm. 21–24a
Rewrite one octave higher.

B. Transcribe these melodies into the clef specified without changing octaves.

(1) Stephen Foster, "Camptown Races," mm. 1–8
Transcribe the melody into alto clef.

The Camp - town la - dies sing this song, Doo - dah! Doo - dah! The

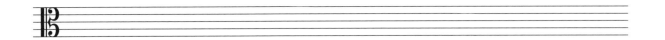

Camp - town race track five miles long Oh! doo - dah day.

(2) Wolfgang Amadeus Mozart, Symphony No. 41 in G minor, fourth movement, mm. 407–411a
Transcribe the melody into treble clef.

(3) Purcell, "Music for a While," mm. 21–22   **3.5** 🎧
Transcribe the bass line for bassoon in tenor clef.

II. Composing melodies

On the staves below, compose two melodies of mostly whole and half steps in any musical style you choose. Begin and end on the same pitch class. You may choose to notate your melodies without rhythm, but be prepared to play them for the class on the instrument of your choice (or to sing). Label all whole and half steps beneath the staff.

A.

B.

Analysis

A. In the musical examples that follow, circle all pitches written with ledger lines, and identify the correct pitch name and octave designation (e.g., C♯5). (When a pitch is repeated in the same measure, you may identify it just once.) Pay attention to clefs!

(1) Anton Webern, String Quartet, Op. 5, third movement, mm. 5–7 (full score)   3.54 🎧

(2) Mozart, Piano Sonata in C Major, K. 545, first movement, mm. 68–73   2.67 🎧

B. The melodies below feature whole and half steps. Circle each whole step, and put a box around each half step. Ignore for now any pair of pitches that does not span a whole or half step. And assume that any accidental applies to all repetitions of a pitch within a measure.

(1) Webern, String Quartet, Op. 5, third movement, mm. 17–19 (violin 1)   **3.54**

(2) Purcell, "Music for a While," mm. 19–21 (vocal line)   **3.5**

their e - ter - - - nal,   e - ter - - - - nal

Beat, Meter, and Rhythm:
Simple Meters

Basic Elements

I. Meter signatures

A. For each of the melodies below, provide the correct meter signature. Next to the signature, write in the meter type (e.g., simple triple). For now, disregard pitch elements and focus only on the rhythm and meter.

(1) Johann Sebastian Bach, *Brandenburg Concerto* No. 4, first movement (flute 1), mm. 1–11

Meter: _____   Meter type: _____

(2) Wolfgang Amadeus Mozart, "Voi, che sapete," from *The Marriage of Figaro*, mm. 9–12   **2.84**

Meter: _____   Meter type: _____

(3) Archangelo Corelli, Preludio, from Trio Sonata in D minor, Op. 4, No. 8, for two violins and continuo, mm. 1–6 (violins)

Meter: _____   Meter type: _____

(4) Stephen Foster, "Jeanie with the Light Brown Hair," mm. 1–2

I   dream   of Jean - ie with the   light   brown_ hair,

Meter: _____   Meter type: _____

B. Using the information given, complete the chart below.

METER TYPE	METER	BEAT UNIT	BEAT DIVISION	FULL BAR DURATION
Simple duple	$\frac{2}{2}$	𝅝	𝅘𝅥 𝅘𝅥	𝅝
Simple duple			𝅘𝅥𝅮𝅘𝅥𝅮	
Simple triple	$\frac{3}{8}$			
Simple triple				𝅘𝅥.
Simple quadruple		𝅗𝅥		𝄶𝅝𝄷
Simple quadruple	$\frac{4}{4}$			

C. Complete the chart below.

METER	METER TYPE	BEAT UNIT	BEAT DIVISION	BEAT SUBDIVISION
$\frac{2}{4}$	simple duple	♩	♫	♬♬
$\frac{3}{16}$				
$\frac{4}{4}$				
$\frac{3}{8}$				
$\frac{2}{2}$				
$\frac{4}{8}$				

II. Divisions and subdivisions with different beat units

The rhythms in each row of the chart below sound the same and are counted the same, but are notated with different beat units (quarter, half, and eighth note). In each blank, write in the rhythm that follows the same counting pattern for that row, using the correct beat unit (quarter, half, or eighth note). The first two rows are completed for you.

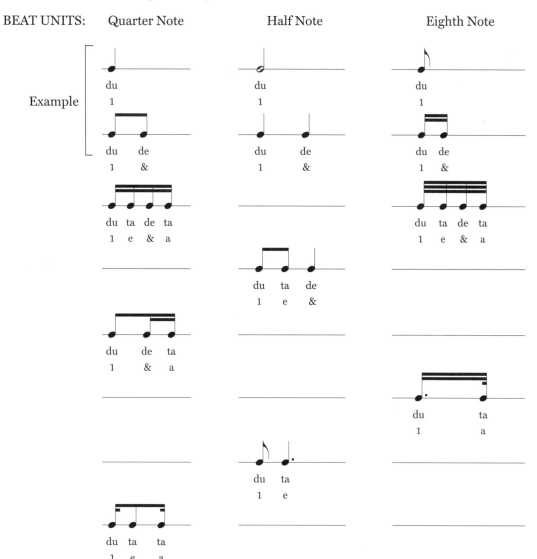

Writing Exercises

I. Incomplete measures (brain teaser)

A. Complete the rhythms below by adding one note value that completes any measure with too few beats (judging from the meter signature). After finishing this exercise, perform each rhythm while conducting the meter. (For now, don't worry about beaming.)

B. Complete the rhythms below by adding rests to complete any measure with too few beats. Then perform each rhythm while conducting the meter.

II. Anacrusis notation

Each of these pieces begins with an anacrusis. What note value (or note value plus rest) could the composer use to fill the last measure of the composition correctly?

A. Franz Joseph Haydn, Scherzo, from Piano Sonata No. 9 in F Major, mm. 1–2   **2.17**

Final note value: _____

B. "Wayfaring Stranger," mm. 1–2

Final note value: _____

C. Fanny Mendelssohn Hensel, "Neue Liebe, neues Leben," mm. 1–3   **2.22**

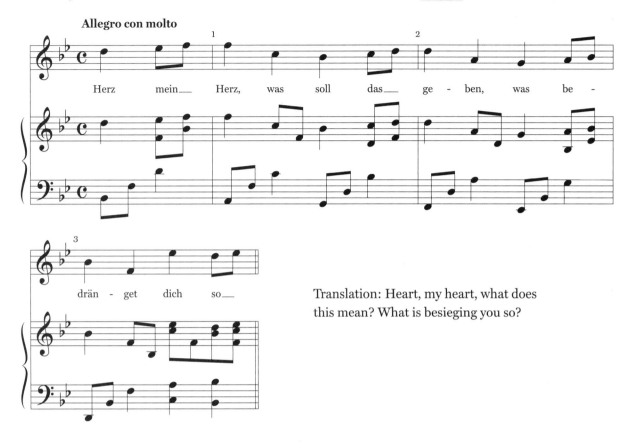

Herz mein— Herz, was soll das— ge - ben, was be -

drän - get dich so—

Translation: Heart, my heart, what does this mean? What is besieging you so?

Final note value: _____

III. Dots and ties

A. Renotate the following rhythms with ties instead of dotted notes.

(1)

Renotated _____

(2)

Renotated _____

(3)

Renotated _____

B. Renotate the following rhythms without ties.

(1)

Renotated ───

(2)

Renotated ───

(3)

Renotated ───

IV. Beaming to reflect the meter

Vocal music, especially in older editions, is often written with beaming that corresponds to syllables of the sung text. Rebeam each of these vocal lines (with beams instead of flags) to reflect the meter and beat unit instead. (We will learn more about beaming in Chapter 10.)

A. Robert Schumann, "Im wunderschönen Monat Mai," from *Dichterliebe*, mm. 5–10a   **3.38**

Im wun – der schö – nen Mo – nat Mai,   als

al – le Knos – pen sprang - en,   da ist in mei - nem Her - zen

Translation: In the lovely month of May, when all the buds were bursting, then within my heart [love broke forth].

B. Foster, "Camptown Races" (chorus, mm. 9–16)

V. Inserting bar lines

Using the meter signature given, add bar lines to the following melodies.

A. Schumann, "Widmung," mm. 18–25

Translation: You were granted to me by heaven. That you love me makes me feel worthy, your glance has transformed me in my own eyes; you raise me [above myself].

B. Mozart, "Quam olim Abrahae" (bass part), from *Requiem,* mm. 44–49

Translation: Which was promised to Abraham and his descendants.

VI. Rhythmic compositions

We will compose rhythmic canons for performance, in four parts, with classmates. Begin by performing the canon given below as an example. One group begins with line 1; as they continue with line 2, a second group begins with line 1 (just like "Row, row, row your boat"). Write a text for each of the four lines of your own composition, including different rhythmic patterns in each phrase for contrast. Use rhythms that emphasize different beats or offbeats, and add contrasting dynamics in each line to make an interesting and musical effect in performance. (You might enjoy listening to some published rhythmic compositions, such as Ernst Toch's *Geographical Fugue.*)

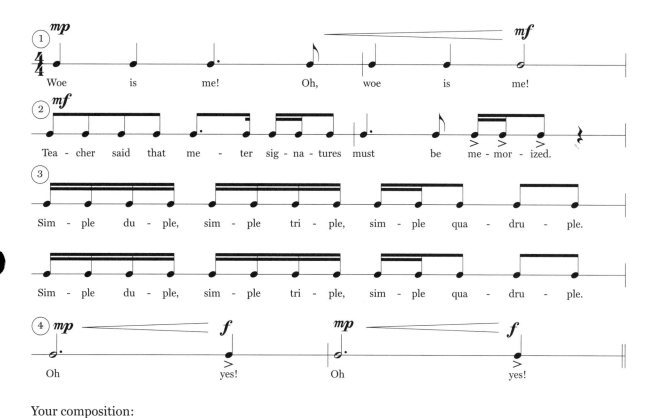

Your composition:

_____

_____

_____

_____

Analysis

A. For each of the melodies below, name the meter type (e.g., simple duple). Then, above the staff, write in the rhythmic syllables (e.g., "1-and, 2-and," "1-te, 2-te," or "du-de, du-de" as your teacher directs) for the primary melody line.

(1) Schumann, "Widmung," mm. 1–5a

Meter type: _____

Translation: You my soul, you my heart, you my joy, O you my pain.

Why might Schumann have chosen $\frac{3}{2}$ instead of $\frac{3}{4}$?

(2) Richard Rodgers and Lorenz Hart, "My Funny Valentine," from *Babes in Arms*, mm. 1–4

Meter type: _____

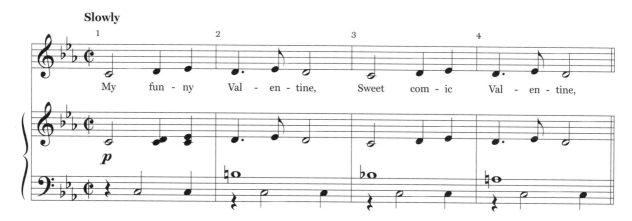

What might the composers' choice of meter imply for performance?

(3) Frédéric Chopin, *Grande Valse brillante*, mm. 1–8a

Meter type: _____

How does meter work to create the mood of this piece? How do accents temporarily disrupt the meter?

Chapter 2 Beat, Meter, and Rhythm: Simple Meters   **21**

B. For each of the works below, circle all syncopations, and explain what rhythmic features create the syncopations.

(1) Scott Joplin, "Solace," mm. 69–72   **2.36** 🎧

What creates the syncopations?

(2) "The Riddle" (traditional American folk tune), mm. 1–2

What creates the syncopations?

(3) Alan Menken and Tim Rice, "A Whole New World," from *Aladdin*, mm. 4–6

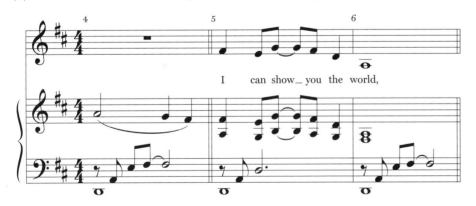

What creates the syncopations?

Pitch Collections, Scales, and Major Keys

Basic Elements

I. Writing scales

A. Chromatic scales: Write a chromatic scale beginning and ending with the given pitches. Use sharps for ascending chromatic scales and flats for descending.

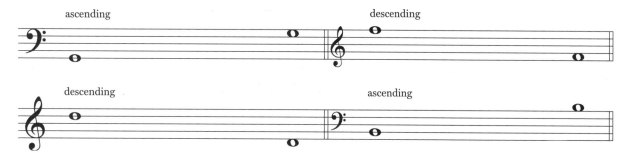

B. Major scales: Beginning on the pitch given, build a major scale by adding flats or sharps where needed, following the pattern of whole and half steps we learned in this chapter: W-W-H-W-W-W-H. (Alternatively, think of two major tetrachords separated by a whole step.) Label the whole and half steps as shown in the example.

Example:

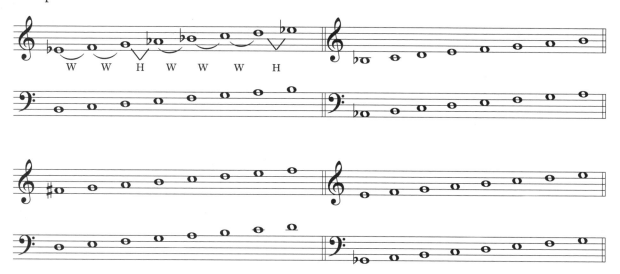

II. Key signatures

A. Warm-up: On a piece of staff paper, practice writing the seven sharps and seven flats in order until you can write the whole sequence in both clefs quickly and easily. As you write each sharp or flat, say the name of the major key that goes with that signature.

B. On the blank staves below, write the correct key signature for each major key indicated. (Be sure that the sharps and flats appear in the correct order and octave.)

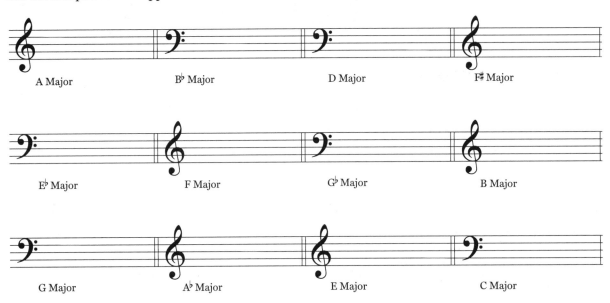

A Major   B♭ Major   D Major   F♯ Major

E♭ Major   F Major   G♭ Major   B Major

G Major   A♭ Major   E Major   C Major

C. Identify the name of the major key associated with each of the key signatures given below.

III. Scale degrees

A. Given the scale degree notated below, write the rest of the scale to which it belongs. Begin by writing whole notes on the lines and spaces above and below the given pitch, then fill in the necessary accidentals (either by the whole- and half-step method or by knowing the key signatures). Do not change the given pitch.

B. For each key listed below, write the pitch-class name of the scale degree requested.

Eb Major: 6̂   _____

B Major: supertonic   _____

F# Major: dominant   _____

E Major: 3̂   _____

B♭ Major: subdominant   _____

D Major: leading tone   _____

F Major: $\hat{4}$ _____

B Major: $\hat{5}$ _____

IV. At your instrument

A. Play (sing) a chromatic scale starting with the lowest pitch of your instrument and ending with the highest pitch you can play.

B. Play (or sing on letter names) a major scale starting on these pitches: E♭, G, B♭, E, F, B.

Writing Exercises

I. Writing melodies from scale degrees

Each of the sequences of scale degrees or solfège syllables below represents a well-known melody. (Solfège is notated with abbreviations: *d* = *do*, *r* = *re*, *m* = *mi*, and so on.) An underlined symbol shows a pitch below the tonic. On the staff, in the key requested, write out the melody (and correct key signature). (For now, rhythm is optional.) If you know the name of the tune, write it in the blank provided (optional). In each sequence, identify one of the following designs, based on the position of the major pentachord and its surrounding pitches: P (pentachord), P+ (a pentachord with an extra pitch above or below, or both), PT (a pentachord beneath a tetrachord), or TP (a tetrachord beneath a pentachord).

A. $\hat{1}$ – $\hat{1}$ – $\hat{2}$ – $\underline{\hat{7}}$ – $\hat{1}$ – $\hat{2}$ – $\hat{3}$ – $\hat{3}$ – $\hat{4}$ – $\hat{3}$ – $\hat{2}$ – $\hat{1}$- $\hat{2}$ – $\hat{1}$ – $\underline{\hat{7}}$ – $\hat{1}$

  d – *d* – *r* – *t̲* – *d* – *r* – *m* – *m* – *f* – *m* – *r* – *d*- *r* – *d* – *t̲* – *d*

A Major
Circle one: P   P+   PT   TP   Name of melody: _____

B. $\hat{3}$ – $\hat{2}$ – $\hat{1}$ – $\hat{3}$ – $\hat{2}$ – $\hat{1}$ – $\hat{5}$ – $\hat{4}$ – $\hat{4}$ – $\hat{3}$ – $\hat{5}$ – $\hat{4}$ – $\hat{4}$ – $\hat{3}$

  m- *r* – *d* – *m* – *r* – *d* – *s* –*f* – *f* – *m* – *s* – *f* – *f* – *m*

E♭ Major
Circle one: P   P+   PT   TP   Name of melody: _____

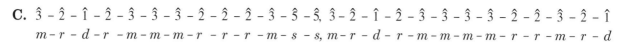

C. $\hat{3}$ – $\hat{2}$ – $\hat{1}$ – $\hat{2}$ – $\hat{3}$ – $\hat{3}$ – $\hat{3}$ – $\hat{2}$ – $\hat{2}$ – $\hat{2}$ – $\hat{3}$ – $\hat{5}$ – $\hat{5}$, $\hat{3}$ – $\hat{2}$ – $\hat{1}$ – $\hat{2}$ – $\hat{3}$ – $\hat{3}$ – $\hat{3}$ – $\hat{3}$ – $\hat{2}$ – $\hat{2}$ – $\hat{3}$ – $\hat{2}$ – $\hat{1}$

m – r – d – r – m – m – m – r – r – r – m – s – s, m – r – d – r – m – m – m – m – r – r – m – r – d

D Major
Circle one: P   P+   PT   TP   Name of melody: _____

D. $\hat{1}$ – $\hat{1}$ – $\hat{2}$ – $\hat{3}$ – $\hat{1}$ – $\hat{3}$ – $\hat{2}$ – $\underline{\hat{5}}$ – $\hat{1}$ – $\hat{1}$ – $\hat{2}$ – $\hat{3}$ – $\hat{1}$ – $\underline{\hat{7}}$, $\hat{1}$ – $\hat{1}$ – $\hat{2}$ – $\hat{3}$ – $\hat{4}$ – $\hat{3}$ – $\hat{2}$ – $\hat{1}$ – $\underline{\hat{7}}$ – $\underline{\hat{5}}$ – $\underline{\hat{6}}$ – $\underline{\hat{7}}$ – $\hat{1}$ – $\hat{1}$

d – d – r – m – d – m – r – <u>s</u> – d – d – r – m – d – <u>t</u>, d – d – r – m– f – m– r – d – <u>t</u> – <u>s</u> – <u>l</u> – <u>t</u> – d – d

B♭ Major
Circle one: P   P+   PT   TP   Name of melody: _____

II. Composing your own melody in a major key

Compose a folk-like melody in a major key, using the melodies given above as examples. Notate your tune on a staff, in solfège, or on scale-degree numbers. (Again, rhythm is optional.) Use scale segments where possible, keeping the melody simple enough that you can sing it. As your teacher directs, either turn the melody in or trade it with another student to sing from your notation.

Analysis

I. Brief analysis

A. Scale-degree analysis of melodies

The vocal melodies below all contain prominent scales or scale segments. First determine the key by examining the key signature. Then write in the scale-degree numbers or solfège above each note of the vocal line. Mark the prominent scale segments with brackets, and circle the appropriate design: P (pentachord), P+ (embellished pentachord), TP (tetrachord beneath pentachord), or PT (pentachord beneath tetrachord). Finally, sing the melodies alone or with your classmates.

(1) Richard Rodgers and Oscar Hammerstein II, "Do, Re, Mi," from *The Sound of Music*, mm. 9–20

Circle one: P   P+   PT   TP

(2) "Come, Follow Me" (anonymous); perform as a round

Circle one: P   P+   PT   TP

(3) Rodgers and Hammerstein, "The Sound of Music," from *The Sound of Music,* mm. 9–16a

Circle one: P   P+   PT   TP

B. Scale and key identification

Each of the following pieces features a prominent scale or scale segment as part of its melody. Consider both the treble and bass melodies. Write the scale on the staff below. Is it chromatic or major? If major, name the key.

(1) Wolfgang Amadeus Mozart, Piano Sonata, K. 333, first movement, mm. 8–10a

Scale type or major key: _____

(2) Scott Joplin, "The Ragtime Dance," mm. 61–64

Scale type or major key: _____

(3) Modest Mussorgsky, "Great Gate of Kiev," from *Pictures at an Exhibition,* mm. 47–50

Scale type or major key: _____

II. Extended analysis

Excerpts from the beginning of two contrasting songs are shown below. First, play each melody at the piano or other instrument. On the staves below the excerpts, write out the collection of pitch classes used (in both voice and piano), arranged in ascending order. You may choose any octave. As you will see, both songs include all or most of the full chromatic collection, yet one clearly sounds "in a key" (B♭ Major), and the other does not. On your own paper, write a paragraph describing musical features that, in your opinion, work to establish a strong sense of key or not.

A. Mel Leven, "Cruella de Ville," from *101 Dalmations*, mm. 1–3

Chromatic collection: _____

B. Anton Webern, "Herr Jesus mein," from *Three Songs*, Op. 23, No. 3, mm. 2b–4

Translation: Lord Jesus mine, every morning you enter [this house].

Chromatic collection: _____

Chapter 3 Pitch Collections, Scales, and Major Keys **31**

CHAPTER 4

Minor Keys and the Diatonic Modes

Basic Elements

I. Writing minor scales: Relative major and minor

A. For each major key requested below, write out the major scale in the left column, using the correct key signature. Circle scale-degree 6̂. Then, in the right column, write out a new scale that begins on the pitch class you circled (you may have to move it down an octave) and that takes the same key signature. Write the name of this relative-minor scale on the line indicated.

Example:

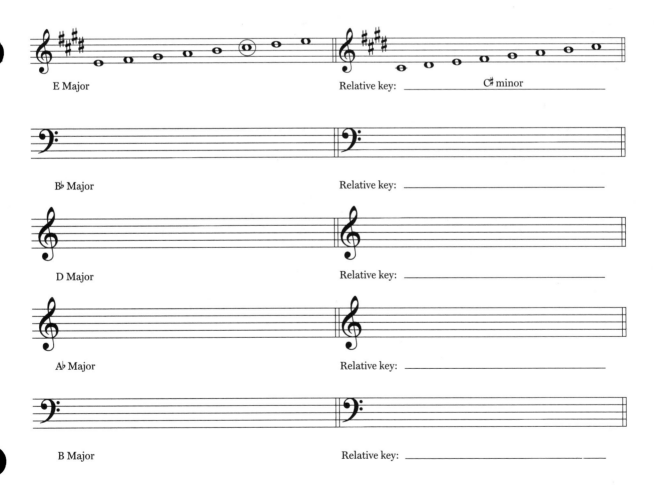

E Major

Relative key: _____ C♯ minor _____

B♭ Major

Relative key: _____

D Major

Relative key: _____

A♭ Major

Relative key: _____

B Major

Relative key: _____

B. Beginning on the pitch given, build a (natural) minor scale by determining the key signature of its relative major. Add flats or sharps in front of the remaining pitches, according to that key signature. (Hint: The relative major's tonic lies three half steps—and three letter names—above the minor-key tonic.) On the right-hand side of the staff, write the key signature of the relative major, and name the key. Then write out that major scale.

Example:

F♯ minor   Relative major: _____A Major_____

G minor   Relative major: _____

B minor   Relative major: _____

C♯ minor   Relative major: _____

E minor   Relative major: _____

F minor   Relative major: _____

C. For each of the key signatures given below, identify its major key in the top row of blanks and its relative-minor key in the bottom row of blanks, as shown in the example.

Example:

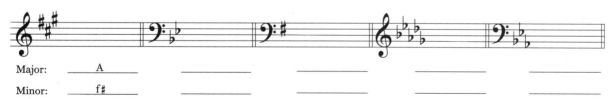

Major: _____A_____   _____   _____   _____   _____

Minor: _____f♯_____   _____   _____   _____   _____

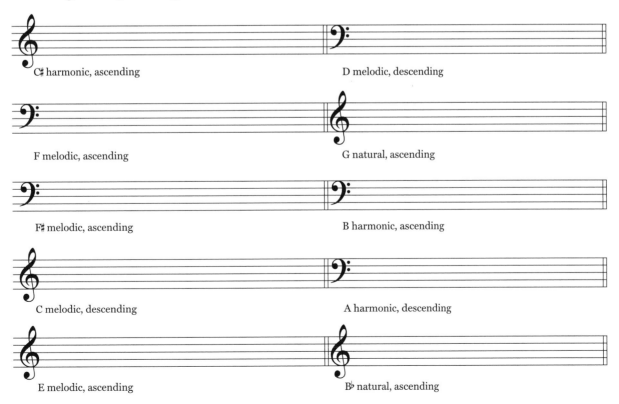

Major: _____ _____ _____ _____ _____

Minor: _____ _____ _____ _____ _____

D. Fill in the blanks with the missing information.

The relative minor of E♭ Major is . . .   _____

The parallel major of E minor has how many sharps?   _____

The relative major of F minor has how many flats?   _____

The relative minor of D Major is . . .   _____

The relative major of D minor is . . .   _____

The parallel major of F♯ minor has how many sharps?   _____

The relative minor of B Major is . . .   _____

II. Forms of the minor scale

On the blank staves below, write the correct key signature for each minor key indicated. (Place the sharps and flats in the correct order and octave!) Then write out the scale requested, ascending or descending, altering scale-degrees $\hat{6}$ and $\hat{7}$ as needed.

C♯ harmonic, ascending   D melodic, descending

F melodic, ascending   G natural, ascending

F♯ melodic, ascending   B harmonic, ascending

C melodic, descending   A harmonic, descending

E melodic, ascending   B♭ natural, ascending

III. Writing the diatonic modes

A. As scales

Beginning on the pitch given, write the mode requested by placing flats or sharps in front of the remaining pitches. (Hint: Does the mode more closely resemble major or natural minor in sound? Write accidentals according to the major- or minor-key signature, then alter selected scale degrees as described in the chapter.)

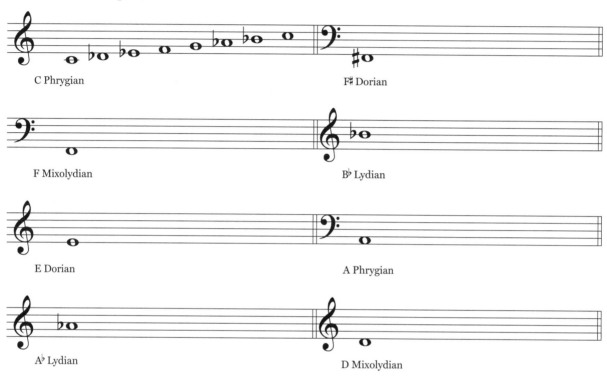

B. With key signatures

Write the correct key signature for the mode requested. (Hint: Think of the modes as rotations of the major scale. For example, since Phrygian begins on scale-degree $\hat{3}$, B Phrygian would have the same key signature as G Major, a major third below.)

IV. Scale degrees in minor

A. Given the scale degree notated and labeled below, write the rest of the minor scale to which the pitch belongs. Use natural minor, unless the raised submediant or leading tone is requested. Begin by writing whole notes on the lines and spaces above and below the given pitch, then fill in the necessary accidentals. Do not change the given pitch.

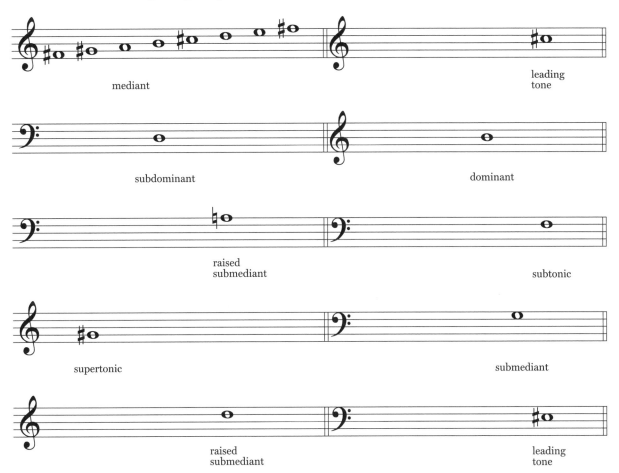

B. For each key listed below, write the pitch-class name of the scale degree requested.

B minor: supertonic   _____

E minor: $\hat{3}$ _____

F minor: subdominant   _____

C minor: $\hat{6}$ _____

D minor: subtonic   _____

E♭ minor: $\hat{4}$ _____

C♯ minor: leading tone   _____

E minor: raised submediant   _____

V. Playing and singing minor scales

A. Play (or sing on letter names) natural minor scales for each of the tonics listed in the previous exercise.

B. Sing each of the forms of the minor scale, ascending and descending, using numbers or inflected solfège, as shown below. Practice singing in many keys.

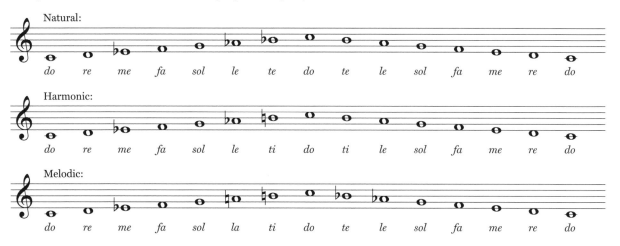

Writing Exercises

I. Writing melodies from scale degrees

Each of the sequences of solfège syllables below represents a minor-key melody. If you are not used to reading solfège, refer to the previous exercise. An underlined syllable indicates a pitch below the tonic. On the staff, in the key requested, write out the melody (rhythm is optional). If you know the name of the tune, write it in the blank provided (optional). In each sequence, identify one of the following: P, P+, PT, or TP.

A. 1̂ – 1̂ – 5̂ – 5̂ – 4̂ – 3̂ – 2̂ – 1̂ – 7̲̂ – 1̂ – 2̂ – 3̂ – 4̂ – 5̂
    do – do – sol – sol – fa – me – re – do – te – do – re – me – fa – sol

D minor
Circle one: P   P+   PT   TP   Name of melody: _____

B. $\hat{1}$ – $\underline{\hat{5}}$ – $\hat{1}$ – $\hat{1}$ – $\hat{1}$ – $\hat{2}$ – $\hat{3}$ – $\hat{2}$ – $\hat{3}$ – $\hat{1}$ – $\underline{\hat{7}}$ – $\underline{\hat{5}}$ – $\underline{\hat{7}}$

  do – <u>sol</u> – do – do – do – re – me – re – me – do – <u>te</u> – <u>sol</u> – <u>te</u>,

  $\hat{1}$ – $\underline{\hat{5}}$ – $\hat{1}$ – $\hat{1}$ – $\hat{1}$ – $\hat{2}$ – $\hat{3}$ – $\hat{2}$ – $\hat{3}$ – $\hat{4}$ – $\hat{5}$ – $\hat{3}$ – $\hat{5}$

  do – <u>sol</u> – do – do – do – re – me – re – me – fa – sol – me – sol

$\colon$ ──────────────────────────────

$\colon$ ──────────────────────────────

C♯ minor

Circle one: P P+ PT TP   Name of melody: _____

C. $\underline{\hat{5}}$ – $\hat{3}$ – $\hat{3}$ – $\hat{2}$ – $\hat{2}$ – $\hat{3}$ – $\hat{3}$ – $\hat{1}$ – $\underline{\hat{5}}$ – $\underline{\hat{5}}$ – $\underline{\hat{7}}$ – $\underline{\hat{7}}$ – $\hat{1}$

  <u>sol</u> – me – me – re – re – me – me – do – <u>sol</u> – <u>sol</u> – <u>ti</u> – <u>ti</u> – do

F minor

Circle one: P P+ PT TP   Name of melody: _____

II. Composing your own melodies in minor keys

Compose a folk-like melody in a minor key, taking the melodies given above as examples. Notate your tune on a staff, in solfège, or on scale-degree numbers. Be sure to indicate the raised or lowered status of scale-degrees $\hat{6}$ and $\hat{7}$ in your notation. (Again, rhythm is optional.) Use scale segments where possible, keeping the melody simple enough that you can sing it. As your teacher directs, either turn the melody in or trade it with another student to sing from your notation.

Analysis

I. Brief analysis

A. Major, minor, or modal?

Play or sing each of the traditional folk-song melodies below. Then, on the blank provided, indicate the major key, minor key, or mode that is used in the melody. Provide both the scale type and letter name of the first scale degree (for example, G Dorian).

(1) "Swallowtail Jig"

Name of key or mode: _____

(2) "Kesh Jig"

Name of key or mode: _____

(3) "Scarborough Fair"

Name of key or mode: _____

B. Scale and key identification

Each of the following pieces features a prominent scale or scale segment as part of its melody. Name the key. If it's minor, be sure to name the form of minor scale used in the passage.

(1) George Frideric Handel, Chaconne, from *Trois Leçons*, Variation 6, mm. 53–56   **2.2** 🎧

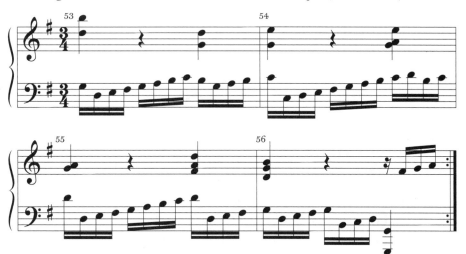

Key and scale type: _____

(2) Johann Sebastian Bach, Invention No. 4, mm. 1–5   **1.14** 🎧

Key and scale type: _____

(3) Franz Schubert, "Erlkönig," mm. 1–4 (piano introduction)   **3.25** 🎧

Key and scale type: _____

(4) Bach, Invention No. 3, mm. 1–4

Key and scale type: _____

II. Extended analysis

In musical compositions, it is often not possible to determine a single minor-key scale type (natural, harmonic, or melodic) for an entire work or movement. You may find more than one scale type within the course of a few measures. The two excerpts below, from the Bach Inventions, are cases in point. Determine the key of each, and discuss ways in which the excerpts shift between minor-scale types. Are there passages that work against our expectations (for example, the ascending form of melodic minor in a descending passage)? On your own paper, write a paragraph that describes your analysis, citing specific measures.

A. Bach, Invention No. 2, mm. 1–5a

B. Bach, Invention No. 7, mm. 1–3a

Beat, Meter, and Rhythm:
Compound Meters

CHAPTER 5

Basic Elements

I. Meter signatures

A. For each of the melodies below, provide the correct meter signature. Then write in the meter type (e.g., compound triple). For now, disregard pitch elements and focus only on the rhythm and meter.

(1) Wolfgang Amadeus Mozart, "Sull' aria," from *The Marriage of Figaro*, mm. 1–6

Translation: On the breeze, what a gentle zephyr [will whisper].

Meter: _____   Meter type: _____

(2) Robert Schumann, "Die Lotusblume," mm. 1–3

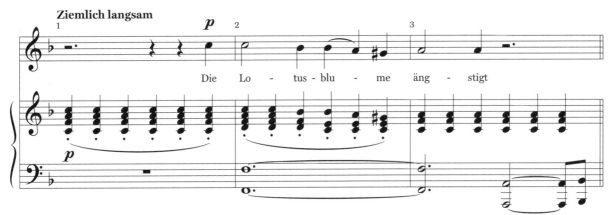

Die Lo - tus - blu - me äng - stigt

Translation: The lotus flower is anxious.

Meter: _____   Meter type: _____

(3) Johann Sebastian Bach, Prelude in A minor, from *The Well-Tempered Clavier*, Book I, mm. 1–2

Meter: _____   Meter type: _____

(4) Bach, Loure, from Violin Partita No. 3 in E Major, mm. 5–8

Meter: _____   Meter type: _____

B. From the information given, complete the chart below.

METER TYPE	METER	BEAT UNIT	BEAT DIVISION	FULL-BAR DURATION
Compound duple	$\frac{6}{4}$	𝅗𝅥.	♩ ♩ ♩	𝅝.
Compound duple			♪♪♪	
Compound triple				𝅗𝅥. 𝅗𝅥.
Compound triple	$\frac{9}{4}$			𝅝. 𝅗𝅥.
Compound quadruple		♩.		
Compound quadruple	$\frac{12}{16}$			

C. Complete the chart below.

METER	METER TYPE	BEAT UNIT	BEAT DIVISION	BEAT SUBDIVISION	BORROWED DIVISION (DUPLETS)
$\frac{9}{8}$	Compound triple	♩.	♪♪♪	𝅘𝅥𝅯𝅘𝅥𝅯𝅘𝅥𝅯𝅘𝅥𝅯𝅘𝅥𝅯𝅘𝅥𝅯	♪♪
$\frac{6}{4}$					
$\frac{12}{16}$					
$\frac{6}{8}$					
$\frac{9}{4}$					

II. Divisions and subdivisions with different beat units

In the blanks below, write in rhythms that follow the same counting pattern as those in the same row. The first two rows are completed for you.

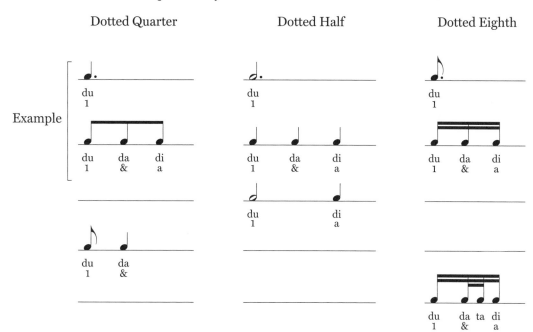

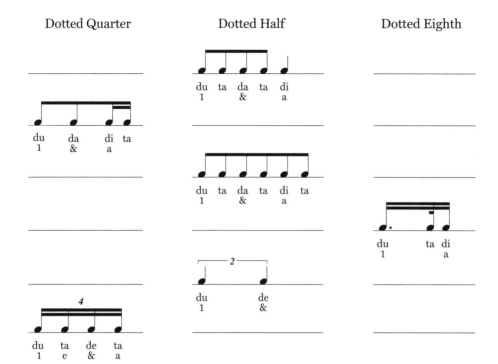

Dotted Quarter	Dotted Half	Dotted Eighth

Writing exercise notation follows:

Writing Exercises

I. Incomplete measures

A. Complete the rhythms below (in compound or simple meters) by adding one note value that completes any measure with too few beats (judging from the meter signature). In some instances, vocal notation (flags instead of beams) has been given. After completing the exercise, perform each rhythm while conducting the meter.

B. For any measure with too few beats, add a combination of one rest and one note value to complete the measure.

II. Anacrusis notation

Each of the pieces below begins with an anacrusis. Write a rhythm that the composer might have used to fill the last measure of the composition correctly (pick notes and/or rests that sum to the correct number of beats).

A. Schumann, "Wilder Reiter," mm. 1–5

Possible final measure rhythm: _____

B. Bach, Loure, from Violin Partita No. 3 in E Major, mm. 1–4

Possible final measure rhythm: _____

C. "Down in the Valley," mm. 1–2

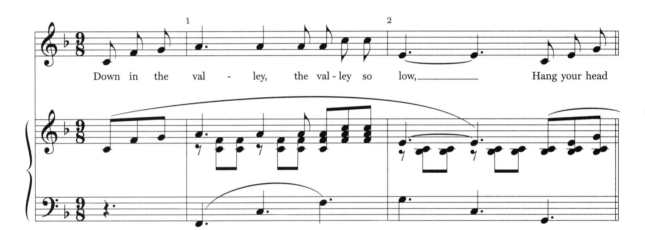

Down in the val - ley, the val - ley so low,_____ Hang your head

Possible final measure rhythm: _____

III. Beaming to reflect the meter

Vocal music, especially in older editions, is often written with beaming that corresponds to syllables of the sung text. Rebeam each of these vocal lines (with beams instead of flags) to reflect the meter and beat unit instead. We will learn more about beaming in Chapter 10.

A. Schumann, "Ich hab' im Traum geweinet," from *Dichterliebe*, mm. 10–17

Translation: [Tears] flowed down my cheeks. I wept in my dream; I dreamed you had abandoned me.

B. Mozart, "Lacrimosa," from *Requiem*, mm. 9–12 (soprano part)

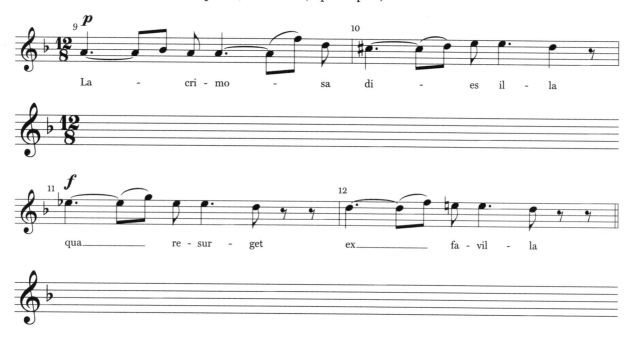

Translation: That day of tears and mourning, when all shall arise from the ashes.

IV. Inserting bar lines: Simple and compound meters

In the melodies below, note the meter signature, then add bar lines. Since the melody in exercise C begins with an anacrusis, the first bar line is given, and the last bar is shortened to account for the upbeat. This melody also features triplets.

A. Bach, Fugue in F♯ minor, from *The Well-Tempered Clavier*, Book I, mm. 1–4

B. Béla Bartók, String Quartet No. 2, first movement, mm. 25–29 (cello)

C. Ralph Vaughan Williams, Agnus Dei, from Mass in G minor, mm. 1–5

A - gnus De - i   qui tol - lis pec - ca - ta mun - di, mi - se - re - re no - bis____

Translation: Lamb of God, who takes away the sins of the world, have mercy upon us.

V. Rhythmic compositions

We will compose compound-meter rhythmic canons for performance, in three parts, with classmates. Begin by performing the canon below as an example. Divide into three groups. One group begins with line 1; as they continue with line 2, the second group begins with line 1 (just like "Row, row, row your boat"), and so on. Write a text for each of the lines of your composition, including different rhythmic patterns in each phrase for contrast. Use rhythms that emphasize different beats or offbeats, and add contrasting dynamics in each line to create an interesting and musical effect in performance.

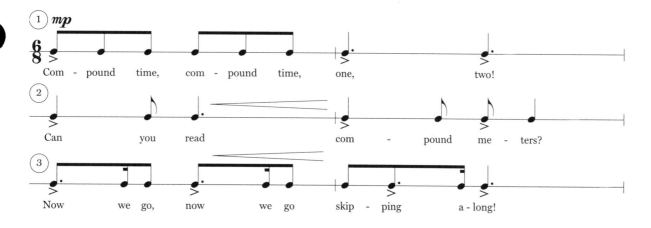

Your composition:

_____

_____

_____

Analysis

For each of the excerpts below, name the meter type (e.g., compound duple). Then, the above the staff, write in the rhythmic syllables (e.g., "1-and-a, 2-and-a" or "du-da-di, du-da-di") for the primary melodic line and any portion of the piece that's bracketed. Finally, answer the questions beneath the excerpt.

A. George Frideric Handel, "Rejoice greatly," from *Messiah* (alternate version), mm. 9–14

Meter type: _____

re - joice_____ great - ly, O daugh - ter of Zi - on,

Compare this setting with the simple-meter version in your anthology (p. 107). How does Handel's compound-meter version compare in mood? Do you think it is simpler or more difficult to sing? Why?

B. Franz Schubert, "Erlkönig," mm. 1–3 and 15–19   **3.25**

Meter type: _____

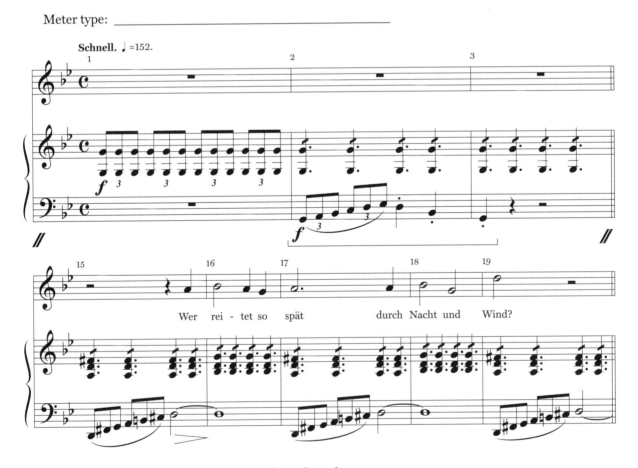

Wer rei - tet so spät   durch Nacht und Wind?

Translation: Who's riding so late through night and wind?

With so many triplets, Schubert might have chosen to write the piano accompaniment in what compound meter? _____ On the staff provided, write out the vocal line for measures 15–19 in that compound meter.

C. Andrew Lloyd Webber and Tim Rice, "Don't Cry for Me Argentina," mm. 1–8

Meter type: _____

Although the meter is notated as $\frac{4}{4}$, the triplet in measure 8 is easier to perform if you think of the meter as $\frac{2}{2}$. Why? What other notational features suggest a duple-meter interpretation?

Pitch Intervals

CHAPTER 6

Basic Elements

I. Writing generic intervals (melodic)

In the exercises below, we concentrate on melodic intervals. Write a whole note on the correct line or space to make each generic interval as specified. Do not add sharps or flats.

A. Write the specified generic melodic interval *above* the given note.

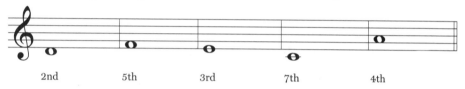

| 2nd | 5th | 3rd | 7th | 4th |

B. Write the specified generic melodic interval *below* the given note.

| 7th | 5th | 3rd | 2nd | 4th |

II. Writing major and perfect pitch intervals

To write an interval *above* the given pitch, first write out the generic interval as you did in Exercise I. Now imagine the major-key signature associated with the bottom pitch. Use that key signature to add a flat or a sharp, if necessary, to the upper pitch to make the correct interval quality. When writing intervals *below* the given note, first write the generic interval. Does the upper note fit in the major-key signature of the lower note? If not, you need to add an accidental to the bottom note (which will change the key signature you are using to spell the interval). Do not change the given pitch.

A. Melodic intervals

(1) Write the specified melodic interval *above* the given note.

| M6 | P5 | M3 | M7 | P4 |

(2) Write the specified melodic interval *below* the given note.

B. Harmonic intervals

(1) Write the specified harmonic interval *above* the given note.

(2) Write the specified harmonic interval *below* the given note.

III. *Writing major, minor, and perfect pitch intervals (harmonic)*

In the exercises below, we concentrate on harmonic intervals. First write out major or perfect intervals as you did in Exercise II. When a minor interval is requested, add an accidental to the major interval you have just spelled, in order to make it smaller in size. As before, do not change the given pitch.

A. Write the specified harmonic interval *above* the given note.

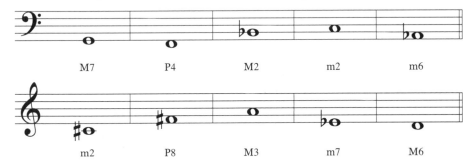

B. Write the specified harmonic interval *below* the given note.

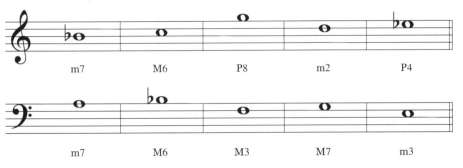

IV. Writing diminished and augmented pitch intervals (melodic)

In the exercises below, we concentrate again on melodic intervals. First write out major, minor, or perfect intervals as you did in Exercise III. When an augmented interval is requested, start with a perfect or major interval, then add an accidental to make it a half step larger. When a diminished interval is requested, start with a perfect or minor interval, then add an accidental to make it a half step smaller. As always, do not change the given pitch.

A. Write the specified melodic interval *above* the given note.

B. Write the specified melodic interval *below* the given note.

V. Enharmonically equivalent intervals

For each interval given below, write three intervals beside it that sound the same but are spelled differently. Name each interval you write.

Example:

VI. Interval inversion

A. In the space provided, invert each given interval by repeating the second note, followed by the first note transposed up an octave (as shown in the example). Then identify both intervals.

Example:

P5   P4   ___   ___   ___   ___

___   ___   ___   ___   ___   ___

B. In the space provided, invert each given interval by repeating the second note, followed by the first note transposed down an octave (as shown in the example). Then identify both intervals.

Example:

m3   M6   ___   ___   ___   ___

___   ___   ___   ___   ___   ___

Tip for spelling large intervals: When you are asked to spell a sixth or seventh, it may be easier to imagine its inversion (a third or second) to decide the correct accidentals.

VII. Interval class

For each of the following intervals, identify its name and class (1 to 6).

Example:

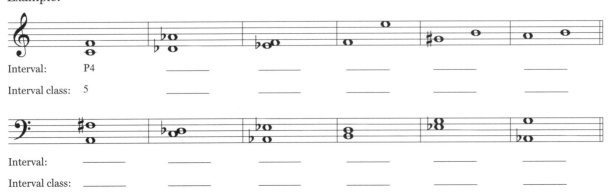

Interval: P4   ___   ___   ___   ___   ___

Interval class: 5   ___   ___   ___   ___   ___

Interval: ___   ___   ___   ___   ___   ___

Interval class: ___   ___   ___   ___   ___   ___

Writing Exercises

Writing intervals

Write out the following series of melodic intervals, starting with the given pitch. Use the second pitch of the interval you have just written as the first pitch of the next melodic interval. Check each interval carefully before writing the next. When you have finished, play or sing the pitches you have written. Each melody is the first line of a traditional song—which song?

A.   ↑M6 ↓M2 ↓M2 ↑M2 ↓M2 ↓m3 ↑M2 ↓m3

Key: _____

Song: _____

B.   PU   ↑P5 PU   ↑M2 PU   ↓M2 ↓M2 PU   ↓m2 PU   ↓M2 PU   ↓M2

Key: _____

Song: _____

C.   PU   ↑P4 ↑M2 ↑M2 ↓M3 ↓m2 ↓M2 ↑m6 PU   PU

Key: _____

Song: _____

D.   ↓m3 ↓M3 ↑M3 ↑m3 ↑P4 ↑M3 ↓M2 ↓M2 ↓m6 ↑M2 ↑m2

Key: _____

Song: _____

Analysis

I. Harmonic and melodic intervals

A. Johann Sebastian Bach, Gavotte II ("La Musette"), from English Suite No. 3 in G Major, mm. 1–4

This little dance movement features a melody and accompaniment part above a sustained bass note, G3 (a pedal tone used to represent the "musette" instrument). Begin by playing these measures or singing the melody against a sustained G3. Between the staves, label each of the harmonic intervals formed between the treble-clef melody and the pedal G3. Identify both size and quality (for example, m3), and label compound intervals as though they were simple.

B. Ludwig van Beethoven, Piano Sonata in C minor, Op. 13 (*Pathétique*), second movement, mm. 1–8   **1.41**

(1) Begin by listening to this passage on your CD. Then write the size and quality of each melodic interval below the staff in the spaces provided.

What types of melodic intervals are used the most?

(2) Listen to the passage again, focusing on the bass line shown below. Then write the size and quality of each melodic interval in the bass line below the staff in the spaces provided.

Do the bass line and melody feature the same types of intervals? Which intervals appear more in the bass line than in the melody?

(3) Now consider the harmonic intervals created when the bass line and melody of the same passage are played together. Listen again, or play the version given below at the keyboard. Identify each harmonic interval in the blanks marked "Interval" between the staves. Contract all compound intervals to simple intervals (e. g., M10 becomes M3). Remember that a new harmonic interval is created each time one of the voices changes pitch. In the blanks marked "Type," write PC (for perfect consonance), IC (for imperfect consonance), or D (for dissonance).

Which type of intervals appears the most: IC, PC, or D?

II. Melodic intervals, compound intervals, and interval class

Anton Webern, "Herr Jesus mein," from *Three Songs*, Op. 23, No. 3, mm. 2b–8
Begin by playing the melody, given below, on the piano or on your own instrument.

(a) Write the pitch names above the staff, including octave designation (C4 = middle C). (If necessary, review Chapter 1.) The first few answers have been provided for you.

(b) Label each melodic interval in the blanks below the staff. Circle the pitch pairs that make intervals larger than an octave (compound intervals).

(c) Below each interval you have named, indicate the interval class.

(a) Pitches: A♭5   E♭5   G4   ___   ___   ___ ___   ___

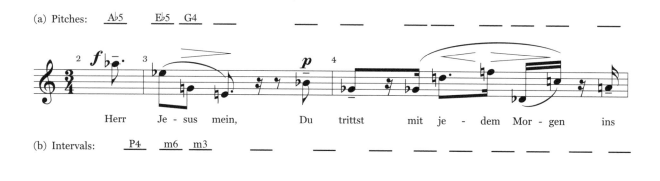

(b) Intervals: P4   m6   m3   ___   ___   ___   ___ ___

(c) Interval class: 5   4   3   ___   ___ ___ ___   ___

(a) Pitches: ___   ___ ___ ___   ___   ___ ___ ___

(b) Intervals: ___   ___ ___ ___   ___ ___   ___ ___

(c) Interval class: ___   ___ ___ ___ ___ ___   ___ ___ ___

(a) Pitches: ___ ___ ___ ___ ___ ___ ___

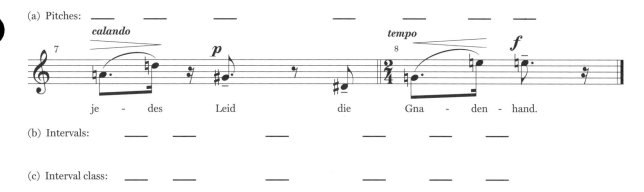

je - des   Leid   die   Gna - den - hand.

(b) Intervals: ___ ___ ___ ___ ___ ___

(c) Interval class: ___ ___ ___ ___ ___ ___

Translation: My Lord Jesus, every morning you enter this house, in which hearts are beating, and soothe each sorrow with your gracious hand.

(d) Write a paragraph discussing Webern's vocal writing. Include answers to these questions: What are the highest and lowest pitches? What types of melodic intervals do you find, and which interval classes appear most often? What pitch-class collection is used? (See Chapter 3.) Are any pitch classes omitted?

Triads and Seventh Chords

CHAPTER 7

Basic Elements

I. Building triads above a scale

Start this exercise by writing in the key signature for the key and mode indicated. Then notate the requested scale with whole notes (show the ascending scale only). Above each scale degree, write in the third and fifth to make a triad. When writing minor-scale triads, use the raised $\hat{7}$ (leading tone) of the harmonic minor scale for the triads built on $\hat{5}$ and $\hat{7}$. Write M (major), m (minor), d (diminished), or A (augmented) under each triad to show the chord quality.

D: ___ ___ ___ ___ ___ ___ ___

E♭: ___ ___ ___ ___ ___ ___ ___

g: ___ ___ ___ ___ ___ ___ ___

e: ___ ___ ___ ___ ___ ___ ___

II. Spelling isolated triads

For each of the exercises below, write the requested triad stacked in thirds, following one of the methods described in the chapter. Do not change the given pitch. An example is shown for each, with the starting note indicated by an arrow.

A. Each pitch below is the *root* of a triad.

Example:

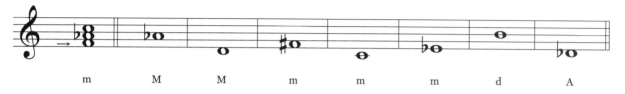

B. Each pitch below is the *third* of a triad.

Example:

C. Each pitch below is the *fifth* of a triad.

Example:

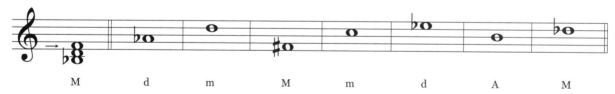

III. Scale-degree triads

Write triads stacked in thirds above the given roots using the pitches in the indicated key. In minor keys, take the raised $\hat{7}$ (leading tone) from harmonic minor to spell triads built on $\hat{5}$ and $\hat{7}$. (You may therefore need to alter the given note in minor keys.) Underneath each triad, write its Roman numeral. Use upper- and lowercase Roman numerals and the symbols $^+$ and $^{\circ}$ to show each triad's quality and its position in the scale (for example, I or vii$^{\circ}$). Then write in the triad's scale-degree name (for example, tonic or submediant) above the staff.

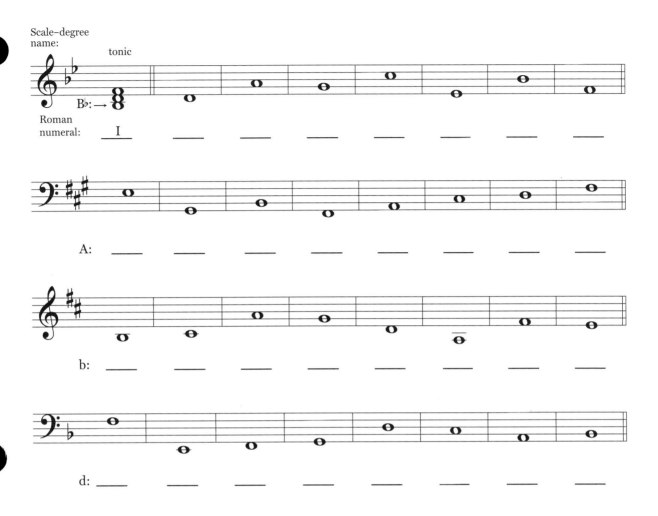

Scale–degree name: tonic

B♭: → I

Roman numeral: I ___ ___ ___ ___ ___ ___

A: ___ ___ ___ ___ ___ ___ ___

b: ___ ___ ___ ___ ___ ___ ___

d: ___ ___ ___ ___ ___ ___ ___ ___

IV. Building seventh chords above a scale

Start this exercise by writing the key signature indicated. Then notate the requested scale in whole notes (ascending scale only). Above each scale degree, write in the third, fifth, and seventh to make a seventh chord. Use the raised $\hat{7}$ (leading tone) of the harmonic minor scale in the minor-scale triads built on $\hat{5}$ and $\hat{7}$. Write one of these abbreviations to show the chord quality of each seventh chord: MM7 (major-major), Mm7 (major-minor), mm7 (minor-minor), $^{\varnothing}$7 (half diminished), and $^{\circ}$7 (fully diminished).

F: ___ ___ ___ ___ ___ ___ ___

G: ___ ___ ___ ___ ___ ___ ___

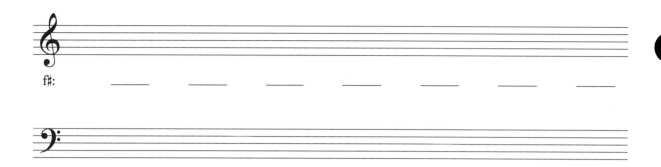

V. Spelling isolated seventh chords

A. Each pitch given is the *root* of a seventh chord. Fill in the seventh chord by one of the methods described in the chapter. Do not change the given pitch.

Example:

B. Each pitch given is the *third* of a seventh chord.

Example:

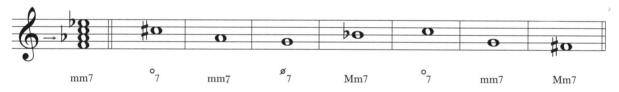

C. Each pitch given is the *fifth* of a seventh chord.

Example:

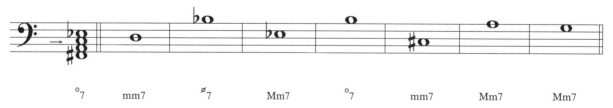

D. Each pitch given is the *seventh* of a seventh chord.

Example:

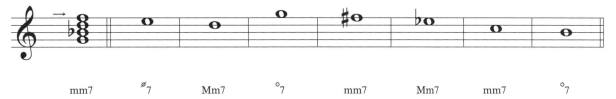

| mm7 | ⌀7 | Mm7 | °7 | mm7 | Mm7 | mm7 | °7 |

VI. Scale-degree triads and seventh chords in inversion

A. For each of the Roman numerals in the keys indicated below, notate the inverted triad on the staff. In minor keys, use the raised $\hat{7}$ (leading tone) from harmonic minor to spell the chords built on $\hat{5}$ and $\hat{7}$.

Example:

| G: | I⁶ | IV⁶ | V⁶₄ | ii⁶ | vi⁶ | I⁶₄ | vii°⁶ |

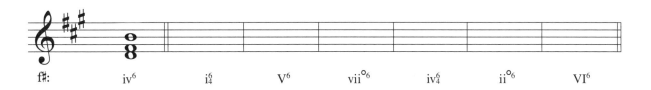

| f♯: | iv⁶ | i⁶₄ | V⁶ | vii°⁶ | iv⁶₄ | ii°⁶ | VI⁶ |

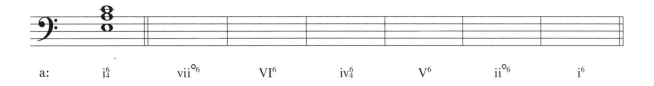

| a: | i⁶₄ | vii°⁶ | VI⁶ | iv⁶₄ | V⁶ | ii°⁶ | i⁶ |

B. For each of the Roman numerals in the keys indicated below, notate the inverted seventh chord on the staff. In minor keys, use the raised $\hat{7}$ (leading tone) from harmonic minor to spell the chords built on $\hat{5}$ and $\hat{7}$.

Example:

B♭:   V$_5^6$ V$_3^4$ ii$_5^6$ IV$_5^6$ V$_2^4$

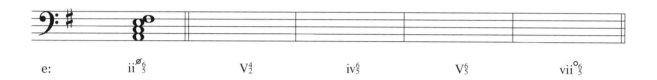

e: ii^ø$_5^6$ V$_2^4$ iv$_5^6$ V$_5^6$ vii^o$_5^6$

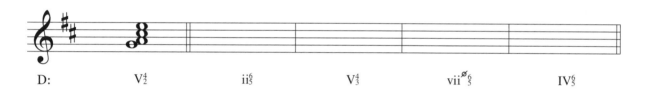

D: V$_2^4$ ii$_5^6$ V$_3^4$ vii^ø$_5^6$ IV$_5^6$

Analysis

I. Brief analysis

Fill in the requested information for each of the musical examples below.

(1) Look at each chord in the excerpt (in both treble and bass clefs). Write the triad or the seventh chord on which it is based in close spacing (stacked in thirds above the root) on the first staff below the example.

(2) Draw an arrow pointing to the chord member of the triad or seventh that is in the bass part in the example.

(3) For inverted chords, use the second staff below the example to renotate the triad or seventh in the correct inversion, taking as your bass the pitch to which the arrow points.

(4) Underneath the staff, write in the Roman numeral that represents the triad's or seventh chord's scale step and quality.

(5) Add figures to the Roman numeral to show an inversion: no figure for root position, ^{6} for first-inversion triads, $_5^6$ for first-inversion seventh chords, etc.

A. Johann Pachelbel, Canon for Three Violins and Keyboard in D Major, mm. 1–2

Triads and seventh chords

(1) Root position:

    (2)

(3) Inversion
    (if needed):

(4, 5) Roman numerals: D: I

B. Wolfgang Amadeus Mozart, "Voi, che sapete," from *The Marriage of Figaro*, mm. 5–12 **2.83** 🎧

Begin by listening to this passage on your CD. Embellishing tones are circled; do not include them in the chords. Most measures feature only one chord, but measures 7 and 11 have two. Can you find seventh chords in this example?

Triads and seventh chords

(1) Root position:

(2)

(3) Inversion:

(4, 5) Roman numerals: B♭: I   ii⁶

9 Cherubino   10   11   12

Voi,   che sa - pe - te   che   co - sa è a - mor,

Translation: You who know what love is, . . .

(1) Root position:

(3) Inversion:

(4, 5) Roman numerals:

II. Examining a lead sheet

"Rich and Rare" (traditional Irish melody), arranged by Joel Phillips

Look at the lead sheet for "Rich and Rare" on the next page. Examine each chord symbol. Write pitches that belong in that chord on the staff underneath each measure.

PART II

Linking Musical Elements in Time

CHAPTER 8

Intervals in Action (Two-Voice Composition)

Basic Elements

I. Opening and closing patterns in note-against-note counterpoint

A. Opening patterns: For each of the opening intervallic progressions below, add a note to complete the second pair, then label the new interval. For some of these exercises, there is more than one correct answer. Check the melodic and harmonic intervals formed by each connection. Beneath the staff, label your voice-leading C (contrary), S (similar), P (parallel), or O (oblique).

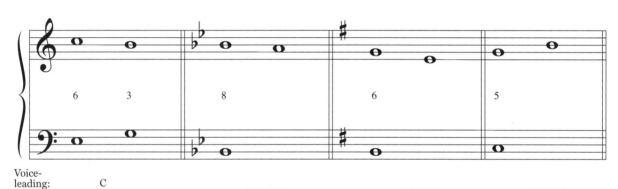

B. Closing patterns: For each of the closing intervallic progressions below, add a note to complete the first or second pair, then label the new interval. For some of these exercises, there is more than one correct answer. Check the melodic and harmonic intervals formed by each connection. Label your voice-leading C (contrary), S (similar), P (parallel), or O (oblique).

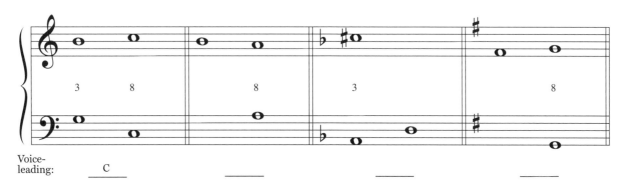

Voice-
leading: C   _____   _____   _____

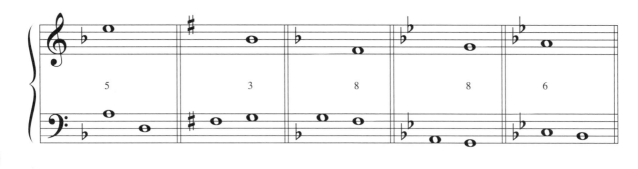

_____   _____   _____   _____   _____

II. The resolution of chordal dissonances

Begin by identifying the given dissonant intervals below (d5, A4, or m7), then resolve them as described in the text chapter. Keys are given for you.

d5 → 3: both voices move in by step.
A4 → 6: both voices move out by step.
m7 → 3: the lower voice skips up a P4 or down a P5; the upper voice moves down by step.

Between the parts, write the numbers of the new generic harmonic intervals you have created.

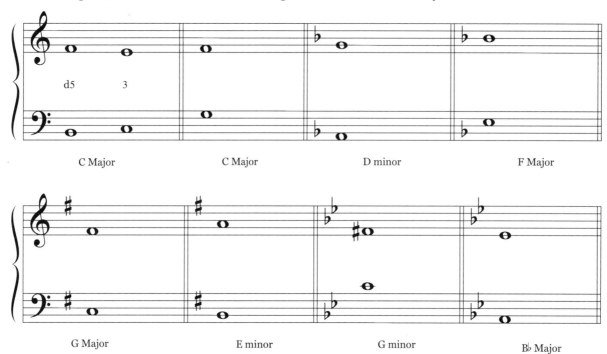

C Major   C Major   D minor   F Major

G Major   E minor   G minor   B♭ Major

III. Note-against-note to 2:1 counterpoint

In each of the given note-against-note frameworks, add an eighth note beamed to either the upper or lower voice to make a correct 2:1 embellishment. Many of these exercises have more than one correct answer. Write in the numbers of the generic harmonic intervals between the parts, and label the embellishment you have added (N for neighbor, P for passing, CS for chordal skip).

Writing Exercises

About the counterpoint exercises

In these exercises (and similar ones in Chapter 9), we will write counterpoint above or below a given melody, called a *cantus firmus*. The third melody in each set is notated in the alto clef (review Chapter 1), as students in Mozart's time would have practiced counterpoint. While whole notes are traditional for notating cantus firmus melodies, we will practice our counterpoint using a variety of note values. The cantus firmus melodies in this book are traditional ones, from Fux's *Gradus ad Parnassum* and from early twentieth-century counterpoint exercises by Knud Jeppesen and Heinrich Schenker.

Write a note-against-note counterpoint above or below each cantus firmus as specified, following the instructions given in the text chapter. Between the staves, write in the numbers for the generic harmonic intervals formed between the voices. Above the staff, label the type of motion between adjacent harmonic intervals: O (oblique), S (similar), C (contrary), or P (parallel). Check your work against the KEY CONCEPT guidelines in the chapter. Always play your counterpoint at the keyboard (or play one line while singing the other), to check your work with your ears!

I. Writing note-against-note counterpoint

A. Above a given line:

(1) Write half notes above each half note in the cantus firmus.

(2) Write quarter notes above each quarter note in the cantus firmus.

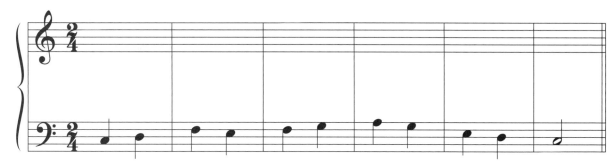

(3) Write whole notes above each whole note in the cantus firmus.

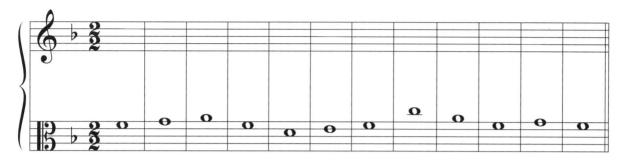

B. Below a given line:

(1) Write quarter notes below each quarter note in the cantus firmus.

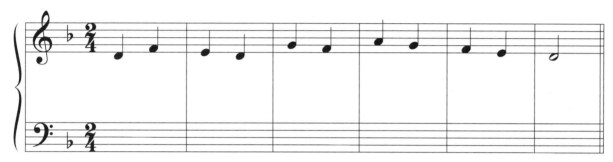

(2) Write half notes below each half note in the cantus firmus.

(3) Write whole notes below each whole note in the cantus firmus.

II. *Writing 2:1 counterpoint*

A. Above a given line:

Write a 2:1 counterpoint above each cantus firmus below. As before, label generic intervals between the staves and the type of motion (O, S, P, or C) above the staff. Play (or play and sing) your counterpoint when it is complete.

(1) Write eighth notes above each quarter note in the cantus firmus.

(2) Write quarter notes above each half note in the cantus firmus.

(3) Write half notes above each whole note in the cantus firmus.

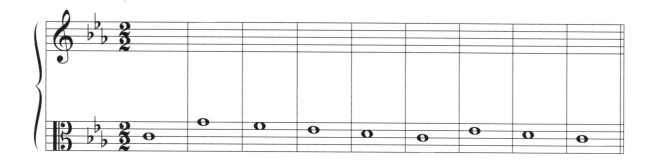

B. Below a given line:

Write a 2:1 counterpoint below each cantus firmus below. Label as in Exercise A, and perform your solution.

(1) Write quarter notes below each half note in the cantus firmus.

(2) Write eighth notes below each quarter note in the cantus firmus.

(3) Write half notes below each whole note in the cantus firmus.

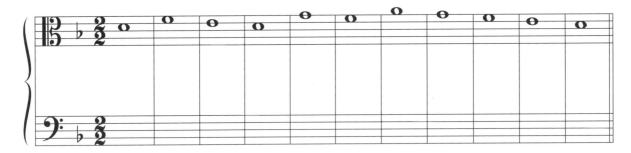

Analysis

I. Analysis of note-against-note counterpoint

For each counterpoint example below:

- Label the generic harmonic intervals between the staves.

- Label each melodic interval in the bass and soprano as a step, skip, or leap (st, sk, or lp).

- Be ready to discuss the relationship between the two voices: are skips or leaps in one voice accompanied by a step or repeated pitch in the other?

- Above the staff, mark each harmonic intervallic connection with O (oblique), S (similar), C (contrary), or P (parallel). Consider which types of motion are used most, and fill in the blank beneath the example.

- Compare the counterpoint in each example with the guidelines given in the chapter.

A. Ludwig van Beethoven, Piano Sonata in C minor, Op. 13 (*Pathétique*), second movement, mm. 1–4 (outer voices only, adapted) **1.41**

Begin by playing through the excerpt or listening to the CD performance. Even though there are both quarter notes and eighth notes in this example, the counterpoint is note-against-note throughout.

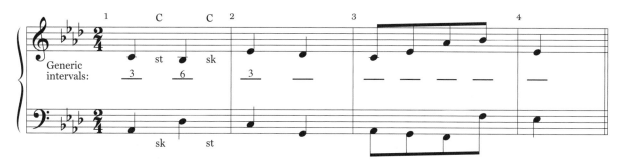

(1) Types of motion used most often: _____

(2) Does the counterpoint follow the chapter guidelines? _____ If not, discuss the differences.

B. Beethoven, Piano Sonata in C Major, Op. 53 (*Waldstein*), first movement, mm. 35–42a (outer voices only)   **1.53**

Play the example, or listen to the passage on your CD. Like the previous excerpt, this passage also features two durations—quarter and half notes—but the counterpoint is note-against-note, except for measures 38 and 41. The circled pitch in measure 41 is a passing tone.

(1) Types of motion used most often: _____

(2) Does the counterpoint follow the chapter guidelines? _____ If not, discuss the differences.

(3) What is the relationship of measures 35–36 to 39–40?

C. Leonard Bernstein and Stephen Sondheim, "One Hand, One Heart," from *West Side Story*, mm. 25–40a

Examine the counterpoint between the vocal solo line and the bass part of the accompaniment. Write in the number of each generic harmonic interval. The circled quarter notes on "last" (m. 35), "-ly" (m. 37), and "will" (m. 38) are incomplete neighbor tones, which will be considered in a later chapter. For now, you may leave them out, yielding a note-against-note framework.

(1) Types of motion used most often: _____

(2) Does the counterpoint follow the chapter guidelines? _____ If not, discuss the differences.

II. Analysis of 2:1 counterpoint

For each 2:1 counterpoint example below:

- Play through the passage slowly at the keyboard.

- Label the generic harmonic intervals between the staves.

- Label embellishing tones as P (passing) or N (neighboring).

- Above the staff, mark each harmonic intervallic connection with O (oblique), S (similar), C (contrary), or P (parallel). Consider which types of motion are used most, and fill in the blank beneath the example. Measure 1 of Example A has been completed for you.

- Compare the example's counterpoint with the guidelines given in the chapter.

A. Johann Sebastian Bach, Fugue in E♭ for Organ (*St. Anne*), mm. 3–5a (rebarred)

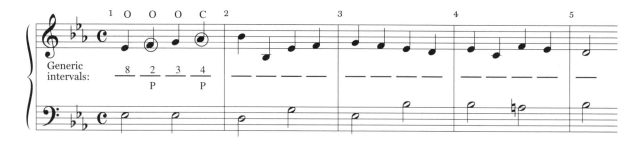

(1) Types of motion used most often: _____

(2) Does the counterpoint follow the chapter guidelines? _____ If not, discuss the differences.

B.   Bach, Invention No. 1 in C Major, mm. 1–4a

Treat this passage as a 2:1 setting, with two sixteenth notes to each eighth note. (Ignore beats where the upper voice temporarily has no counterpoint beneath it.)

(1)   Types of motion used most often: _____

(2)   Does the counterpoint follow the chapter guidelines? _____ If not, discuss the differences.

Melodic and Rhythmic Embellishment in Two-Voice Composition

Basic Elements

I. From note-against-note to 4:1 or 3:1

For each of the given note-against-note frameworks below, rewrite to create groups of four sixteenth notes or three triplet eighth notes on the first beat, in correct 4:1 or 3:1 style. All of these exercises have more than one correct answer. Label the generic harmonic intervals between the parts, and circle and label the dissonant intervals you have written. After you have completed your setting, compare your choices with those of your classmates—which solutions sound the best?

A. Make the upper voice 4:1 or 3:1 on beat 1.

B. Make the lower voice 4:1 or 3:1 on beat 1.

II. Chains of suspensions

Chains of suspensions in two parts are easy to make; they are rhythmic displacements of a series of parallel thirds or sixths. Three series of parallel thirds and sixths are shown below. On the staff to the right, revise each to make a chain of suspensions that ends in the chord given in half notes. The preparation and the first suspension of each chain are completed for you. You may write either tied or rearticulated suspensions. Write in the generic-interval numbers below the staff to label your suspensions.

Two blank staves, (d) and (e), have been provided for you to write your own suspension chains. Use thirds or sixths, as in (a)–(c), but write your suspension chain in a key other than C Major. Play your suspension chains at the keyboard, or sing or play them as a duet with a partner.

(d)

(e)

III. Suspensions from note-against-note

For each note-against-note framework, make a dissonant suspension as shown below. Between the staves, write in the generic-interval numbers for both the note-against-note framework and your suspension pattern. Above the staff, label each of the three parts of the suspension: preparation (P), dissonant suspension (S), resolution (R). Include at least one bass suspension.

Example:

Writing Exercises

I. Writing 4:1 counterpoint

Write a 4:1 counterpoint for each cantus firmus shown below, following the instructions given in the text chapter. Write in the numbers for the generic harmonic intervals formed between the voices. Check your work against the KEY CONCEPT guidelines in the chapter. Be sure to check for parallel perfect intervals between consecutive pitches, beat-to-beat pitches, and off-beat-to-on-the-beat pitches—if you find any, revise! Play (or play and sing) your completed counterpoint at the keyboard. (These exercises may also work for 3:1 counterpoint if your teacher assigns it.)

A. Above a given line:

B. Below a given line:

(1)

(2)

(3)

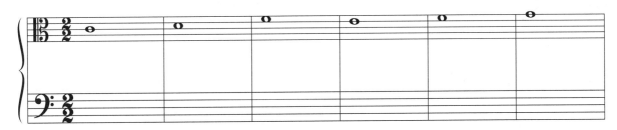

II. Writing a fourth-species counterpoint

Write a fourth-species counterpoint (using suspensions) for each cantus firmus shown below, following the instructions given in the chapter. You may "break species" (write 2:1 counterpoint instead of a suspension on a beat) as necessary, but include as many suspensions as possible, and take advantage of opportunities to write chains of suspensions. Write in the numbers for the generic harmonic intervals formed between the voices. Check your work against the KEY CONCEPT guidelines in the chapter, and perform it once it is complete.

A. Above a given line:

(1)

(2)

B. Below a given line:

Analysis

I. Brief analysis

For each counterpoint example below:

- Play it through at the keyboard (or listen to it on your CD).

- Label the generic intervals between the voices.

- Circle and label all dissonances.

- Fill in the blanks beneath the example.

  (1) Is there a balance of contrary, oblique, parallel, and similar motion, or are one or two types of motion used more frequently?

  (2) Compare the example's counterpoint with the guidelines outlined in the chapter.

A. Johann Sebastian Bach, Cantata No. 140 ("Wachet auf"), second movement, mm. 25b–27a (outer voices only)

(1) Types of motion used most often: _____

(2) Does the counterpoint follow the chapter guidelines? _____ If not, discuss the differences.

(3) What is the most common type of dissonance? _____

B. George Frideric Handel, Chaconne in G Major, from *Trois Leçons*, Variation 6, mm. 49–56a   2.2 🎧

Listen to this variation on your CD. Then label the generic intervals between the highest note of the chords in the right hand and the sixteenth-note 4:1 counterpoint in the left. Consider the top pitch on the downbeat in the right hand to extend through the quarter rest. Circle and label the dissonances.

(1) Types of motion used most often: _____

(2) Does the counterpoint follow the chapter guidelines? _____ If not, discuss the differences.

(3) What is the most common type of dissonance? _____

C. Ludwig van Beethoven, Piano Sonata in C Major, Op. 53 (*Waldstein*), first movement, mm. 204–207a   **1.58** 🎧

Begin by listening to this passage on your CD. Then label the generic intervals between the highest line (the triplets) and the lowest note of the chords in the left hand—these parts make a 3:1 setting. Label all embellishing tones. This passage is an elaboration of the note-to-note counterpoint we considered in the exercises for Chapter 8 (mm. 35–42). (That setting was in E Major; this one is in C Major.)

(1) Types of motion used most often: _____

(2) Does the counterpoint follow the chapter guidelines? _____ If not, discuss the differences.

(3) What is the most common type of dissonance? _____

II. Extended analysis

Handel, "Rejoice greatly," from *Messiah* (p. 107)   **2.10** 🎧

Begin by listening to the opening of this aria on your CD, while following the score in your anthology. Then label generic intervals between voices, circle and label dissonances, and answer the questions below the examples.

This aria provides many passages that illustrate the contrapuntal principles we have been studying. For now, we consider only selected portions of the aria, and we will examine the counterpoint between the highest and lowest lines of the accompaniment (which sometimes doubles the soprano's melody). After you have analyzed the measures below, listen to the aria again while following the score, to see how these passages fit into the entire movement.

A. Mm. 7b–8a   **2.11** 🎧

B. Mm. 11b–12a   **2.12** 🎧

C. Mm. 20–22   **2.14** 🎧

D. Mm. 24–25a   **2.15**

E. Mm. 83b–84a

(1) For each of the excerpts, which types of motion (contrary, similar, parallel, or oblique) are used most often?

A. _____ B. _____ C. _____

D. _____ E. _____

(2) Which embellishing tones are used most often?

A. _____ B. _____ C. _____

D. _____ E. _____

(3) Does the counterpoint follow the chapter guidelines? _____ If not, discuss the differences.

CHAPTER 10

Notation and Scoring

Basic Elements

Beams and flags in vocal and instrumental music

A. "Michael Finnigin"

Begin by singing through this melody with numbers, solfège syllables, or the text. Then on your own staff paper, renotate it for instrumental performance, beaming the music to show the beat groupings.

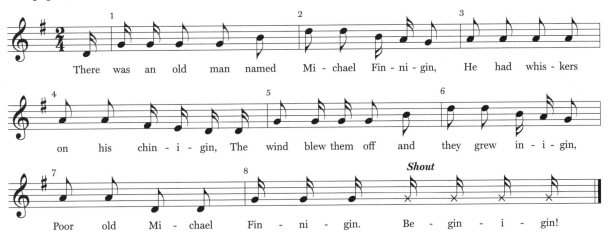

B. "Kookaburra" (Australian round)

Sing through the melody first, then renotate it for vocal performance, beaming the music to reflect how the words correspond with the melody pitches.

Writing Exercises

Making an open score from a keyboard four-voice score

Write out the selected measures from each of the following national anthems in open score on the staves below. Sing these pieces in class, from the open score as well as from the keyboard score. What aspects are easier with open score? Which are more challenging?

A. Francis Scott Key, "The Star-Spangled Banner," mm. 1–4a

B. Calixa Lavallée and Robert Stanley Weir, "O Canada," mm. 1–4

Analysis

I. Studying rounds

A. "Come, Follow Me"

Begin by singing the following round with two other students or as a class, divided into three groups. The circled numbers in the score indicate when the next group should enter.

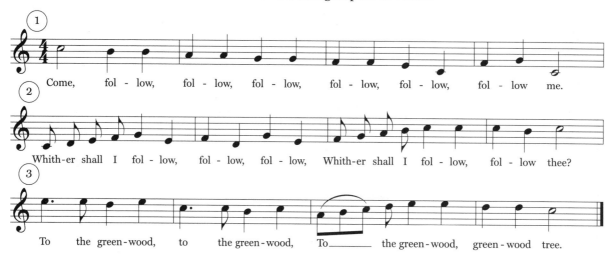

We can study the counterpoint in these rounds by writing out what happens when the pairs or groups of voices are singing together.

(1) On your own staff paper, write phrase 1 with stems up and, on the same staff and in the same measures, phrase 2 with stems down. Then write the numbers beneath the staff for the intervals formed by the combination of melodies. Examine the dissonant intervals—are these passing tones, neighbor tones, or other embellishments? Circle and label embellishing tones. If one of the melodies is sung by women's voices and the other by men's, these intervals may be inverted; the counterpoint in the round must work with either part in the higher voices.

(2) Now do the same for phrases 2 and 3—use stems down for phrase 2, stems up for phrase 3. Examine the dissonant intervals. Circle and label embellishing tones.

(3) When the three parts combine, chords are formed. Although it is possible to distinguish three individual parts on the same staff with stems (we saw this in the Purcell accompaniment in Example 10.2), the notation can be hard to read. To consider all three parts, simply write in the note heads (without stems) for each part with the beats aligned, to represent the combination of phrases 1, 2, and 3. Using your analysis of the embellishing tones in the paired phrases, circle the embellishing tones in the combination, then identify the triad or seventh chord that underlies each measure. Label the chords with Roman numerals underneath the staff.

B. "Kookaburra"

In this round, shown in "Basic elements" I/B, four groups of singers may participate (phrase 2 begins on m. 3, phrase 3 on m. 5, and phrase 4 on m. 7, as marked), making the pattern shown below.

Group 1: phrase	1	2	3	4	(1)	(2)	(3)...
Group 2: phrase		1	2	3	4	(1)	(2)...
Group 3: phrase			1	2	3	4	(1)...
Group 4: phrase				1	2	3	4

Follow the instructions for steps (1) and (2) in the previous exercise to consider the combinations of phrases 1 and 2 and phrases 3 and 4. Follow the instructions for step (3) to consider phrases 1-2-3 and 2-3-4.

II. Examining four-part settings

The U.S. and Canadian national anthems are again given on the following pages, each shown in a four-part keyboard setting. Such songs are often sung SATB from this type of setting, with keyboard accompaniment. For each, do the following.

- Circle all the places where two voice parts sing in unison. Indicate beside your circles (by writing in S, A, T, or B) which parts are in unison.

- Examine the range of each voice part. Does each range conform to the guidelines given in the text chapter? Draw a square around any pitches that are out of range for that voice part.

- Check the spacing between the soprano and alto, and alto and tenor parts—is it always an octave or less? Draw an arrow pointing to any chords that do not have the correct spacing between all parts.

- Answer the questions that follow the score.

A. Key, "The Star-Spangled Banner"

"The Star-Spangled Banner" is considered difficult to sing—why? Which voice types may have problems with the melody as written?

B. Lavallée and Weir, "O Canada"

Is "O Canada" as difficult to sing as "The Star-Spangled Banner"? Does it fall within a comfortable range for all voice types?

Voicing Chords in Multiple Parts:

Instrumentation

Basic Elements

I. Doubling in triads

Write the half-note triads requested below in four parts (SATB) on the staves provided, using the doublings suggested in Chapter 11 of the text. Write in any accidentals that are needed to make the correct chord quality. Carefully check stem direction and doubling. Make sure each part is in the proper voice range, that the spacing is correct, and that you have written no crossed voices.

A. Root position

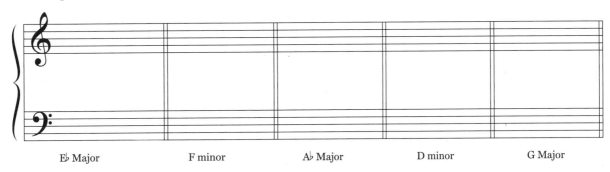

| Eb Major | F minor | Ab Major | D minor | G Major |

B. First inversion

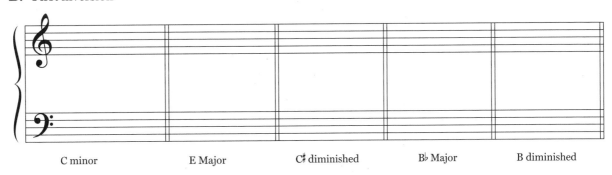

| C minor | E Major | C# diminished | Bb Major | B diminished |

C. Second inversion

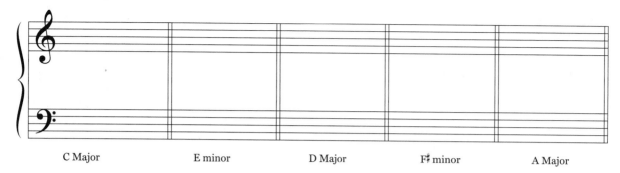

C Major   E minor   D Major   F♯ minor   A Major

II. SATB seventh chords

Write the half-note seventh chords requested below in four parts (SATB) on the staves provided. Be sure to include any accidentals that are needed to make the correct chord quality. Carefully check that each seventh chord member is present, that each part is in the proper voice range, and that no voices are crossed.

A. Root position

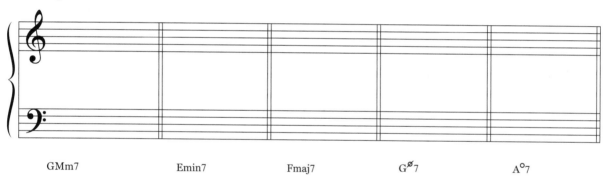

GMm7   Emin7   Fmaj7   G^ø7   A°7

B. First inversion

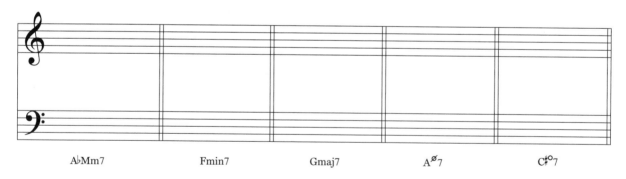

A♭Mm7   Fmin7   Gmaj7   A^ø7   C♯°7

C. Second inversion

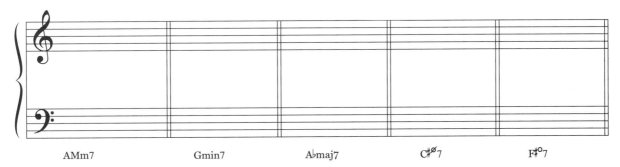

AMm7   Gmin7   A♭maj7   C#ø7   F#°7

D. Third inversion

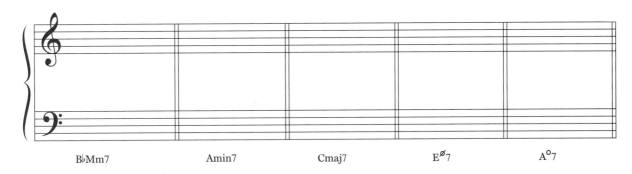

B♭Mm7   Amin7   Cmaj7   Eø7   A°7

III. Voicing and doubling

Play each of the following pieces at the keyboard, or sing with your class. Then examine each chord in the piece as described below.

- Write each chord stacked in thirds on the treble staff provided, and label its root and quality beneath (triad or seventh chord; e. g., D minor, F Mm7). Embellishing tones have been circled; do not include them in the chords.

- Check each chord in the piece for doubling. Does the chord follow the doubling guidelines for that type of chord and inversion? Write an asterisk (*) above any triad or seventh chord that does not. Explain possible reasons for any chord doubling that diverges from the guidelines.

- Based on stem direction, are there any places where voices cross? Circle the spot(s), and be ready to discuss why you think the composer set the line that way.

A. William Billings, "Chester"

Let ty-rants shake their i - ron rod, And Slav'-ry clank_____ her

C   A   G
Major minor Major

gall - ing chains, We fear them not,_____ we trust_____ in God,

New_____ Eng - land's God_____ for - ev - er reigns.

B. Katharine Lee Bates, "America the Beautiful"

IV. Voice-leading

Select one phrase from one of the songs in section III. Write in a numeric analysis of the generic intervals between the bass line and each of the three upper voices, then examine these intervals and the connections between them. Where and how are skips used? Which intervals appear the most? Do the three upper voices vary in terms of intervals and voice-leading connections? Which types of voice-leading (similar, contrary, or oblique) are most common?

On your own paper, write a paragraph describing your observations and conclusions. Compare the phrase you studied with others considered by classmates—is each piece consistent in the use of intervals and voice-leading connections?

Writing Exercises

Making a quartet setting from SATB

The following assignments may be completed as a class or group project, as well as individually. If possible, have students or "guest artists" perform your setting in class.

A. Billings, "Chester"

Prepare a setting of "Chester" for clarinet quartet (three B♭ clarinets and bass clarinet), saxophone quartet (two altos, tenor, and baritone), or brass quartet (two trumpets, horn, and trombone; or two trumpets and two trombones; or two trumpets, trombone, and tuba) using the SATB version given in "Basic Elements" III/A. Assign each instrument to one of the original SATB voice-leading strands, then transpose the parts as needed. Write out the parts in a transposing score, and prepare individual parts for each instrument.

B. Bates, "America the Beautiful"

Prepare a setting of "America the Beautiful" for string orchestra using the SATB version given in "Basic Elements" III/B. The original setting is in C Major; set yours in D Major (as you set each voice-leading strand, transpose it up a whole step to D).

Set the melody for the first violins, the alto part for second violins, the tenor part for violas (don't forget—use the alto clef!), and the bass part for cellos. String basses may also play the cello line, with the basses sounding an octave lower. (While this makes a series of "parallel" octaves between the cellos and basses, these are not intended to be separate voice-leading strands, and thus do not create inappropriate parallel intervals in the counterpoint. They are called "sonority doublings.")

Analysis

Reading a full score

A. Johannes Brahms, Variations on a Theme by Haydn, mm. 1–29 (theme)

Before continuing with this assignment, listen to a recording of this piece while following the score on pages 262–65 of this workbook.

Were you able to keep your place in the score? If you are not used to reading full scores, you probably had some difficulty! (Most people cannot follow a full score on their first few tries; they have to learn how.) While reading a full score may seem confusing at first, there are some techniques you can learn to make the process easier.

One technique is to figure out which instruments are performing the same part. Look first for lines with the same rhythm and contour. If the instruments play in the same key, the task is easy—they will be playing the same notated pitches or pitches an octave apart (for a doubling at one or more octaves). If there are instruments in different keys (for example, flute, E♭ alto saxophone, and B♭ clarinet), you will need to transpose a few pitches of the non-C instruments to concert key to determine which pitches sound.

On your own paper, answer the following questions, then check your answers by listening to the measures in question.

(1) Which instruments play the same part in measures 1–10? How many different parts are there?

(2) Now look at measures 15–18. How many different parts are there?

(3) Compare measures 1–10 with 19–23. How many different parts are in 19–23?

(4) In measures 23–29, which parts are doubling?

B. Wolfgang Amadeus Mozart, Symphony in C Major, K. 551 (*Jupiter*), fourth movement, mm. 1–8

(1) One way to make reading a full score easier is to make a pitch reduction. (We won't worry here about representing the exact rhythms.) Look at measures 1–8 of this Mozart symphony, given below. Make a pitch reduction of these measures on the blank grand staff on page 116. Start by writing in the pitches played in whole notes by the first violin in measures 1–4 and those in the viola, cello, and basses in measures 5–6. Represent each pitch in the correct octave. Watch out for the alto clef and instruments whose pitches sound an octave lower than written!

In measures 1–7, the violin 2 part looks complicated at first because of all the eighth notes, but how many different pitches does it play in each measure? Represent the pitches of the violin 2 part in simultaneous whole notes in measures 1–6 (so that they make a chord with the violin 1's whole notes), but use half notes for measure 7, where the chords change in mid-measure. The violin 1, viola, cello, and bass also change pitches in measure 7—write those in using half notes. The first two measures have been completed for you.

Finally, complete the violin 1 part by examining measures 5–8. This melody has repeated pitches, and an embellishing scale figure in measure 6. Show it with one whole note each in measures 5 and 6 to represent the primary melody pitches (leaving out the scale figure) and two half notes in measure 7.

Tip: This excerpt includes only string parts, but in many full orchestral scores, the strings carry the essence of the harmonies, and the kind of reduction we are making here will allow you to follow the piece more easily without having to transpose the wind or brass parts.

(2) Label the chords in each measure with Roman numerals representing the scale degree that triad or seventh chord is built on, and indicate inversions with figures. (This movement is in C Major.) Some of the seventh chords in measures 1–4 include only three of the usual four parts—what chord member is missing in each?

(3) The reduction you made is not the same as a short score. Why not? What would be different in a short score?

The Phrase Model

PART III

CHAPTER 12

The Basic Phrase Model:
Tonic and Dominant Voice-Leading

Basic Elements

I. Spelling tonic and dominant

Write the requested tonic and dominant triads in root position or inversions in the keys indicated, using SATB voicing as described in Chapter 11. In minor keys, remember to raise the third of dominant triads to make the correct chord quality.

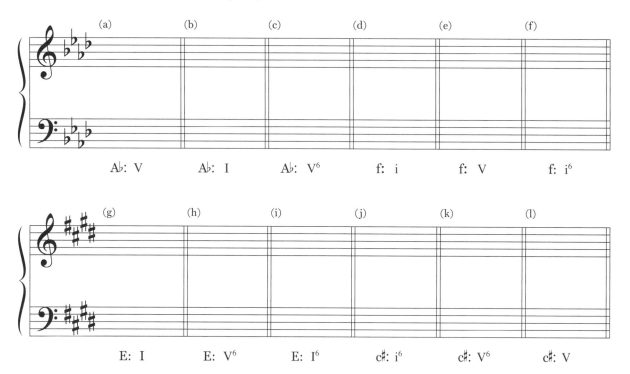

(a) (b) (c) (d) (e) (f)

Ab: V   Ab: I   Ab: V⁶   f: i   f: V   f: i⁶

(g) (h) (i) (j) (k) (l)

E: I   E: V⁶   E: I⁶   c#: i⁶   c#: V⁶   c#: V

II. Spelling dominant seventh chords

For each of the following keys, write dominant seventh chords in root position or inversions as indicated, taking the soprano pitch provided. Use SATB voicing as described in Chapter 11. In minor keys, remember to use the leading tone in dominant seventh chords to make the correct chord quality. Write in all necessary accidentals.

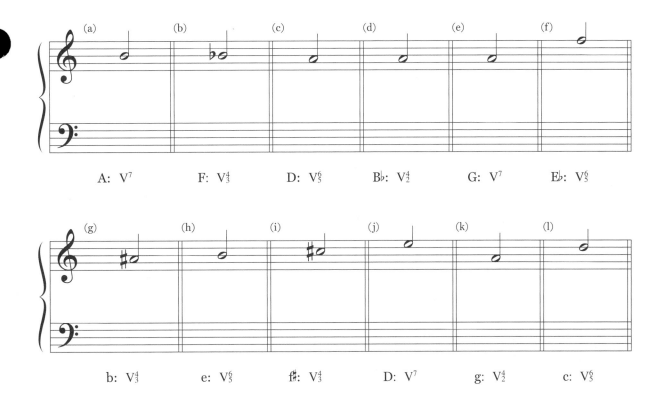

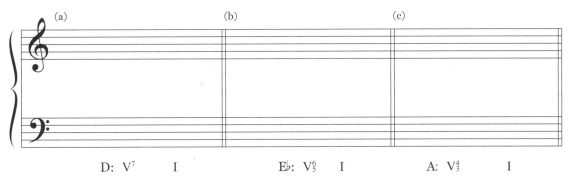

III. Resolution of V⁷

Part-write the progressions in the specified keys below, using SATB voicing. Draw arrows to show the resolution of leading tones up and chordal sevenths down. Write in all necessary accidentals, or provide the correct key signature.

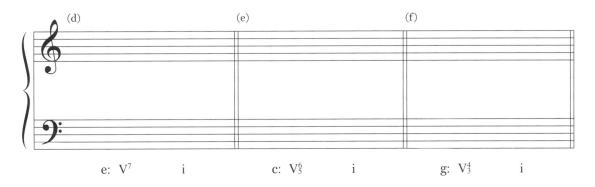

IV. Cadences with I and V or V⁷

Part-write the two-chord cadences as indicated below, with SATB voicing in the specified key. Draw arrows to show the resolution of leading tones up and chordal sevenths down. Analyze with Roman numerals and figures. Provide the correct key signature for each measure.

A. Write a perfect authentic cadence (PAC) using V or V⁷.

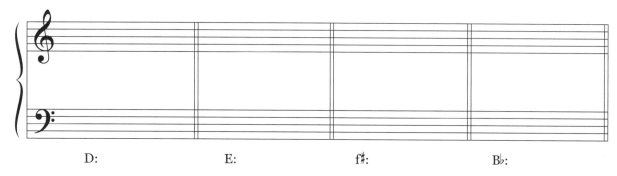

D: E: f♯:   B♭:

B. Write an imperfect authentic cadence (IAC) using V or V⁷ in root position.

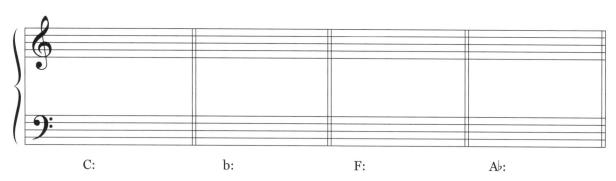

C: b: F: A♭:

C. Write an imperfect authentic cadence (IAC) using V⁷ in an inversion.

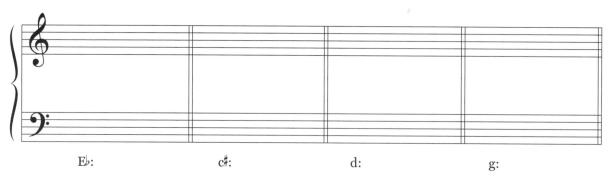

E♭:   c♯:   d: g:

D. Write a half cadence (HC).

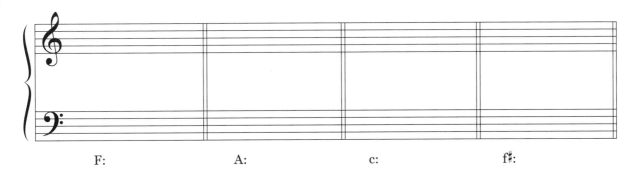

F: A: c: f♯:

Writing Exercises

I. Basic phrases

On your own staff paper, write the following basic four-measure phrase progressions in the keys indicated.

- Use one chord per measure.

- Start by writing the bass line, in the inversions requested. Then compose a soprano line that makes good counterpoint with the bass. Finally, fill in the chords.

- Check the doubling in each chord, and mark the resolution of leading tones up and chordal sevenths down with arrows.

- Beneath your Roman numeral analysis, indicate the functional areas with T or D.

- Place a bracket over the cadence, and label its type (PAC, IAC, HC).

(1) F: I I^6 I V, $\frac{2}{4}$

(2) D: V I V I, $\frac{3}{8}$

(3) B♭: I I V I, $\frac{3}{4}$

(4) A: I I V^7 V^7, $\frac{3}{8}$

(5) G: V^7 V^7 I I, $\frac{2}{4}$

II. Melody harmonization

Each of the melodies below can be harmonized with one (or more) of the phrase progressions provided above: (1), (2), (3), (4), or (5). Reread the instructions for harmonizing a melody in Chapter 12. Following these guidelines, write a Roman numeral harmonization beneath the staff of each melody. (Hint: You may set an anacrusis with a dominant or tonic harmony, or you may leave it unaccompanied.)

A. "Hush, Little Baby"

Hush,   lit - tle   ba - by,   don't   say   a   word,

Ma - ma's going   to   buy   you   a   mock - ing - bird.

B. "The More We Get Together"

The   more   we get to - ge - ther, to - ge - ther, to - ge - ther, the

more   we get to - ge - ther   the   hap - pier   we'll   be.

C. Waltz tune

III. Piano arrangement

On your own staff paper, take two of the melodies you harmonized for Exercise II above and make a piano accompaniment for each. Use an arpeggiation pattern for the first one, and a jump-bass accompaniment pattern for the second.

IV. Creative writing

A. Take one of the melodies and accompaniments you set in Exercise III (or one of the other melody settings from Exercise II) and recast it in the parallel minor. Change the key signature, and write in needed accidentals (don't forget the leading tone in V chords!).

B. Use your settings of the melodies in Exercises III and IV/A (or combine your settings with those of several of your classmates who set the same melody) to make a sectional variation set. Arrange the variations with the simplest one first (perhaps a block-chord setting), followed by the others in order of complexity. Insert the minor variations as a group in the middle of the major ones. Then play the settings as a variation set.

Analysis

I. Brief analysis

One place where tonic and dominant chords are typically reiterated in common-practice compositions is at the conclusion of a movement. These repeated V–I progressions don't make a complete phrase, but instead serve to "put the brakes on" at the end of a long, active piece. Our brief analyses are all drawn from closing passages.

A. Wolfgang Amadeus Mozart, Piano Sonata in C Major, K. 545, first movement (p. 149)   **2.57** 🎧

Listen to this movement on your CD. Write a Roman numeral analysis of measures 70–73 (track 68) beneath the score in your anthology. Write in arrows to show the resolution of any leading tones and chordal sevenths.

(1) Copy your analysis into the following chart.

	m. 70	71	72	73	
Roman numerals:					
Key: _____					

(2) The last complete phrase in this piece ends with the cadence from measures 70–71 (the rest is a codetta, or closing passage); what type of cadence is this? _____

B. Ludwig van Beethoven, Sonatina in F Major, Op. Posth., second movement (p. 52)   **1.60** 🎧

Listen to this piece on your CD while following the score in your anthology, and pay particular attention to the ending. The V⁷–I from the second half of measure 89 to measure 90 ends the last complete phrase, which is followed by a brief codetta. Mark the Roman numerals for measures 87–94 (track 62) in your score. Use one chord per measure, and don't worry for now about changes in inversion. Write in arrows that show the resolution of any leading tones or chordal sevenths in the dominant harmonies.

(1) Copy your Roman numeral analysis into the chart below.

	m. 87	88	89	90	
Roman numerals:					
Key: _____					

Roman numerals:

(2) What harmonic and rhythmic elements set the codetta apart from the phrase that precedes it?

II. Extended analysis

A. Mozart, "Sull' aria" ("Letter Duet"), from *The Marriage of Figaro*, mm. 1–10

Sing through the vocal parts of this aria while playing the bass line of the piano accompaniment. Then repeat, this time playing the treble line of the accompaniment. Each of the chords in the accompaniment (and in the vocal parts, too) is arpeggiated. To identify the triads and seventh chords, consider all the pitches in each dotted-quarter-note beat, then label each beat with a Roman numeral and figures under the bass staff.

Key:

Translation: On the breeze, what a gentle zephyr [will whisper].

What is the musical effect of the alternation of chords in this passage? How does this effect relate to the text?

B. Mozart, Symphony No. 41 in C Major (*Jupiter*), fourth movement, mm. 408–423

Listen to a recording of this passage in your library. Following a PAC in measures 407–408, there is an extended closing passage that brings the movement (and the whole symphony) to a close. All the prevailing harmonies in these measures are either tonic or dominant, but passing and neighboring embellishments have been added in some measures. In measures with eighth notes, begin by circling the passing and neighboring embellishments to identify which triad (tonic or dominant) is being arpeggiated in each measure. Write a I for tonic or V for dominant (it is not necessary at this point to consider inversions) under the bottom bass staff, then copy the analysis for each measure into the chart on p. 131 to turn in. Except for measures 416–418, your analysis should consist of one Roman numeral per measure. Circle and label each melodic embellishment on the score, and be prepared to discuss your analysis.

(1) Mozart, *Jupiter* Symphony

	m. 408	409	410	411	
Roman numerals:					

Key: _____

	412	413	414	415	
Roman numerals:					

	416	417	418	419	
Roman numerals:					

	420	421	422	423	
Roman numerals:					

(2) How does Mozart extend harmonies across more than one measure?

CHAPTER 13

Embellishing Tones

Basic Elements

I. Labeling embellishing tones

In the following excerpts, the embellishing tones have been circled for you. Next to the line that extends above or below the circle, place the correct abbreviation for each tone: P for passing tone, N for neighbor, IN for incomplete neighbor, A for anticipation, Ped. for pedal point, R for retardation, and S for suspension.

For suspensions and retardations, indicate the intervals involved (i.e., 7–6) as well as the abbreviated label. Begin by playing or listening to each excerpt. Then after you have finished the labeling, play or listen to each excerpt again to hear how the embellishments you have identified enrich the passage. For now, don't worry about completing a Roman numeral analysis.

A. Scott Joplin, "Pine Apple Rag," mm. 5–12   **2.29**

B. Johann Sebastian Bach, "Jesu, meine Freude" ("Jesus, My Joy," Chorale No. 138)

C. Richard Rodgers and Lorenz Hart, "My Funny Valentine," mm. 13–18a

(1) Here, the chord symbols above the staff help us determine which pitches might be considered embellishing tones. After you label them, write a sentence or two beneath the example to discuss the dissonance treatment of any suspension you find. While the suspended pitches in "sus" chords are often treated more freely in popular music than in common-practice style, is that the case here?

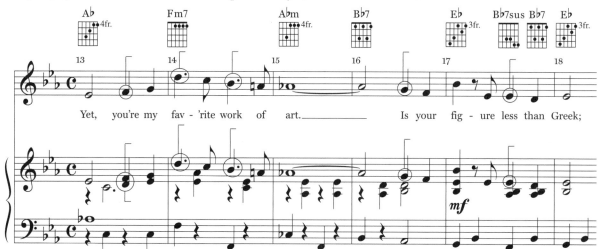

(2) Extra challenge! Look in the library for two or three different interpretations of this oft-recorded song. Compare the embellishments used by each singer or instrumentalist. Think not just about the embellishments in this chapter, but also pitch bends, vibrato, rhythmic hesitations, and pitch changes or substitutions. On your own paper, write a paragraph that briefly compares the performances. Discuss how these embellishments color your reaction to the performances.

II. Writing embellishing tones

Add embellishing tones as specified on the offbeat between the given chords. Do not change the voicing or spacing.

A. Add a passing tone. (Hint: Look for a chordal skip to fill in.)

B. Add a neighbor tone. (Hint: Look for a repeated pitch.)

C. Add double passing tones (in two examples) and double neighbor tones (in two examples).

D. Add an anticipation. (Hint: Look for an upper-voice part where a chord member can arrive early—usually found at a cadence.)

E. Rewrite these short progressions on the blank staff below in order to add a suspension or retardation. (Hint: For a suspension, look for a voice-leading connection that moves down by step between two chords. Place a retardation at a cadence where $\hat{7}$ steps up to $\hat{1}$ in the soprano part.) Write a different type of suspension in each measure.

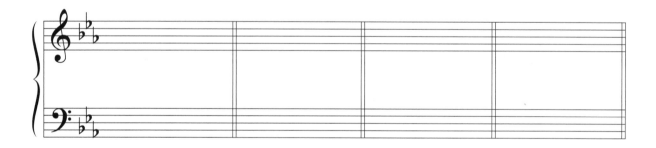

Writing Exercises

I. Part-writing

Write the requested basic phrase progressions below. Begin by filling in the bass line as specified by the Roman numerals, then compose the SAT parts. Plan your setting to include some passing tones, neighboring tones, suspensions, retardations, and anticipations. When a chord is repeated, you may change the voicing of the upper three parts to incorporate consonant skips that may be filled in with passing tones. You may also include single consonant skips, but for this exercise do not use arpeggiation.

Label each embellishing tone in your setting, using the abbreviations described above. Strive for eighth-note motion in at least one part within each beat.

A. Include passing tones, neighbor tones, and other melodic embellishments. Remember that when V_2^4 moves to I^6, a common voicing of the soprano is to skip from $\hat{2}$ to $\hat{5}$.

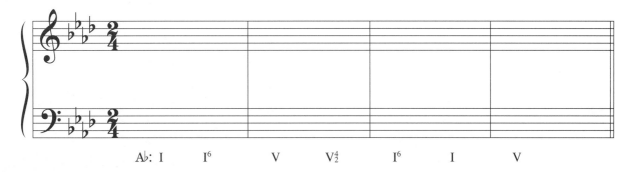

$\text{A}\flat$:   I I^6 V V_2^4 I^6 I   V

B. Include passing tones, neighbor tones, and at least one suspension or retardation.

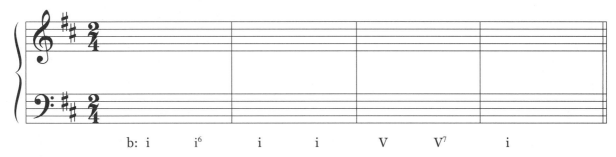

b: i i^6 i   i   V V^7 i

II. Folk melody harmonization

Each of the following melodies may be harmonized with tonic and dominant harmonies. Start by singing or listening to the melody. Determine the harmonic rhythm, then select chords. Which melody pitches are embellishing tones? Circle and label each embellishing tone. On your own staff paper, set the melody for solo instrument or vocalist, and keyboard or guitar accompaniment.

The first example features a more contemporary method of vocal notation. Instead of using flags to denote syllables of the text, modern editions often employ standard beaming for syllabic settings, but add slurs to show where several pitches are to be sung to one syllable (as in "merry").

A. "Hey, Ho, Nobody Home"

(Hint: This one sounds best if the accompaniment pattern is kept simple—either block chords, strummed guitar chords, or arpeggiations. This melody, with its modal structure, features a $\flat\hat{7}$. Harmonize it with a minor v.)

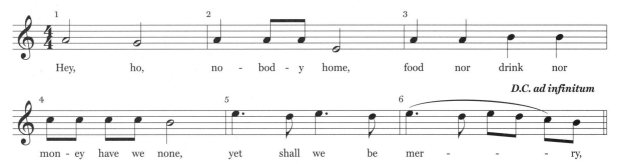

B. "Alouette"

(Hint: A "jump-bass" accompaniment works well with this song.)

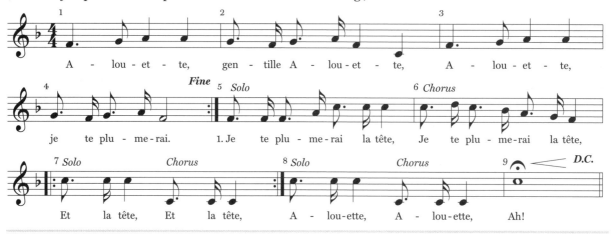

A - lou-et - te, gen - tille A - lou-et - te, A - lou-et - te,

je te plu - me-rai. 1. Je te plu - me-rai la tête, Je te plu - me-rai la tête,

Et la tête, Et la tête, A - lou-ette, A - lou-ette, Ah!

Analysis

I. Brief analysis

A. Wolfgang Amadeus Mozart, String Quartet in D minor, K. 421, fourth movement, mm. 1–4

Make a reduction of the chords in measures 1–4 on the grand staff provided below. Write the main chord members of each half measure, in dotted-quarter notes; keep each pitch in the correct octave to preserve Mozart's voice-leading plan. Play through your reduction.

(1) Label each embellishing tone in measures 1–4, but omit them from the reduction. What types of embellishing tones appear in this excerpt? _____

(2) Label the chords in your reduction with Roman numerals and figures. What type of cadence ends this phrase? _____

B. George Frideric Handel, "Rejoice greatly," from *Messiah* (p. 107)   **2.10**

Listen to measures 49–52 on your CD (track 16). Despite the key signature of two flats, this passage begins with an authentic cadence in C minor on "heathen." Circle and label all embellishing tones in your anthology.

(1) What is the most prominent embellishing tone in measures 50–52? _____

(2) Without doing a thorough Roman numeral analysis, decide on the prevailing triad or seventh-chord type for each bar (e.g., F Major), and list these on the chart below.

	m. 50	51	52	
Chord type:				

II. Extended analysis

A. John Barnes Chance, Variations on a Korean Folk Song, Variation 1 (p. 59)   **1.66**

Listen to the opening of this piece on your CD while following the score in your anthology. In measures 1–8, the clarinet section plays in unison the first strain (we can call it phrase **a**) of a melody that is the basis for the set of variations. After the second strain (mm. 9–16, phrase **b**), the initial melody returns with an accompaniment in measures 17–24.

(1) Look at the melody in measures 1–8. From the musical context, try to determine which tones are embellishing. Then turn (in the anthology) to the return of this melody with an accompaniment in measures 17–24 to check your intuition against the harmonized version. Once you have checked, circle the embellishing tones below.

(2) What is the underlying framework of the melody? Look at it with the embellishing tones removed. How does that framework relate to the accompaniment? Write a paragraph explaining your answer.

B. Jerry Gray and Eddie de Lange, "A String of Pearls," mm. 5–11a

At the keyboard, play through the score that follows, or find a recording in your library.

(1) Write Roman numerals in the diagram below to chart the basic harmonic motion of measures 5–11 (ignoring for the present the added sixths and sevenths in this jazz idiom). Provide just one or two Roman numerals per measure. (For now, ignore the F9 chord in m. 10.)

m. 5   6   7   8

Roman numerals:

Key: _____

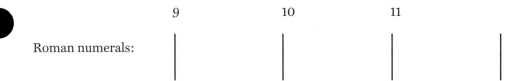

(2) Circle and label each of the embellishing tones in your score. Passing and neighboring tones (and syncopation) are essential to the sound of this piece, which has a surprisingly simple harmonic plan.

C. Bach, *Brandenburg Concerto* No. 4, first movement, mm. 1–21

Listen to the opening measures of this concerto (given below) on a recording from your library. Once you can hear it in your head when you look at the score, you are ready to begin analyzing the passage.

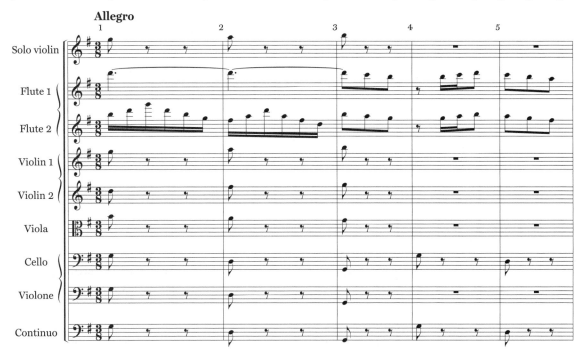

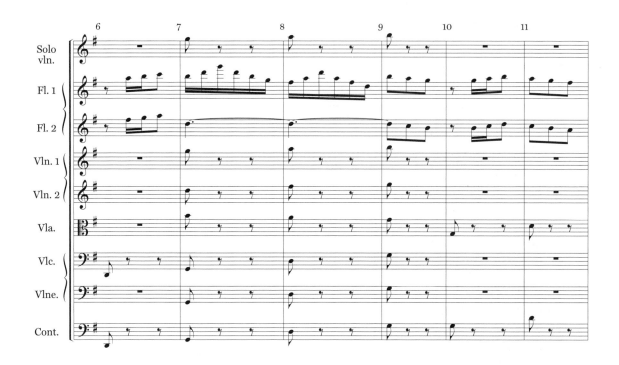

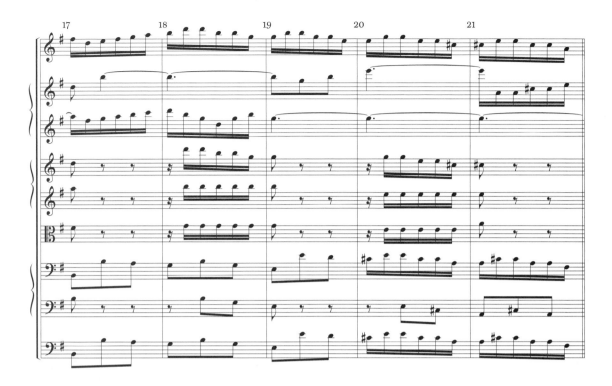

(1) Compare measures 1–6 with 7–12. What is alike? What is different?

(2) Make a harmonic reduction of measures 1 to the downbeat of 13 on the grand staves below. Start by writing in the bass line in dotted-quarter notes from the continuo part, then add in the other parts in their proper octaves. Arpeggios may be written as simultaneous chords. If one instrumental part has exactly the same pitches as another or plays exactly the same part up or down an octave, you only need to write that voice-leading strand in one octave. As you examine each measure, circle and label embellishing tones in your full score, then omit them from the reduction.

(3) What type of embellishing tones did you find? Which involve dissonant intervals, and which are consonant (made from chord members)?

(4) Play your reduction at the keyboard. Write in the Roman numerals underneath the bass line to indicate the harmonies. Play or listen again after completing your analysis—can you hear the change of harmonies?

CHAPTER 14

Chorale Harmonization and Figured Bass

Basic Elements

I. Setting melodic fragments

Set each of the following melodic cadential patterns with one chord per melody pitch. Start by singing the melody line with scale-degree numbers or solfège. Decide the cadence type, then select appropriate bass notes that also make a good counterpoint with the melody. Write in the Roman numerals and figures, then label the cadence type (PAC, IAC, HC). As a last step, fill in the inner voices, following the voice-leading guidelines outlined in the text.

145

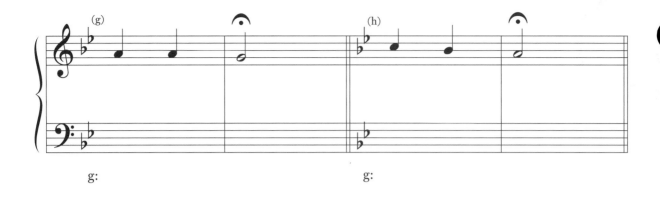

g: g:

II. Cadences with figured bass

Realize each of the figured basses below, following the guidelines in Chapter 14 of the text. Write in the key and Roman numeral analysis, and label the cadence type (PAC, IAC, HC).

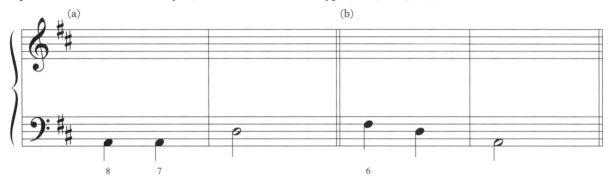

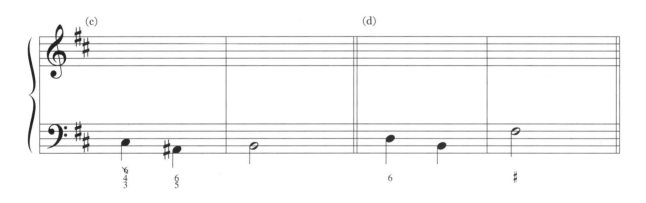

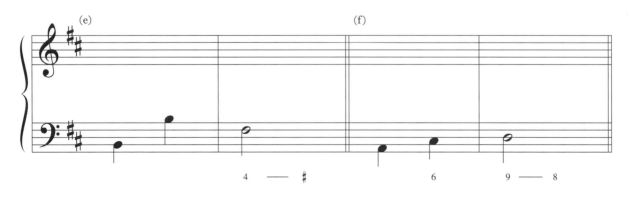

Writing Exercises

I. Chorale melody harmonization

Follow the steps outlined in Chapter 14 to harmonize the melodies below. Use tonic and dominant harmonies (I or i, V or V⁷, and their inversions) only. Remember to complete the soprano-bass counterpoint first, and carefully check the intervallic connections before filling in the inner voices. Analyze your harmonizations with Roman numerals and figures. (If you like, add embellishing tones, but watch out for parallels.) Play through your completed harmonization.

A. Johann Sebastian Bach, "O Haupt voll Blut und Wunden" (Chorale No. 80), phrase 6 (mm 10b–12)

B. Bach, "Liebster Jesu" ("Blessed Jesus," Chorale No. 131), phrases 1 and 2 (mm. 1–5)

Think carefully about your setting of measure 3. How can the repeated pitch in the melody be set in an interesting way?

C. Bach, "Heut' ist, O Mensch" ("Today Is, O Mankind," Chorale No. 168), phrase 1 (mm. 1–3a)

(Hint: This G-minor melody uses the subtonic [♭7̂]; set it with a minor v. We will set phrases 2 and 3 in Chapter 17. With what kind of cadence does this phrase end?)

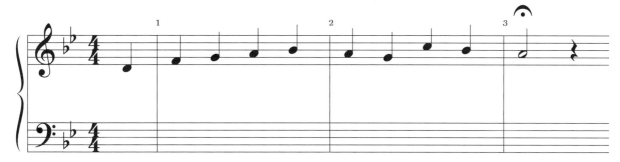

g:

II. Embellished chorales

Start with the basic chorale melody settings you completed in Exercise I. After checking the voice-leading and doubling in your completed SATB setting, add embellishing tones to inner voices or the bass line. Listen carefully to measures where you have added embellishing tones—does each fit naturally into the voice-leading strand? Check the counterpoint between voices to ensure that the embellishing tones do not create voice-leading problems with any other voices (particularly parallel unisons, fifths, or octaves).

III. Figured-bass realization

Follow the steps for realizing figured bass outlined in Chapter 14. If the soprano is not provided, complete the soprano-bass counterpoint first, then fill in the inner voices.

Figured basses A and B include chords we have learned to identify with Roman numerals, but whose use we have not yet studied in detail. You should be able to part-write these, however, following the guidelines in the chapter. For these exercises, think about the chords as intervals above the bass; it is not necessary to provide a Roman numeral analysis. Embellishing tones have been labeled for you. Play through the completed harmonizations.

A. Bach, "So wünsch ich mir zu guter" ("I So Wish to Be Better," Riemenschneider Chorale No. 66), phrase 1 (mm. 1–2a)

Use SATB texture.

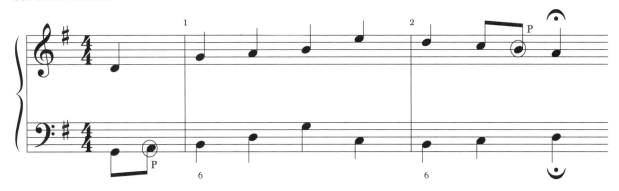

B. Bach, "Liebster Immanuel" ("Blessed Savior," Riemenschneider Chorale No. 54), phrase 1 (mm. 1–4)

Use SATB texture.

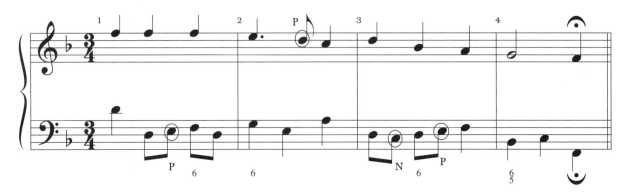

C. Antonio Vivaldi, *Gloria*, sixth movement, mm. 7–11a

Realize the figured-bass continuo part provided on the grand staff below. Use keyboard spacing—that is, write all three of the upper voice-leading strands in the treble-clef right-hand part on the grand staff—and provide a chord on each beat of the $\frac{12}{8}$ meter. You may revoice the upper parts when a chord is repeated to make the keyboard part more interesting, but connect each chord to the next following the voice-leading guidelines. The soprano solo part is also shown on a staff above the grand staff, but you need not follow the solo melody when writing your soprano part in the accompaniment.

After you have completed your realization, write in the Roman numerals under the bass line (this example is in C Major). What type of cadence is found in measures 10–11? _____

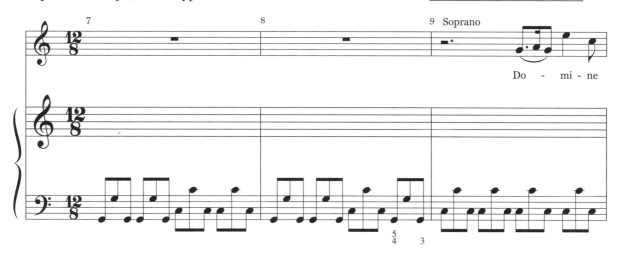

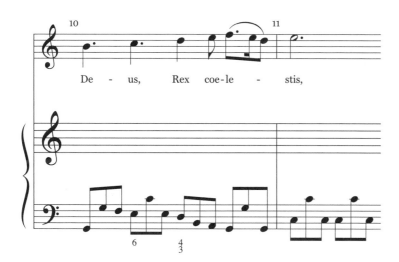

Translation: Lord God, heavenly king.

Expanding the Basic Phrase:
Leading-Tone, Predominant, and ⁶₄ Chords

CHAPTER 15

Basic Elements

Part-write the progressions below in the keys indicated, using SATB voicing. Start by writing the key signature and filling in the bass, then add the upper parts. Draw arrows to show the resolution of leading tones up and chordal sevenths down; check the resolution of each leading tone and chordal seventh.

I. Writing and resolving vii°⁶

Check for the correct resolution of the leading tone.

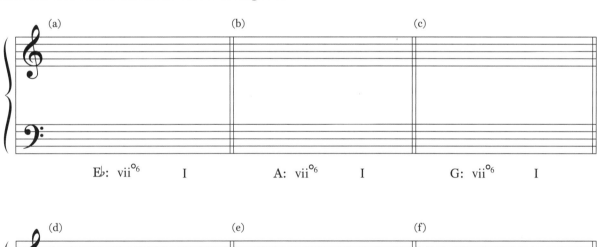

(a)   (b)   (c)

E♭: vii°⁶   I   A: vii°⁶   I   G: vii°⁶   I

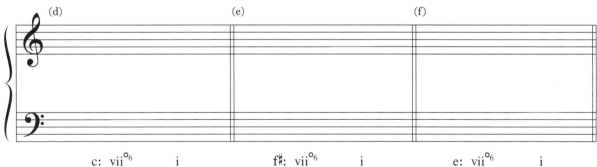

(d)   (e)   (f)

c: vii°⁶   i   f♯: vii°⁶   i   e: vii°⁶   i

II. Writing and resolving *vii*^{ø7} and *vii*^{o7} and their inversions

For each leading-tone chord, examine the resolution of the tritone ($\hat{7}$ and $\hat{4}$). Which guideline for resolution does each follow? (Hint: See Chapter 15, pp. 258–60.)

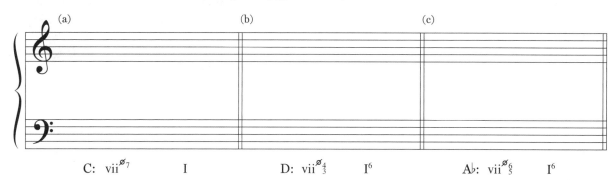

(a)   (b)   (c)

C: vii^{ø7}   I   D: vii^{ø4/3}   I⁶   A♭: vii^{ø6/5}   I⁶

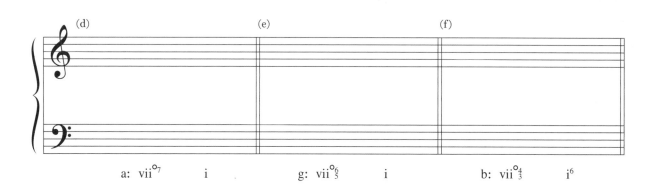

(d)   (e)   (f)

a: vii^{o7}   i   g: vii^{o6/5}   i   b: vii^{o4/3}   i⁶

III. More leading-tone chords (*vii*^{o6}, *vii*^{ø7}, and *vii*^{o7} and their inversions)

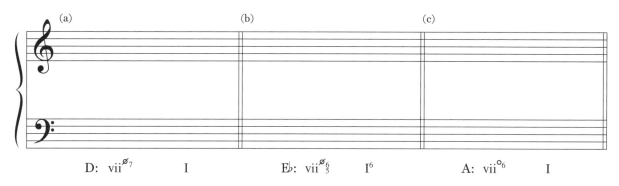

(a)   (b)   (c)

D: vii^{ø7}   I   E♭: vii^{ø6/5}   I⁶   A: vii^{o6}   I

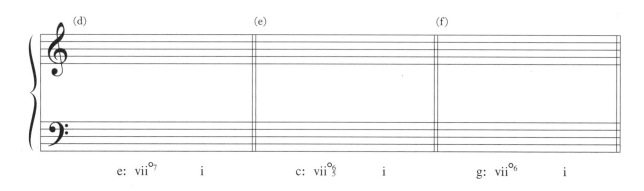

(d)   (e)   (f)

e: vii^{o7}   i   c: vii^{o6/5}   i   g: vii^{o6}   i

IV. Predominant chords

On your own paper, part-write the progressions in the keys indicated, using SATB voicing. Start by filling in the bass, then add the upper parts. For each, add a second layer of analysis (contextual) following the T–PD–D–T model.

A. F Major, $\frac{2}{4}$: I IV | V I ‖

B. G minor, $\frac{2}{4}$: i iv^6 | V i ‖

C. F♯ minor, $\frac{3}{4}$: i ii^{o6} V^7 | i ‖

D. E♭ Major, $\frac{3}{4}$: I ii V | I ‖

V. Voice exchange with predominants

On your own paper, part-write the chords in the specified keys below, using SATB voicing. Where possible, include a voice exchange between the bass and soprano voice parts on the PD harmonies, and mark the exchange with lines between the staves. For each progression, the rhythmic context is ♩ ♩ ♩ in a measure of $\frac{4}{4}$.

A. D: ii^7 ii$^6_5$ V

B. E♭: ii$^6_5$ ii^7 V

C. A: IV^6 ii$^6_5$ V

D. B♭: ii ii$^6_5$ V

VI. Cadential $^6_4$

Fill in the missing voices from the figured bass or Roman numerals provided, using smooth voice-leading.

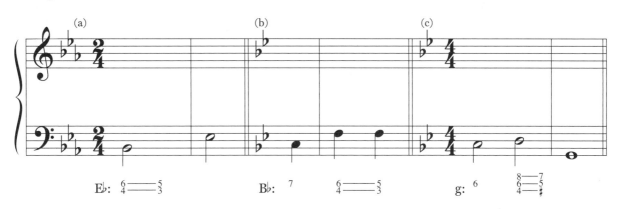

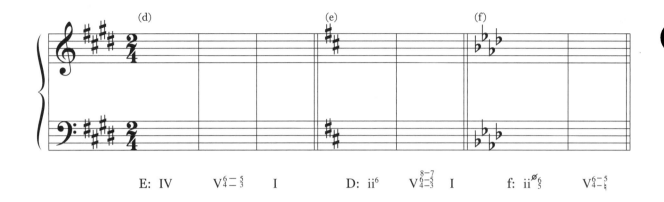

E: IV   V$^{6-5}_{4-3}$ I   D: ii^6 V$^{8-7}_{\substack{6-5\\4-3}}$ I   f: ii$^{\varnothing 6}_{5}$ V$^{6-5}_{4-\sharp}$

VII. Other $^6_4$ chords

Each three-chord succession below expands a single harmony. Part-write each example. Where Roman numerals are not given, provide a two-level analysis.

A. Passing $^6_4$

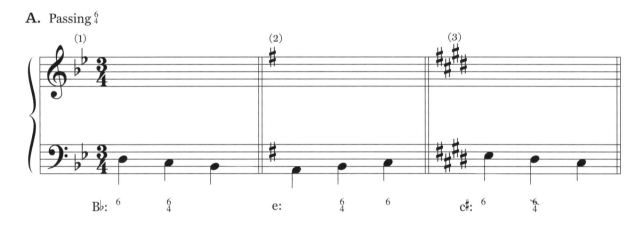

B♭:   6 $^6_4$ e: $^6_4$ 6   c♯:   6 $^6_4$

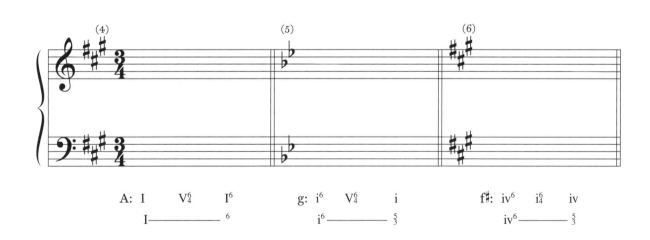

A: I   V$^6_4$ I^6 g: i^6 V$^6_4$ i   f♯: iv^6 i$^6_4$ iv

   I————— 6   i^6————— $^5_3$ iv^6————— $^5_3$

B. Neighboring $^6_4$

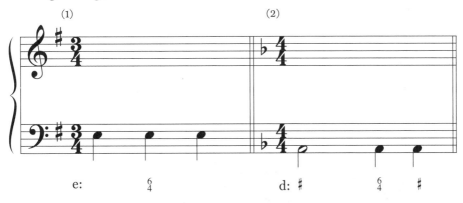

e: $^6_4$ d: ♯ $^6_4$ ♯

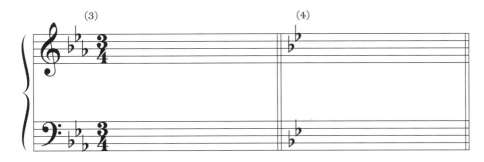

E♭:   I   IV$^6_4$ I   g: i   iv$^6_4$ i

I ———————   i ———————

C. Arpeggiating $^6_4$

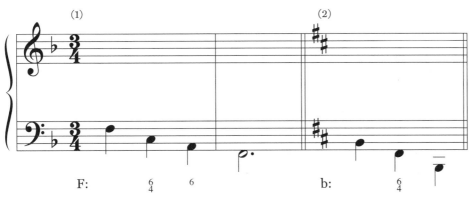

F: $^6_4$ 6   b: $^6_4$

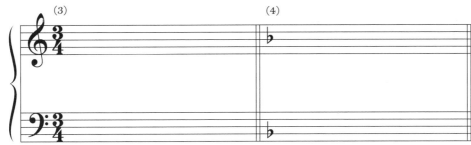

C: IV   IV$^6_4$ IV^6 d: i   i$^6_4$ i

IV ——————— 6   i ———————

Writing Exercises

I. Folk melody harmonization

On staff paper, harmonize the melodies below in simple folk style, following the basic phrase model. First pencil in block chords with correct voice-leading, then arrange the chords for piano.

A. "Scotland the Brave"

B. Johannes Brahms, "Lullaby" (although this melody was composed by Brahms, it is now so well known that some consider it a folk tune)

II. Chorale melody harmonization

On staff paper, harmonize each chorale melody below, following guidelines outlined in Chapter 14. Use diatonic triads and seventh chords. Remember to complete the soprano-bass counterpoint first, and carefully check the intervallic connections before filling in the inner voices. After you have checked your four-part setting, incorporate suspensions, passing tones, and neighbor tones. Check each embellishment to make sure it does not create inappropriate parallels. Play your harmonization at the keyboard.

A. Johann Sebastian Bach, "O Haupt voll Blut und Wunden" (Chorale No. 80), phrases 5 and 6 (mm. 9–12)

We harmonized the last phrase of this chorale in Chapter 14 using only I and V$^{(7)}$. In this setting, include at least one predominant-function chord in each phrase.

B. Bach, "Liebster Jesu" ("Blessed Jesus," Chorale No. 131), phrases 1 and 2 (mm. 1–5)

We set measures 1–5 using only I and V or V$^{(7)}$ in Chapter 14. In this setting, include at least one predominant-function chord in each phrase. In measure 3, what additional options are available with predominant harmonies?

C. Extra: On staff paper, write several different accompaniment settings to the "Liebster Jesu" chorale tune (B) to make variations. You may want to embellish the melody differently in each variation. Arrange your settings from the simplest in texture and rhythmic activity to the most complex, and play them one after the other as a set of sectional variations. You may include a setting of the melody in the parallel minor if you like. Compare your variations with those of other classmates.

III. Figured-bass realization

Realize the figured basses below. For each, use SATB spacing, with one chord per beat in the specified meter. Write in a two-level Roman numeral analysis underneath the bass staff that shows where harmonies have been expanded. Play through your realizations at the keyboard.

IV. Figured-bass realization from music literature

Realize the Vivaldi figured basses below. For each:

- Use keyboard spacing: three voice-leading strands in the right-hand part and one (the given bass) in the left.

- Place one chord on each beat in the given meter, revoicing the upper parts as needed to fit smoothly with the arpeggiations in the bass line.

- Write in a Roman numeral analysis underneath the bass staff.

- Follow any specific instructions included with the individual exercises.

A. Antonio Vivaldi, *Gloria*, fifth movement, mm. 15–19

Realize this figured-bass continuo part on the grand staff below.

(1) Before beginning the realization, examine the figures—what type of $^6_4$ chords are these? What type of cadence will you write to end the movement in measure 19? Label the $^6_4$ chord types and cadence in the example.

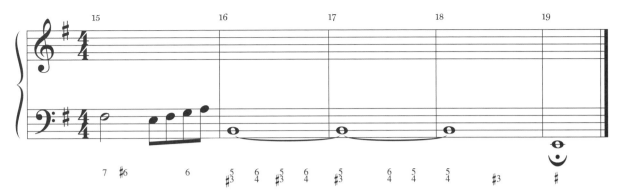

(2) After completing your realization, listen to this movement with the orchestra and chorus on a recording from your library. Why does this passage contain so many $^6_4$ chords?

B. Vivaldi, *Gloria*, sixth movement, mm. 27–31

Realize this figured-bass continuo part on the grand staff below. Begin by sight-singing the soprano solo in a comfortable register while playing the bass line at the keyboard. Avoid parallel unisons, fifths, and octaves between the accompaniment's soprano part and the solo melody. This example is in C Major.

Translation: God the father almighty.

(1) What type of $^6_4$ chord is featured in this passage?

(2) What is another name for this type of progression, over an unchanging bass?

Analysis

A. Archangelo Corelli, Allemanda, from Trio Sonata in A minor, Op. 4, No. 5 (p. 78)   **1.78** 🎧

Start this exercise by writing out a keyboard continuo part above the given figured bass for measures 1–3a on the blank staff in your anthology, then write in the Roman numerals and figures. Circle all passing and neighbor melodic embellishments in the bass line. Now listen to the performance on your CD.

(1) Copy your Roman numeral analysis on the chart below, and label the functional areas with T, PD, and D.

	m. 1	2	3a	
Roman numerals:				
Key: _____				

(2) The figures $^{9-6}$ in measure 2 indicate a melodic embellishment—what type?

(3) In this piece, as in many Baroque instrumental pieces, a cadential pattern is not always followed by a break in the melodic-harmonic motion. This flowing, continuous texture is called *Fortspinnung*— "spinning out." What type of cadence ends the harmonic thought from the end of measure 2 to measure 3?

B. Wolfgang Amadeus Mozart, String Quartet in D minor, K. 421, third movement (p. 157)   **2.74** 🎧

Listen carefully to this movement on your CD. Then make a reduction of the two opening phrases of the Trio (mm. 39b–47a; track 79) on staff paper to turn in. For the violin 2, viola, and cello parts, write each pitch in the octave it sounds. You may represent arpeggiations in the cello part by the pitch sounding on the downbeat. Write the Roman numerals and figures for each chord beneath your reduction.

(1) What cadence type ends each phrase?

(2) Three types of melodic embellishments are featured in the violin 1 part. What are they? Where are they? Give measure numbers.

(3) For the violin 1 part, identify any embellishing tones, and label them in your score. There are some places where chord members act like one of these melodic embellishments—where?

(4) Now look at measures 55b–63a. What do you notice about these measures?

C. Scott Joplin, "Solace" (p. 131)   **2.33** ∩

Listen to "Solace" on your CD while following the score in your anthology. Then write in the Roman numerals and figures for measures 53–56 in your anthology (track 36), and circle and label all embellishing tones. Measures 53–56 (and 61–64, which are a repetition of the first phrase) are built from progressions you have encountered in this chapter, but you will need to watch for registral displacement and consider the melodic embellishments carefully.

(1) List the measures in which you find each of the following (you need list only one instance).

chromatic passing tone   _____

submediant as a tonic expansion   _____

double suspension   _____

chromatic neighbor tone   _____

incomplete chromatic neighbor tone   _____

unresolved leading tone   _____

(2) Copy your Roman numeral analysis into the chart below. Label the functional areas with T, PD, and D.

                             m. 53   54   55   56

Roman numerals:

Key: _____

D. Muzio Clementi, Sonatina in G Major, Op. 36, No. 5, third movement, mm. 1–16

(1) Play through this passage at the keyboard. Write in the Roman numerals and figures, and circle and label all embellishing tones.

(2) Write a paragraph explaining the function of each vii° or vii^{ø7} chord.

Extra: Some popular songs draw on music from composers of previous eras—a custom that was certainly accepted by eighteenth-century composers as well. This Clementi piece, for example, was used as a source for the song "A Groovy Kind of Love," recorded by the Mindbenders in the 1960s.

Further Expansions of the Basic Phrase:

CHAPTER 16

Tonic Expansions, Root Progressions, and the Mediant Triad

Basic Elements

I. Tonic expansion

Write the following brief progressions from the given Roman numerals. For each, use SATB spacing with one chord per beat in the specified meter. Where possible, include a voice exchange between the soprano and bass voices. Add a second level of Roman numeral analysis to show what is prolonged in each progression.

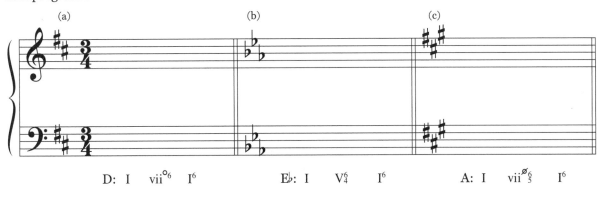

D: I vii°⁶ I⁶   E♭: I V⁶₄ I⁶   A: I vii°ø⁶₅ I⁶

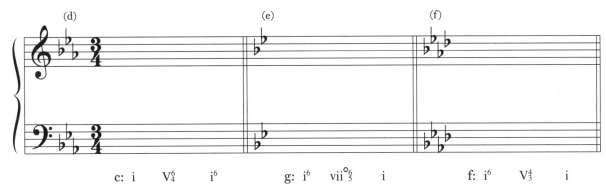

c: i V⁶₄ i⁶   g: i⁶ vii°⁶₅ i   f: i⁶ V⁴₃ i

II. Figured bass with passing chords

Write the following brief progressions from the given figured bass. For each, use SATB spacing with one chord per beat in the specified meter. Write in a Roman numeral analysis underneath the staff. Where possible, include a voice exchange between the soprano and bass voices. Add a second level of Roman numeral analysis to show what harmony is prolonged in each progression.

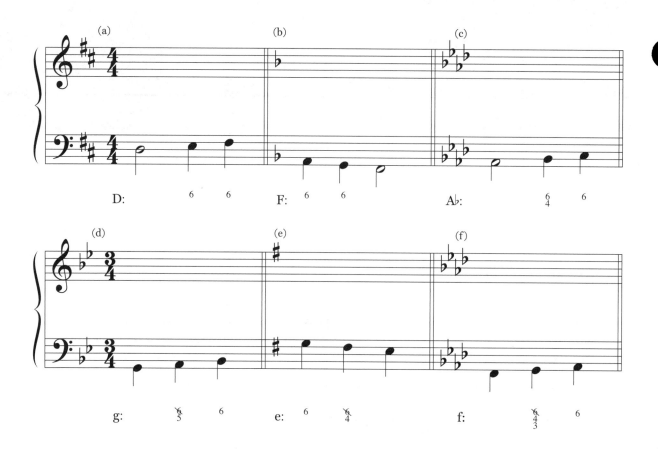

III. Melody fragments

Each of the following melodic fragments is usually harmonized with progressions we have studied in this chapter ("Typical Soprano-Bass Counterpoint"). Set each for SATB using a harmonic rhythm of one chord per melody note.

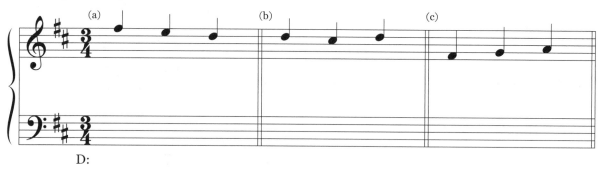

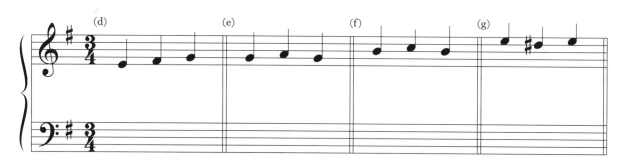

IV. Part-writing with mediants and submediants

In the keys indicated, part-write the progressions below following the given Roman numerals. For each, use SATB spacing and rhythms appropriate to the meter. Play your completed phrase at the keyboard.

A.

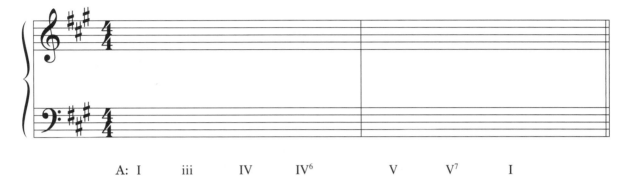

A: I   iii   IV   IV⁶   V   V⁷   I

B.

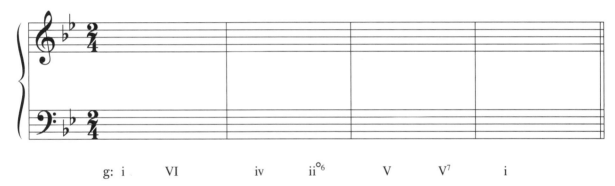

g: i   VI   iv   ii°⁶   V   V⁷   i

V. Part-writing phrases

In the keys indicated, part-write the progressions below, following either the Roman numerals or figured bass. Use SATB voicing. For each, provide a second layer of analysis using the T–PD–D–T model; indicate tonic expansions in your second-level analysis. Play your completed phrase at the keyboard.

A.

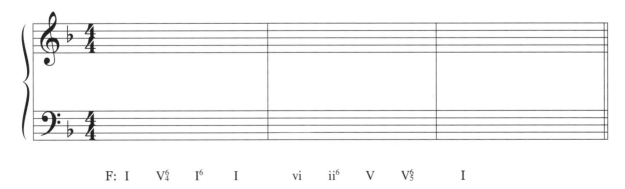

F: I   V⁶₄   I⁶   I   vi   ii⁶   V   V⁶₅   I

B.

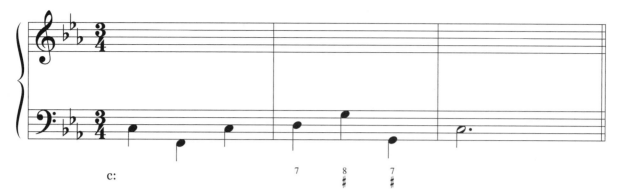

C.

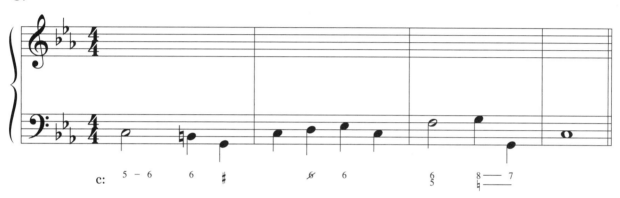

Writing Exercises

I. Melody harmonization

Harmonize the given melodies in an SATB setting, using a harmonic rhythm of one chord per beat. Follow the procedure for harmonization of chorale tunes given in Chapter 14.

A. After harmonizing this melody, compare your chorale-style harmonization with the folk-style one you completed in workbook Chapter 12, "Writing Exercises" II/A.

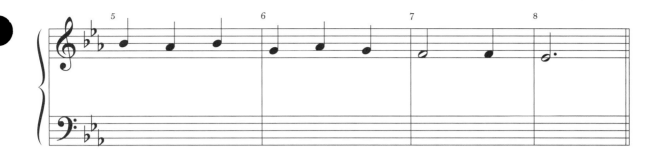

B. This melody is from *Variations on a Korean Folk Song*, by John Barnes Chance. We considered his harmonization of the melody in workbook Chapter 13 ("Analysis" II/A). In your harmonization, use one chord per beat, setting the "embellishing tones" of Chance's melody with dominant or leading-tone passing and neighboring chords. The three accompanying parts may follow the dotted-quarter-plus-eighth rhythm of the soprano part or maintain a quarter-note rhythm. Circle and label the remaining passing and neighboring tones in the melody.

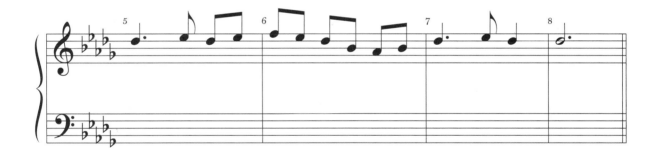

II. Rule-of-octaves harmonization

This is a type of figured-bass exercise that young musicians in the eighteenth century would realize at the keyboard, transposed to each major key, to learn their chord progressions and how to apply them to scalar bass lines. Use keyboard spacing: three voice-leading strands in the right-hand part and one (the given bass) in the left. (Hint: Remember to start the upper voices high enough to have room for the ascending bass line.) After you have completed the realization, write a Roman numeral analysis beneath the bass staff.

A. Ascending

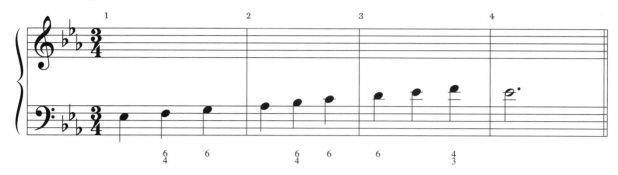

B. Descending

The descending scale, with the leading tone progressing downward, presents special challenges. The figures given here are one way to solve this puzzle—can you think of other progressions that would work as a setting for this bass scale?

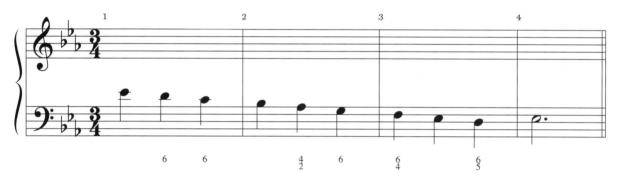

III. Scalar melody harmonization

This is a type of melody harmonization exercise that young musicians in the eighteenth century would complete at the keyboard, transposed to each major key, to learn their chord progressions and how to apply them to stepwise melodic lines.

Harmonize the melodies below on staff paper, using SATB voicing and a harmonic rhythm of one chord per beat in the specified meter. Include passing, neighboring, and cadential $^6_4$ progressions where possible. Provide a Roman numeral analysis for your setting.

A. This melody is based on an ascending major scale.

B. This melody is based on a descending major scale.

C. This melody is based on an ascending minor scale. What might you set differently in this melody as compared with melody A?

D. This melody is based on a descending minor scale. Use a minor v⁶ to set the subtonic scale degree. What might you set differently in this melody as compared with melody B?

Analysis

A. Johann Sebastian Bach, "Wachet auf" (Chorale No. 179) (p. 8)   **1.9** 🎧

Listen to this chorale on your CD while looking at the score in the anthology. Write in the Roman numerals and figures for measures 32b–36 (track 13), and label the embellishing tones in each part.

(1) Copy the Roman numeral analysis into the chart provided below, and identify the functional areas using T, PD, D, and T.

	m. 32b	33	34	35	36
Roman numerals:					

Key: _____

(2) What type of cadence is featured here? _____

(3) What root progressions are used in the phrase? Is each of these typical in its functional area?

(4) Where do seventh chords appear? Is each approached as you would expect? Does each resolve as expected?

B. Wolfgang Amadeus Mozart, *Eine kleine Nachtmusik*, K. 525, first movement, mm. 9–10

Write the Roman numerals and figures in the score below.

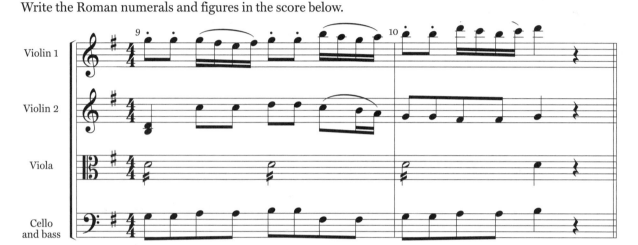

(1) Copy your analysis into the chart below.

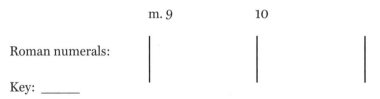

m. 9   10

Roman numerals:

Key: _____

(2) Examine the dominant-quality harmonies carefully—what do you notice about the way Mozart voices these chords? What is prolonged in this passage?

(3) Sing the violin 1 line on scale degrees in a comfortable octave octave while playing the bass line at the keyboard. Circle and label each embellishing tone in the violin 1 part. The melodic embellishments written out here also may be abbreviated with an ornament symbol—which one?

C. Bach, "Aus meines Herzens Grunde" (Chorale No. 1) (p. 6)   **1.5**

Listen to this chorale on your CD, then write in the Roman numerals and figures from the initial anacrusis to measure 7a and for measures 14b–18a in your anthology. Circle and label all embellishing tones. Copy your Roman numeral analysis into the charts below. Label the functional areas with T, PD, and D. (Write anacrusis chords to the left of the bar lines.)

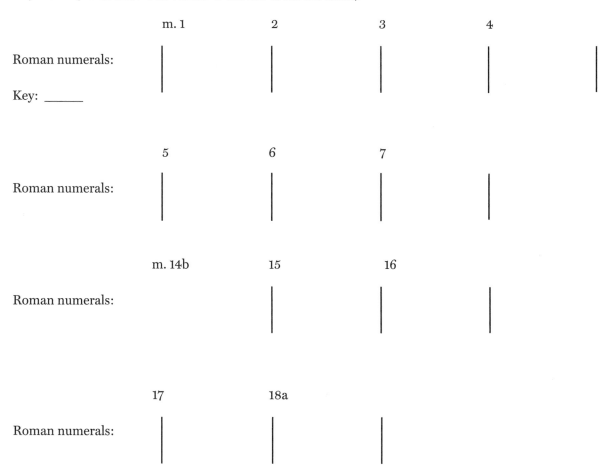

(1) What type of cadence ends each of the two phrases in the first excerpt?

(2) What function does the progression have in measures 14b–16a?

(3) What types of root progressions do you find in measures 17–18a?

(4) What type of cadence ends the second excerpt?

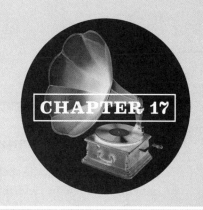

The Interaction of Melody and Harmony:

More on Cadence, Phrase, and Melody

CHAPTER 17

Basic Elements

Part-writing cadences

Part-write the progressions in the keys below, using SATB voicing. Start by filling in the bass, then add the upper parts. Identify each progression as a deceptive, plagal, or Phrygian cadence. Supply either the correct key signature or Roman numeral analysis as necessary. Remember in the deceptive cadence (DC) to resolve the leading tone up (this will result in a doubled third in the tonic chord).

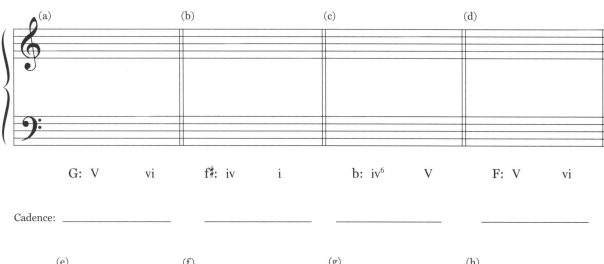

(a)   (b)   (c)   (d)

G: V   vi   f#: iv   i   b: iv^6 V   F: V   vi

Cadence: _____   _____   _____   _____

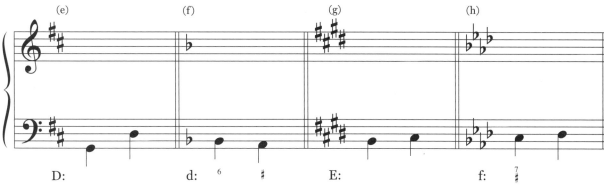

(e)   (f)   (g)   (h)

D: d: ^{6} #   E: f: $^7_\#$

Cadence: _____   _____   _____   _____

Writing Exercises

I. Melody harmonization

Harmonize the melodies below with the harmonic progressions we studied in Chapters 12–16. Start by singing the melody. Determine the appropriate cadences and harmonic rhythm, then select chords.

On your own paper, set the melody for vocal solo (or solo instrument) and keyboard accompaniment. Use appropriate keyboard textures, such as arpeggiated bass, jump bass, or Alberti bass. Prepare a score for class performance.

- Circle and label all embellishing tones in the melody of your arrangement.

- Label each cadence type by name and each period as parallel or contrasting.

A. "Drink to me only with thine eyes" (words by Ben Jonson, 1616)

B. "Believe me, if all those endearing young charms" (words by Thomas Moore, 1808)

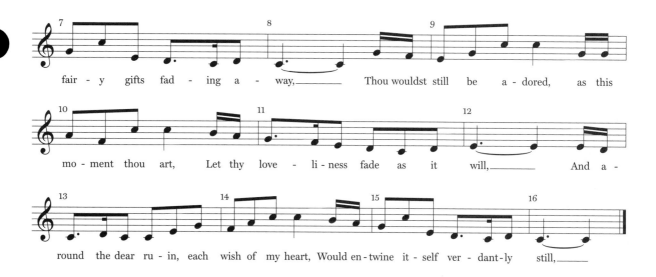

fair - y gifts fad - ing a - way,_____ Thou wouldst still be a - dored, as this

mo - ment thou art, Let thy love - li - ness fade as it will,_____ And a -

round the dear ru - in, each wish of my heart, Would en - twine it - self ver - dant - ly still,_____

II. Writing consequent phrases

Here, we will write antecedent-consequent phrases in Classical style, based on major-key melodies from Mozart piano sonatas. Sing through the antecedent phrases below (ending on a half cadence), then write two possible consequent phrases, each ending on a perfect authentic cadence. For your first solution, write a parallel period; for your second, write a contrasting period. (Then find a score and compare your consequent phrase with Mozart's!)

A. Wolfgang Amadeus Mozart, Sonata in B♭ Major, K. 281, third movement, mm. 1–4a

Antecedent:

Consequent 1 (parallel):

Consequent 2 (contrasting):

B. Mozart, Sonata in D Major, K. 284, third movement, mm. 1–4a

Antecedent:

Consequent 1 (parallel):

Consequent 2 (contrasting):

C. Mozart, Sonata in D Major, K. 311, third movement, mm. 1–4a

Antecedent:

Consequent 1 (parallel):

Consequent 2 (contrasting):

III. Composing complete parallel periods

A. Using block chords in keyboard style, write out a harmonic progression of your choice that follows an antecedent-consequent model: T–PD–D, T–PD–D–T. Plan on parallel phrases in eight measures (four measures for each phrase); the initial harmonies in each phrase are the same. (The harmonic rhythm should be slow: the tonic may extend for several bars before the phrase ending, and the harmonic rhythm should speed up at the cadence.)

B. Play your progression at the piano, vocally improvising melodies that go with it. Use parallel structure; you need to remember the first phrase of your melody in order to sing it at the beginning of the second phrase.

C. When you come up with a melody you like, write it out on staff paper. Prepare two different melodies to turn in (both of which can be harmonized with the progression you composed). Extra challenge: Make a piano setting, with the melody in the right hand and accompanimental patterns in the left.

Analysis

I. Brief analysis

A. Archangelo Corelli, Allemanda, from Trio Sonata in A minor, Op. 4, No. 5 (p. 78)   **1.78**

First listen to the movement while following your anthology score. Write a keyboard continuo part above the given figured bass in your anthology, extending from the second half of measure 9 to measure 12 (track 79) and from the second half of measure 24 to 28 (track 81). These passages are in A minor, the primary key of the movement. Be sure not to double any tendency tone that appears in the melody. The figures ⁵⁶₄ in measures 10 and 11 indicate a 4-3 suspension with a change of bass (to a first-inversion triad) as the suspension resolves.

(1) Write the Roman numerals and figures in the charts below. Where chords are arpeggiated, take the lowest-sounding pitch as the bass note. Mark the suspensions in your score, but your analysis (Roman numerals and figures) does not need to account for them.

m. 9   10   11   12

Roman numerals:

Key: _____

m. 24   25   26   27   28

Roman numerals:

(2) What is the last chord in measure 11? And why is this particular chord quality used here?

(3) What type of cadence ends the first excerpt? _____

(4) The figure 5 in measures 25 and 27 indicates a root-position triad. What chord is it, and what is its function?

(5) What type of cadence ends the second excerpt? _____

B. Fanny Mendelssohn Hensel, "Neue Liebe, neues Leben" (p. 122)   **2.22** 🎧

Listen to the first verse of this song (mm. 1–16), while following your anthology score, then answer the questions below.

(1) Draw a diagram that accurately represents the phrase structure. Include the number of measures in each phrase, alphabet letters to show whether the phrases are parallel or contrasting, and cadence types. What terminology do we use to describe this relationship?

(2) This melody features a melodic sequence. Bracket the initial pattern and each repetition of the sequence in your score. Write a few sentences to describe the sequence. How many repetitions are in each phrase? By what generic interval is each pattern transposed? Are any repetitions incomplete? Why?

II. Extended analysis

A. Mozart, Piano Sonata in B♭ Major, K. 333, third movement, mm. 1–16a

Play this excerpt at the piano, or sight-sing the upper line in a comfortable range while playing the bass-clef lines. Then answer the questions below.

(1) Draw a phrase diagram of all sixteen measures. Include the number of measures in each phrase, alphabet letters to show whether the phrases are parallel or contrasting, and cadence types. How many phrases are in this excerpt? How many periods?

(2) After presenting his initial idea in the opening measures, Mozart continuously develops it. Write a paragraph explaining how the composer varies the opening melody, focusing on types of embellishments. Be specific; give measure numbers.

B. Scott Joplin, "Solace" (p. 131)   **2.33** 🎧

(1) Begin by listening to the entire rag while following the score in your anthology. Draw a diagram that accurately represents the phrase structure of measures 61–68. Include the number of measures in each phrase, alphabet letters to show whether the phrases are parallel or contrasting, and cadence types. What terminology do we use to describe this relationship?

(2) What rhythmic motives can you identify that help contribute to the ragtime character of this piece? Discuss their use in these measures, citing specific instances.

(3) Now look at measures 69–80a. These phrases are in F Major (the primary key of this piece). Label each measure from 69 to 76 with the *one* Roman numeral that best describes its harmonic function. Don't worry about inversion symbols. There are many embellishing tones that may cloud the picture at first; circle and label them. It may help to play through the excerpt as you analyze. Hint: Consider the bass line and left-hand part first, then label the embellishing tones in the upper parts.

When you have completed your analysis of measures 69–72a, you have also analyzed measures 77–80a, which are identical. Now copy your Roman numeral analysis in the charts below, and label the harmonic functions (T, PD, and D).

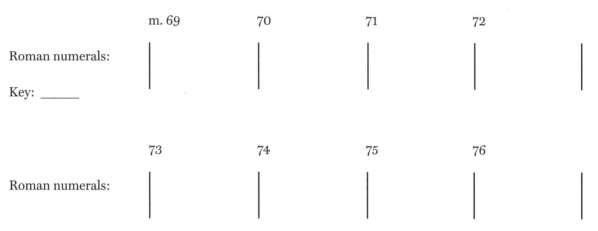

m. 69   70   71   72

Roman numerals:

Key: _____

73   74   75   76

Roman numerals:

(4) What type of cadence appears in measures 75–76? Comment on the strength of the cadence at measures 71–72 in comparison.

C. Franz Schubert, "Der Lindenbaum," from *Winterreise* (p. 194)   **3.16** 🎧

Start by listening to the introduction and first stanza of this song, while following your anthology score.

(1) Draw a phrase diagram of measures 9–24 (track 18). Include the number of measures in each phrase, alphabet letters to show whether the phrases are parallel or contrasting, and cadence types. How many phrases are in this excerpt? How many periods, and of what type?

(2) How does Schubert portray the sense of the text in the introduction? in the first verse?

(3) The introduction features a neighbor-note motive, C♯–B. Is the motive also a part of the verse? Where? Give measure numbers.

Diatonic Sequences

CHAPTER 18

Basic Elements

Writing sequences

A. Three-voice sequences

Each of the exercises below shows an incomplete sequence in three voices. These sequences usually appear in three parts rather than four to avoid the parallels that would occur with the usual doublings for four parts. First, examine the beginning. Locate the linear-intervallic pattern on which the sequence is built. Determine how the chords are voiced in the pattern and the interval (in time) between restatements of the pattern. Then use this information to complete each sequence, connecting to the conclusion shown.

(1)

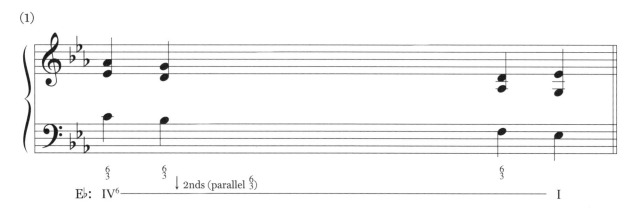

(2)

(3)

B$\flat$: I ————————— $\downarrow$ 2nds (7—6 sus) ————————— V

B. Four-voice sequences

Each exercise below shows an incomplete sequence in four voices. First, examine the beginning. The root motion between chords is specified, as are any inversions. Consider how the chords are voiced and what the interval is between restatements of the pattern. Then use this information to complete the sequence in each, connecting into the conclusion shown.

(1)

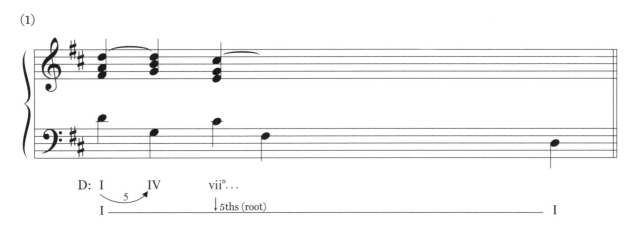

D: I ⟍5⟋ IV   vii°...
I ————— $\downarrow$ 5ths (root) ————————— I

(2)

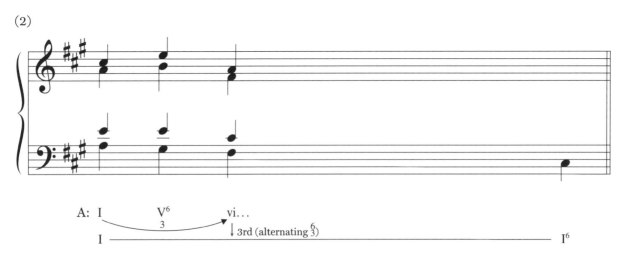

A: I   V^6 vi...
       3
I ————— $\downarrow$ 3rd (alternating $\frac{6}{3}$) ————————— I^6

(3)

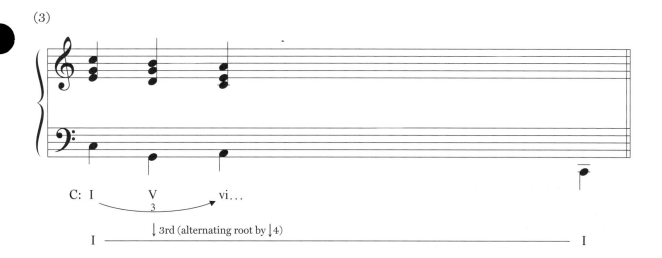

C: I   V   vi…
3

I   ↓ 3rd (alternating root by ↓4)   I

Writing Exercises

I. Creative writing

Write your own sequence-based composition incorporating the sequence frameworks given in Chapter 18 of the text or in the "Basic Elements" section. For each of the composition projects below (A, B, and C), follow this procedure.

- Choose a sequence framework (see, for instance, Examples 18.3, 18.9, 18.13, 18.16b, 18.19, or 18.21).

- Transpose the framework to the key and mode of your choice, then write it out in the new key.

- Precede the sequence with a progression to establish the tonic—a simple tonic expansion—and add a cadence after the sequence concludes.

- You may want to rearrange the upper parts: you can place the voice-leading strands in any part, as long as the entire strand is in the same part and there is one of each strand. The bass lines of these frameworks need to stay in the bass.

- Improvise to embellish your composition—add passing tones between skips, decorate repeated pitches with neighbors, or arpeggiate your SATB chords into a piano accompaniment.

A. Song/solo

Write a song or solo instrumental phrase with keyboard accompaniment, based on one of the sequence frameworks. Establish the tonic at the beginning, before the sequence, and end with a cadence. Exend your composition by repeating the phrase. End the first statement with an inconclusive cadence. End its restatement with a conclusive cadence.

If you are writing for a vocalist, select an appropriate text, and make sure the vocal line falls within an appropriate range for the singer (soprano, alto, tenor, or bass). If writing for an instrument, make sure your solo falls within the range for that instrument. For transposing instruments, prepare both a score for the accompanist and a transposed part for the soloist.

B. Song/solo (variant)

Write your composition for unaccompanied vocalist or solo instrument. This assignment is more difficult, because the solo line will need to capture the sense of the sequence framework through arpeggiation or compound melody, while making a playable/singable line.

C. Keyboard solo

Write a keyboard solo based on one of the sequence frameworks. Follow the instructions in A to create two phrases. Suggested procedure: Start by playing the framework as given, then add melodic/rhythmic embellishments to make an interesting keyboard solo, or work with an arpeggiation pattern. Keep the voice-leading strands of the framework intact to avoid voice-leading problems. Make sure that the parts fall well under the performer's hands and are idiomatic for the keyboard.

II. Figured-bass realization

Realize the figured basses below. For each:

- Use keyboard spacing.
- Place one chord on each beat in the given meter, revoicing the upper parts as needed to cooperate with the arpeggiations in the bass line.
- Provide a Roman numeral analysis, and label cadence types.
- Identify the sequence type, matching it to a framework in Chapter 18 of the text.
- Follow any specific instructions included with the individual exercises.

A. Johann Sebastian Bach, Cantata No. 140 ("Wachet auf"), first movement, mm. 5–9a

(1) Realize the figured-bass continuo part on the grand staff below.

(2) What type of sequence is this? _____
How does it connect to the tonic chord in measure 9? _____
If the sequence had continued into measure 9, what other chord would you have expected there instead?
_____

(3) Listen to a realization of this section on a recording in your library, or perform your realization at the keyboard.

B. Antonio Vivaldi, *Gloria*, first movement, mm. 8–15

(1) Realize the figured-bass continuo part below. First examine the figures. What type of sequence is this? Label it in your analysis. This type is usually voiced with two upper parts instead of three. Write in the two upper parts in keyboard style, with a half-note harmonic rhythm.

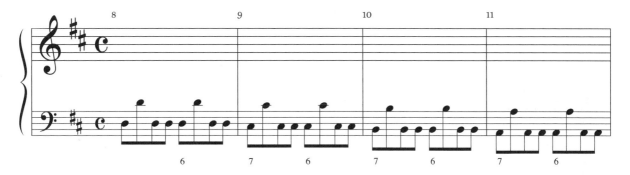

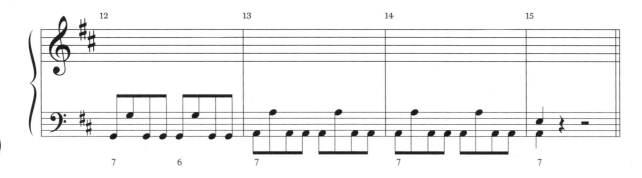

(2) Label the cadence in measures 12–13. After you complete your realization, listen to a recording of the movement in the library, and compare your realization.

C. Vivaldi, *Gloria*, seventh movement, mm. 18–26a

(1) Realize the figured-bass continuo part below. Despite the key signature, this excerpt is in C Major.

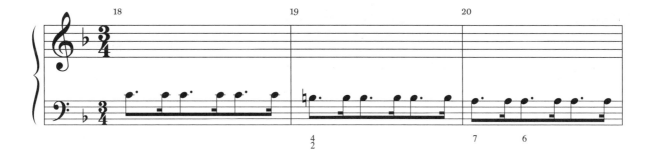

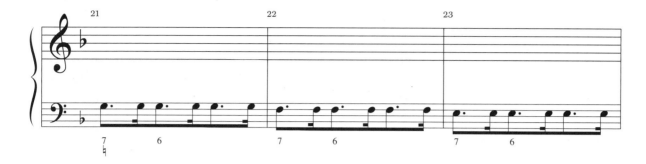

(2) Find a sequence, and label its type with a horizontal line to show the extent of the sequence. After you complete your realization, listen to a recording in your library to hear how the choral parts fit with the accompaniment.

(3) Describe a rhythmic device that is featured in this movement.

Analysis

I. Brief analysis

A. Earl Edwards, Eugene Dixon, and Bernice Williams, "Duke of Earl," mm. 1–4a

Analyze the four-measure chord progression featured in this 1960s song, shown below. Provide a Roman numeral analysis below the staff, and identify the sequence type.

Sequence type: _____

B. Richard Rodgers and Oscar Hammerstein, "My Favorite Things," from *The Sound of Music*, mm. 27–30

Analyze the measures shown below from this well-known musical. Write in the popular-music chord symbols above the staff, one chord per bar. What type of sequence is this?

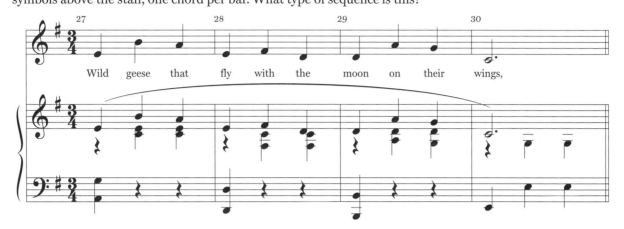

Sequence type: _____

II. Extended analysis

A. Wolfgang Amadeus Mozart, Sonata in C Major K. 545, first movement (p. 149)   **2.57** 🎧

Listen to the opening of this movement, following your anthology score.

(1) Make a reduction of measures 5–12 (track 58) on the grand staff below, with one chord per measure. The first chord has been completed for you. (Note: Although scales are prominent in this excerpt, don't show them in the reduction. They simply decorate the underlying sequence framework.)

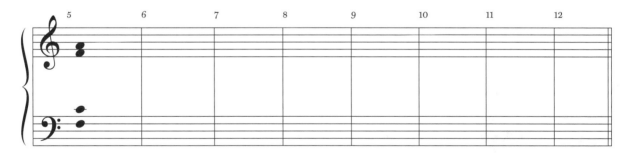

(2) What are the intervals between the outer voices in the sequence?

(3) What clues indicate that measure 9 is not part of the sequence?

(4) What is unusual about the harmonic progression from measure 9 to 10? There is a voice exchange in this passage—where?

(5) How are the arpeggiated chords in measure 11 represented in Roman numerals and figures, and what is their meaning in the phrase?

(6) Make a reduction of measures 18–21 (track 62) on the grand staff below. This passage is in G Major. The harmony changes twice per measure. In the reduction, show only the outer parts for each chord in your reduced framework, but label with Roman numerals that accurately represent each harmony. The first measure has been completed for you.

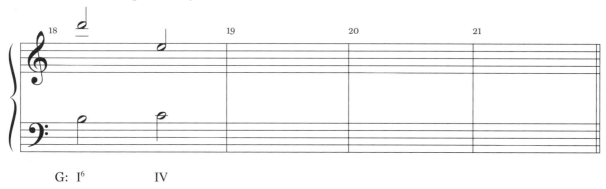

(7) Which of the sequence types we considered in this chapter is featured in these measures?

B. Ludwig Van Beethoven, Sonatina in F Major, Op. Posth., second movement (p. 52)   **1.60** 🎧

Listen carefully to the sequences in measures 49–56 (track 61), while following the score in your anthology. This section is in D minor. Examine measures 49–52 first, then measures 53–56.

(1) Make a reduction on the grand staff below. Include all chord members in their correct octave, but leave out any embellishing tones. Label with Roman numerals.

(2) How long is the pattern in measures 49–52 and in measures 53–56?

(3) What root progressions do you find in the patterns?

(4) What intervals between voices structure this sequence?

(5) What type of cadence concludes this excerpt?

(6) Is this sequence similar to one in the examples in Chapter 18?

Intensifying the Dominant:

Secondary Dominants and Secondary Leading-Tone Chords; New Voice-Leading Chords

CHAPTER 19

Basic Elements

I. Spelling secondary dominant and leading-tone chords to V

On the treble staves below, spell each of the triads or seventh chords requested. Provide the correct key signature, then add any necessary accidentals to adjust the chord quality. (Hint: If it is helpful to you, you may also add the dominant chord of resolution as a "block chord"—don't worry about voice-leading in the resolution for now.)

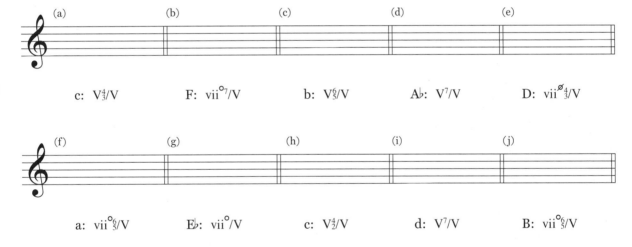

(a) (b) (c) (d) (e)

c: V^4_3/V F: vii°^{7}/V b: V^6_5/V A♭: V^7/V D: vii$^{ø4}_3$/V

(f) (g) (h) (i) (j)

a: vii°$^6_5$/V E♭: vii°/V c: V^4_2/V d: V^7/V B: vii°$^6_5$/V

II. Secondary dominants

Part-write the progressions in the specified keys below, using SATB voicing (and quarter notes). Draw arrows to show the resolution of leading tones up and chordal sevenths down. Compare these progressions with those in Chapter 12, "Basic Elements"/III.

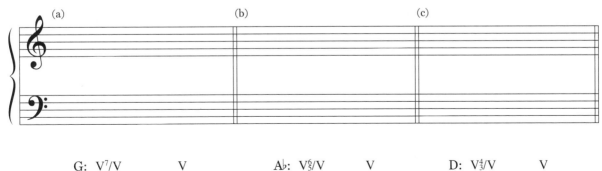

(a) (b) (c)

G: V^7/V V A♭: V^6_5/V V D: V^4_3/V V

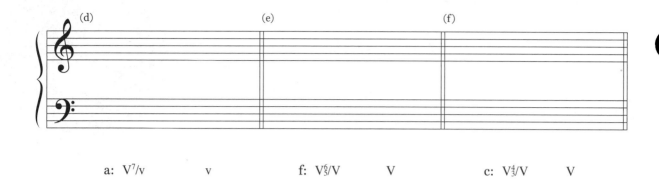

a: V⁷/v   v   f: V⁶₅/V   V   c: V⁴₃/V   V

What is the relationship between each progression in this exercise and the corresponding one in Chapter 12?

III. Secondary leading-tone chords

Part-write the progressions in the specified keys below, using SATB voicing (and half notes). Draw arrows to show the resolution of leading tones up and chordal sevenths down. Compare these progressions with those in Chapter 15, "Basic Elements"/III.

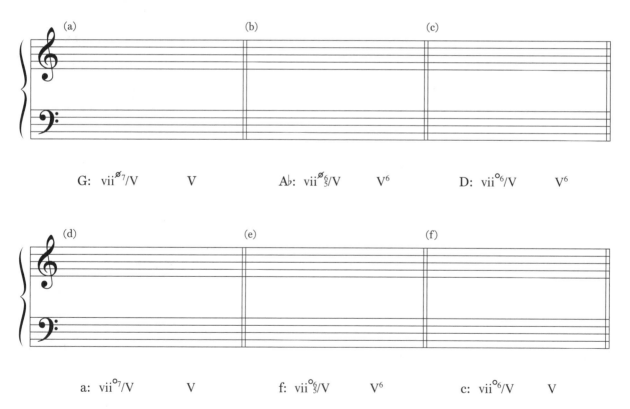

G: vii°⁷/V   V   A♭: vii°⁶₅/V   V⁶   D: vii°⁶/V   V⁶

a: vii°⁷/V   V   f: vii°⁶₅/V   V⁶   c: vii°⁶/V   V

What is the relationship between each progression in this exercise and the corresponding one in Chapter 15?

IV. Dominant expansions

Part-write the dominant expansion progressions in the specified keys below, using SATB voicing (and quarter notes). Draw arrows to show the resolution of leading tones up and chordal sevenths down.

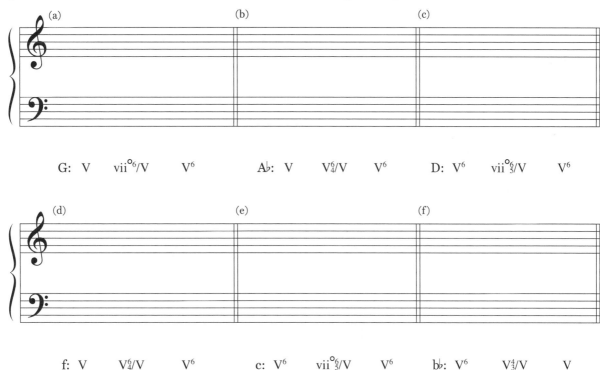

(a) G: V   vii°⁶/V   V⁶   (b) A♭: V   V⁶₄/V   V⁶   (c) D: V⁶   vii°⁶₅/V   V⁶

(d) f: V   V⁶₄/V   V⁶   (e) c: V⁶   vii°⁶₅/V   V⁶   (f) b♭: V⁶   V⁴₃/V   V

V. Chromatic voice exchange

Part-write the chords in the specified keys below, using SATB voicing. Check to see that the ♯4̂ is approached either by a chromatic voice exchange or by chromatic motion in a single voice. Mark the voice exchange between the staves. For each, the rhythmic context is ♩ ♩ ♩ in ⁴₄. Compare these progressions with those in Chapter 15, "Basic Elements"/V.

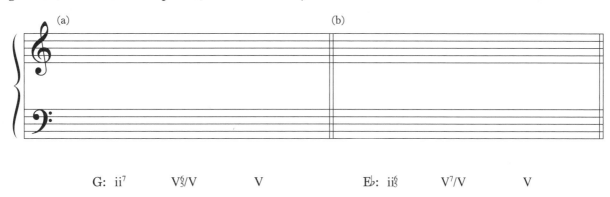

(a) G: ii⁷   V⁶₅/V   V   (b) E♭: ii⁶₅   V⁷/V   V

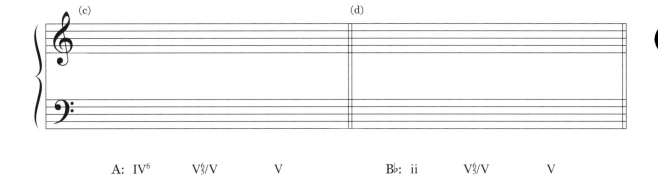

A: IV⁶   V⁶₃/V   V   B♭: ii   V⁶₃/V   V

What is the relationship between each progression in this exercise and the corresponding one in Chapter 15?

Writing Exercises

I. Part-writing

On your own staff paper, part-write the progressions in the keys indicated below, using SATB spacing.

A. G Major, $\frac{2}{4}$: I V⁶₄ I⁶ | ii⁷ V⁶₃/V | V V⁶₅ | I

B. E♭ Major, $\frac{3}{4}$: I V⁶₄ I⁶ | IV ii | V⁶ V⁴₃/V V⁷ | I

C. Elaborate the progression in either A or B into a freer keyboard texture.

II. Melody harmonization

On staff paper, harmonize the melodies in the specified meters below, using SATB voicing and a harmonic rhythm of one chord per beat. Write a secondary dominant or leading-tone chord to harmonize ♯4̂, and include a dominant expansion with a passing chord in each setting.

A.

B. With a harmonic rhythm of one chord per beat, what tempo would be appropriate for this melody? How would you harmonize the tune differently if the $\frac{3}{8}$ meter were conducted with one beat per measure?

C. This chorale tune, "Ein feste Burg" ("A Mighty Fortress," mm. 1–4), can be harmonized in many ways. Use a secondary dominant approach to a half cadence to end the first phrase and a PAC to end the second. After completing and checking your harmonization for part-writing errors, add embellishing tones to make a typical chorale texture. Then compare your harmonization with those of your classmates, and with Bach's.

III. Figured-bass realization

Realize the figured basses below, drawn from Bach's Cantata No. 140, "Wachet auf." For each:

- Use keyboard spacing.
- Place one chord on each beat in the given meter, revoicing the upper parts as needed to cooperate with the arpeggiations in the bass line.
- Write in a Roman numeral analysis underneath the bass staff.
- Follow any instructions included with the individual exercises.
- Listen to realizations of these passages on recordings in your library.

A. First movement, mm. 1–5a

In the space below your analysis, explain the role of each of the $\frac{4}{2}$ chords.

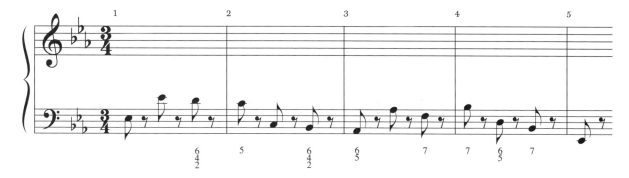

B. Fourth movement, mm. 1–7a

For this example, the unison melody played in the strings is included on a separate staff above the grand staff. In the space below your analysis, explain the role of each $\frac{4}{2}$ chord. Compare the string melody with the block-chord accompaniment you have written. Circle and label all embellishments in the melody.

C. Fourth movement, mm. 7b–12a

Again, the unison melody played in the strings is included on a separate staff above the grand staff. Analyze this portion of the movement in B♭ Major. In the space below your analysis, explain the role of each $\frac{4}{2}$ chord. Compare the string melody with your block-chord accompaniment. Circle and label all embellishments in the melody.

Analysis

I. Brief analysis

A. Jeremiah Clarke, *Trumpet Voluntary* (*Prince of Denmark's March*) (p. 69)   **1.69**

Listen to this piece while following your anthology score, then write in the Roman numerals and figures for measures 55–56 (track 72). Consider the pitches played by both the keyboard and the trumpet. Label the embellishing tones in both the trumpet melody and the accompaniment.

(1) Copy your Roman numeral analysis into the chart below.

	m. 55	56	
Roman numerals:			
Key: _____			

(2) Which two types of embellishing tones appear in the trumpet part?

B. Wolfgang Amadeus Mozart, Piano Sonata in C Major, K. 545, first movement (p. 149)   2.57 🎧

Look at measures 8–12 of this movement in the anthology (track 59). Listen to the passage, then answer the following questions.

(1) What chromatic detail can be interpreted as implying a chord?

(2) Write in Roman numerals and figures for these measures. Beneath, provide a contextual analysis.

m. 8   9   10

Roman numerals: | | | |

Key: _____

11   12

Roman numerals: | | |

(3) What type of cadence is this? _____

C. Clarke, *Trumpet Voluntary* (p. 69)

(1) Look at measure 4 of this score in your anthology. When we examined this phrase in an earlier chapter, we didn't consider the function of the G in the bass line on beat 4. What chord does the G create, and what is its function?

(2) Does this chord connect as expected to the chord at the beginning of measure 5?

II. Extended analysis

A. Mozart, String Quartet in D minor, K. 421, third movement (p. 157)   2.74

Listen carefully to this movement while following the score in your anthology.

(1) Make a reduction of measures 48–55 (from the Trio; track 80) on the grand staff below. For the violin 2, viola, and cello parts, represent each pitch in the octave it sounds. Show arpeggiations in the cello by the pitch sounding on the downbeat.

(2) Write the Roman numerals and figures for each chord underneath your reduction.

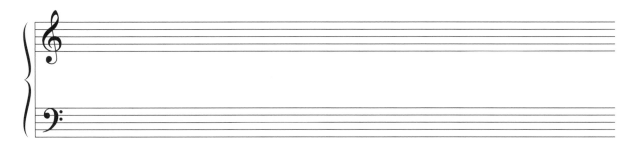

(3) For each secondary dominant, mark the resolution of any tendency tones, and comment beneath the staff if any of them resolve irregularly.

(4) What is the relationship between the violin 1 part and the reduced chords you have shown above? Circle all embellishing tones, and label them. Which embellishing tones appear the most?

B. Clarke, *Trumpet Voluntary* (p. 69)   1.69

Listen to this piece while following the score in your anthology.

(1) Write in the Roman numerals and figures for measures 17–24 in the score (track 73). When analyzing the chords, include both the keyboard and trumpet pitches. Label the embellishing tones in the trumpet melody.

(2) How are the two phrases that make up this passage alike in their harmonic and melodic organization? How do they differ?

(3) Give the measure numbers where you find a secondary dominant chord. What is the function of this chord within the phrase, and how does it impact the cadence?

(4) Write a paragraph contrasting measures 49–56 with measures 41–48. Consider types of embellishing tones, cadences, harmonic rhythm, melodic contour, and other musical features. Give specific examples (and measure numbers).

C. John Philip Sousa, "The Stars and Stripes Forever" (p. 220)   **3.41** 🎧

Listen to this piece while following the score in your anthology.

(1) Write in the Roman numerals and figures for measures 13–20 in the score (track 43).

(2) Provide a diagram below that divides these measures into two phrases. Include measure numbers and cadence types. What is alike and what is different between phrases?

(3) Write a paragraph discussing Sousa's use of "⁶₄ chords." How do you interpret these in your analysis? Give specific examples of each type, with an explanation of your analysis. Do all these ⁶₄ chords carry the same type of structural weight for the performer?

(4) Explain the role of each A♮ in this passage. Should all the A♮s be played the same way? What chord does the G♭ make in measure 18?

D. Alan Menken and Tim Rice, "A Whole New World," from *Aladdin*, mm. 24b–29, 32b–37

Sight-sing the melody in the two phrases below, while accompanying yourself at the keyboard. The chord progressions for the first three measures of each phrase are the same, with some slight changes.

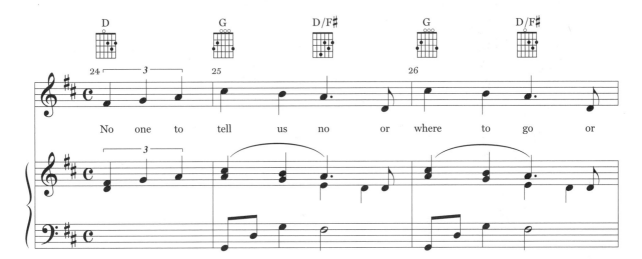

(1) Write in the Roman numerals and figures, and circle and identify all embellishing tones. For now, you may omit the chords on the upbeat of measure 32 and downbeat of measure 36. (We will return to these in Chapter 21.)

(2) What harmonies underly "only dreaming" and "whole new world" (mm. 27–29)? How does the choice of harmonies illustrate the text?

(3) One of the secondary dominants resolves deceptively—to what chord?

(4) Consider the length of these two phrases—what is unusual about them? Why do you think the composer made that choice?

Phrase Rhythm and Motivic Analysis

CHAPTER 20

Basic Elements

I. Connecting and expanding phrases

Play each of the excerpts below, or listen to it on your CD. Number the measures to show the hypermetric structure, then identify the technique illustrated (prefix, elision, *Fortspinnung*, lead-in, and so on). Answer any questions asked about the excerpt.

A. Franz Joseph Haydn, Piano Sonata No. 27 in G Major, first movement, mm. 1–12a

Technique illustrated: _____

(Hint: Where is the first authentic cadence? What happens after that cadence?)

B. George Frideric Handel, "Rejoice greatly," from *Messiah*, mm. 18–25 (p. 107)   **2.13** 🎧

Technique illustrated: _____

(1) How many phrases occur in these measures? With what types of cadences do they conclude?

(2) Identify the harmonic sequences in measures 18–23.

(3) How are the phrases connected in measure 23?

C. Haydn, Piano Sonata No. 13 in E Major, second movement, mm. 1–24

(1) This example is an entire short movement. What type of phrase structure is illustrated in the first eight measures? _____

(2) After numbering the hypermetric structure, you will discover one unit of six measures rather than four. Give measure numbers for this six-measure phrase: _____ What technique of phrase expansion is illustrated here? _____ We can create a coherent four-measure phrase by eliminating two measures; which two? _____

(3) In the final phrase, you will discover a unit of ten measures rather than eight. What technique of phrase expansion is illustrated here? _____ We can create a coherent four-measure phrase by eliminating two measures; which two? _____

II. Motivic transformations

Excerpts from two Bach fugues are given below. Play through each example, or listen to a recording from your library. Name the motivic transformation that each passage illustrates.

A. Johann Sebastian Bach, Fugue in A minor, from *The Well-Tempered Clavier*, Book 1, mm. 1–4, 67–70

Bach's fugue subject appears in the first three measures. How is the subject transformed in measures 67–70? _____

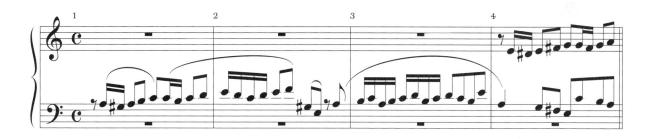

B. Bach, Fugue in C Major for Organ, mm. 1–3a, 27–29a, and 49–52a

The fugue subject appears in the first measure.

(1) What transformation does the subject undergo in measures 27–29a?

(2) What is the relationship of the subject in the organ pedal in measures 49–52a to the original?

(3) In the score, mark any other instance of the subject that you see in measures 49–52a. Label any motivic transformation.

Writing Exercises

Motivic transformations

Each of the motives below is from the first movement of Muzio Clementi's Sonatina in F Major, Op. 36, No. 4. Sing or play each motive, then write an inversion, an augmentation, and a diminution. For the inversion, invert the contour and generic intervals (don't attempt to match the exact intervals). For the augmentation and diminution, double or halve the rhythmic values. Play your solutions to make sure they "make sense" in the key and meter. For some of these, there are several possible solutions. A first note is suggested for the inversions.

A. From mm. 18–19

Motive 1

Inversion

Augmentation

Diminution

B. From mm. 1–2

Motive 2

Inversion

Augmentation

Diminution

C. From m. 13

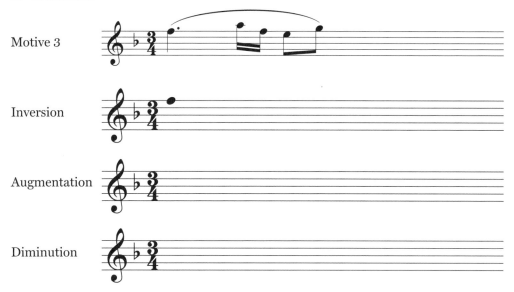

Motive 3

Inversion

Augmentation

Diminution

Analysis

I. Brief analysis

A. Wolfgang Amadeus Mozart, Piano Sonata in C Major, K. 545, third movement (p. 155)   **2.71** 🎧

Listen to the first period of this movement (mm. 1–8) while following your anthology score. Then answer the questions that follow.

(1) Provide a Roman numeral analysis in the chart below, and label each cadence type. (Anacrusis goes to the left of bar line.)

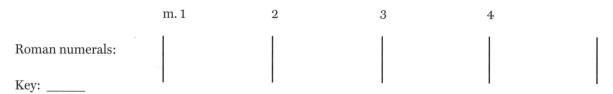

Roman numerals:

Key: _____

Cadence type: _____

Roman numerals:

Cadence type: _____

(2) What makes the harmonic analysis of the upbeat to measures 1 and 5 challenging?

(3) What is the relationship between these phrases called? Be sure to consider Mozart's working out of the opening motive in making your decision. Write a sentence or two that justifies your decision.

(4) Listen to the the rest of the movement. In your score, identify at least two motives in the first eight measures that appear later in the piece. Name them, and write a paragraph describing how Mozart uses them later in the movement. Be sure to cite specific measure numbers.

B. Bach, Prelude, from Cello Suite No. 2 in D minor, mm. 24–36a

Play through this excerpt several times at the piano or on your instrument. Use your ears to identify melodic sequences, step progressions, and phrase structure. You need not do a complete harmonic analysis. Then answer the following questions.

(1) Find two melodic sequences. For each, mark the initial statement and each subsequent pattern. What is the generic interval of transposition for each recurrence?

(2) Find one step progression that implies a compound melody. Circle the pitches to show their stepwise connection.

(3) Identify and label any cadences you hear in the passage.

(4) With your answers to the first three questions as a guide, write a paragraph about performing this passage. Describe the phrase structure, and include one of these terms: sentence structure, *Fortspinnung*, phrase group.

C. John Lennon and Paul McCartney, "Michelle," mm. 34–44a

Listen to a recording of this Beatles song, or sing the melody while playing the bass line at the keyboard. Then answer the questions below.

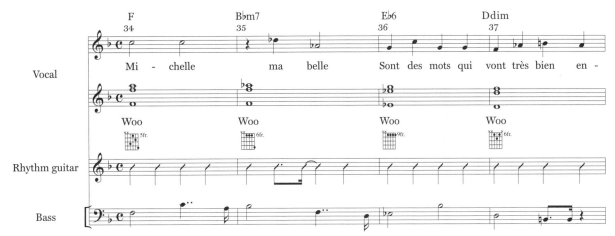

(1) Draw a diagram that represents the phrase structure. Include the number of measures in each phrase, alphabet letters to show whether the phrases are parallel or contrasting, and cadence types. What terminology do we use to describe this relationship?

(2) What causes the uneven phrase lengths? What term describes the technique of phrase expansion?

(3) How is the melody in measures 34–39 constructed?

II. *Extended analysis*

A. Ludwig van Beethoven, Sonata for Violin and Piano in C minor, Op. 30, No. 2, first movement, mm. 1–24a

Listen to the first twenty-four measures of this sonata movement from a recording in your library. These measures present the primary thematic material for this section.

(1) Provide a phrase diagram for the first sixteen measures. Include the number of measures in each phrase, alphabet letters to show whether the phrases are parallel or contrasting, and cadence types. What terminology do we use to describe this relationship?

(2) What is the relationship between the violin and piano in the first sixteen measures? What factors might contribute to the idea that the first eight measures are introductory in nature?

(3) Once the violin enters in measure 9, what factors make us unite the next eight measures (mm. 9–16) into one long phrase rather than two four-bar phrases? What are these four-bar units called? What type of eight-bar phrase does the motivic structure suggest?

(4) Do the remaining eight measures (17–24) form one phrase or two? What is the source of their thematic material?

B. Bach, *Brandenburg Concerto* No. 4, first movement, mm. 1–35

Listen to a recording of this movement from your library. Then make a three-voice reduction of measures 1–13a on your own staff paper. Include the bass line from the continuo part (through the downbeat of m. 13), and select pitches for the upper parts from the solo violin and two flute parts. You may displace these notes into lower octaves if you wish. There is no one right answer for the reduction; it will simply function as a tool for Roman numeral and phrase analysis.

Write the Roman numerals for each chord underneath your reduction, then play your reduction and listen to find phrase beginnings and endings.

(1) Compare the two phrases of the opening section: what is alike and what is different? What is the relationship between the two flute parts? How are the phrases linked?

(2) Look at just the solo violin part in the passage that extends from measure 13 to 22. This melody features melodic sequences. Mark each pattern of the sequence in your score. What is the interval of transposition between patterns? What happens to the sequence in measures 18 and following? Does the interval of transposition change?

(3) Compare measures 1–13 with 23–35. Write a short paragraph about the similarities and differences.

(4) What term best describes the phrase structure in measures 1–35? Why?

C. Bach, Invention No. 8 in F Major

Begin by listening to a recording of this piece from your music library, or play through the work at the piano. Write an essay on its melodic and motivic structure (for now, don't worry about harmonic structure). Over the course of your essay, include answers to the following questions, but don't simply organize your essay as a list of answers.

(1) In the first two measures, identify at least two motives that return over the course of the invention. Give the motives labels, and mark their recurrences in the score. Then discuss how and where Bach uses them, giving specific examples. Do you find any inversions or other transformations?

(2) Does Bach feature period structures or *Fortspinnung* in his melodies? Support your answer by citing specific measure numbers and examples.

(3) Discuss Bach's use of melodic sequence and compound melody, giving at least two examples of each.

PART

Further Expansion of the Harmonic Vocabulary

CHAPTER 21

Tonicizing Scale Degrees Other Than V

Basic Elements

I. Spelling secondary dominant and leading-tone chords

On the treble staves below, spell each of the triads or seventh chords requested. Provide the correct key signature, then add any necessary accidentals to adjust the chord quality. (Hint: If it is helpful, you may also provide the chord of resolution as a block chord; don't worry about voice-leading for now.)

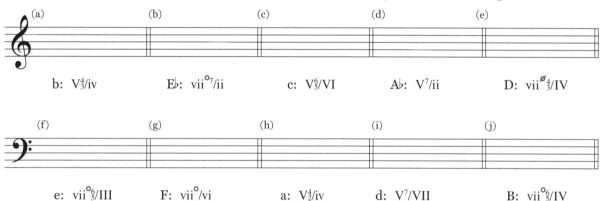

(a) b: V^4_3/iv   (b) E♭: vii°⁷/ii   (c) c: V^6_5/VI   (d) A♭: V^7/ii   (e) D: vii⌀$^4_3$/IV

(f) e: vii°$^6_5$/III   (g) F: vii°/vi   (h) a: V^4_2/iv   (i) d: V^7/VII   (j) B: vii°$^6_5$/IV

II. Resolving secondary dominants

Part-write the progressions in the specified keys below, using SATB voicing. Provide the key signature, and draw arrows to show the resolution of leading tones up and chordal sevenths down. You may want to review voice-leading guidelines for V^7 chords in Chapter 12 of the text (see Example 12.10).

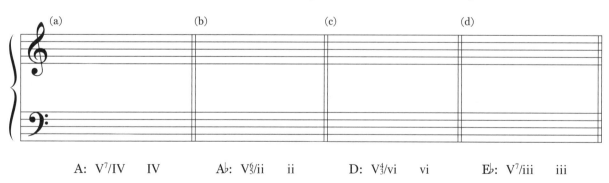

(a) A: V^7/IV   IV   (b) A♭: V^6_5/ii   ii   (c) D: V^4_3/vi   vi   (d) E♭: V^7/iii   iii

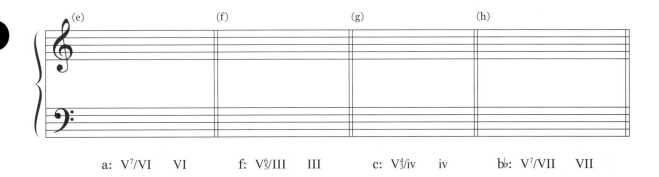

a: V⁷/VI   VI   f: V⁶₅/III   III   c: V⁴₃/iv   iv   b♭: V⁷/VII   VII

III. Resolving secondary leading-tone chords

Part-write the progressions in the specified keys below, using SATB voicing. Provide the key signature, and draw arrows to show the resolution of leading tones up and chordal sevenths down. You may want to review voice-leading guidelines for vii°⁷ chords in Chapter 15 (see Example 15.6).

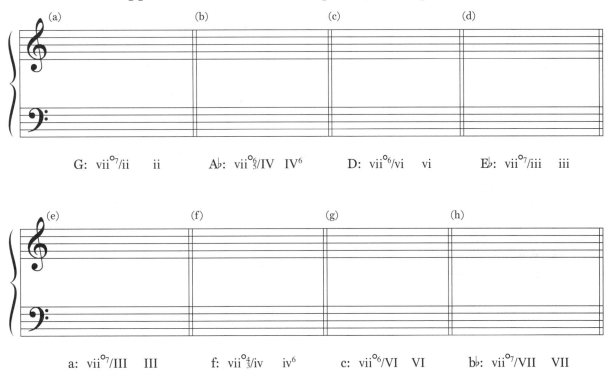

G: vii°⁷/ii   ii   A♭: vii°⁶₅/IV   IV⁶   D: vii°⁶/vi   vi   E♭: vii°⁷/iii   iii

a: vii°⁷/III   III   f: vii°⁴₃/iv   iv⁶   c: vii°⁶/VI   VI   b♭: vii°⁷/VII   VII

Writing Exercises

I. Part-writing

On your own staff paper, part-write the progressions in the keys indicated below, using SATB spacing. For each, identify the parts of the basic phrase T–PD–D–T. Choose one progression to elaborate into a freer keyboard texture.

A. E Major, $\frac{3}{4}$: I V$\frac{4}{3}$/IV | IV^6 V$\frac{4}{3}$/ii | ii^6 V V^7 | I

B. G minor, $\frac{6}{8}$: i V^7/VI | VI V/iv | iv ii$^{\o 6}_5$ V^7 | i

II. Folk melody harmonization

Harmonize the melodies below. Start by singing or listening to the melody, and circle and label each embellishing tone. Set the melody for vocal solo (or instrumental solo) and keyboard accompaniment, with a dotted-quarter-note harmonic rhythm for melody A and an eighth-note harmonic rhythm for melody B. Melody notes indicated by an * take a secondary dominant or leading-tone chord. To determine which applied chord to use, think first about how you will harmonize the following pitch.

We harmonized these same melodies in Chapter 17 of the workbook ("Writing Exercises"/I), without secondary-dominant-function chords; when you have completed your settings, compare your new harmonizations with those in Chapter 17.

A. "Believe me, if all those endearing young charms"

B. "Drink to me only with thine eyes"

III. Chorale harmonization

"Jesu, meine Freude" ("Jesus, My Joy")

This chorale tune may be harmonized in many ways. For this setting, don't modulate (although you may use tonicized half cadences). Set each melody pitch marked with an asterisk with either a secondary dominant or leading-tone chord. After completing and checking your harmonization for part-writing errors, add embellishing tones to make a typical chorale texture.

Bach set this melody many times. Compare your setting with one of his (for example, Chorale No. 138 in workbook Chapter 13, "Basic Elements"/I, or Chorale Nos. 96, 263, 283, 324, or 356), as well as with those of your classmates.

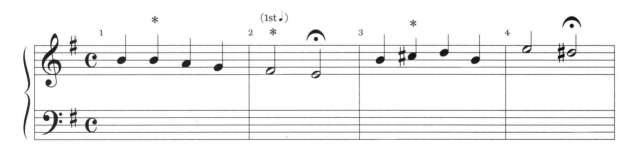

IV. Figured-bass realization

A. Johann Sebastian Bach, "Wachet auf" (Chorale No. 179), mm. 12b–16

Realize the figured bass on the grand staff below, in SATB voicing. Use a harmonic rhythm of one chord per half note in the bass line; passing tones in the bass line have been circled. Write in a Roman numeral analysis, then answer the following questions.

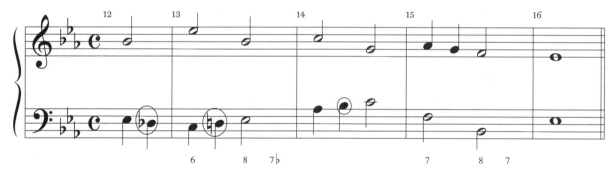

(1) How would you have analyzed the anacrusis if the harmonic rhythm had been one chord per quarter note instead of one chord per half note?

(2) Compare the chords in the anacrusis to those in measure 13b—what is alike, and what is different?

(3) After you have checked your part-writing, you may add embellishing tones as appropriate in chorale style. Then compare your setting with those of your classmates and with Bach's (anthology, p. 8), and listen to the passage on your CD (CD 1, track 9). On your own paper, write a paragraph summarizing the differences; explain why you made the choices you did and why Bach might have made different ones.

B. Antonio Vivaldi, *Gloria*, first movement, mm. 50–61

Realize the figured-bass continuo part on the grand staff below. Use keyboard voicing (three voices in the right hand, the bass line provided in the left) and a whole-note (with one exception) harmonic rhythm. Write in a Roman numeral analysis beneath the bass line, taking the key established at the end of the excerpt as the key for the entire section. In the space below your analysis, explain how each of the secondary dominant or leading-tone chords functions. Listen to a recording in your library to hear a realization with the choral parts.

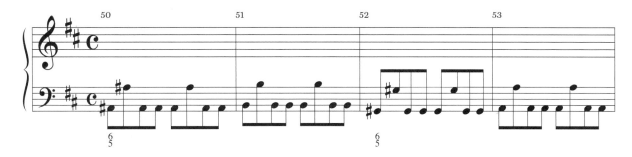

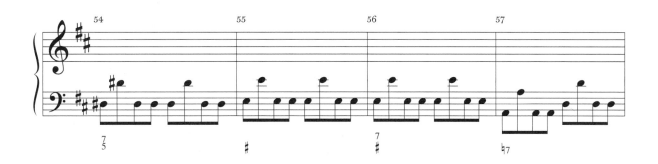

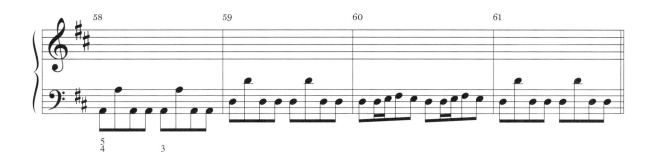

Analysis

I. Brief analysis

A. Scott Joplin, "Solace" (p. 131)   **2.33** 🎧

Listen to this work while following your anthology, and pay close attention to measures 53–60 (track 36). Circle each embellishing tone in these eight measures. The tonal motion of this phrase ends in the first half of measure 60. The final chord in that measure, under the fermata, is an anacrusis to the next phrase.

(1) Write in the Roman numerals and figures for measures 57–60 in your anthology, and copy them into the chart below. (Hint: Measures 58–59 present a two-measure tonicization of a diatonic harmony, including a "cadential $\begin{smallmatrix}8-7\\6-5\\4-3\end{smallmatrix}$" motion in the tonicized area.)

	m. 57	58	59	60	
Roman numerals:					
Key: _____					

(2) Which diatonic triad is tonicized in this phrase? Is this a common choice for a phrase ending?

B. Bach, Prelude in C Major, from *The Well-Tempered Clavier*, Book I (p. 13)   **1.17** 🎧

Follow your anthology score as you listen to this piece, paying special attention to measures 19–31 (track 21). The chord in measure 19 serves as the concluding tonic for the previous phrase and the elided beginning of another. Write in the Roman numerals and figures for this passage in your anthology. Use your analysis to answer the following questions.

(1) What is the chord in measure 20? Describe the resolution of each tendency tone in this chord. Does each resolve as expected? How is it approached?

(2) What is the quality of the chord in measure 21? Does the chord in measure 20 resolve to the chord you would expect? If not, what is unusual here?

(3) What is the quality of the chord in measure 22? What should it resolve to? Find the chord of resolution. (Hint: It is not in measure 23!) Do all the tendency tones resolve as expected?

(4) Explain how the chords in measures 25 and 29 fit within this functional area. What do we call this type of chord?

(5) What type of embellishing tone appears in measures 26 and 30? Where does this dissonance resolve?

(6) You probably noticed that all of the chords in measures 24–31 have the same bass note, G2, which functions as a pedal tone. As is usual with pedal tones, the pedal may or may not be a chord member in the measure's primary harmony. Analyze the chord in measure 28 without considering the pedal tone. What is its quality? How does it function here?

II. Extended analysis

A. Schubert, "Erlkönig" (p. 203)   **3.25** 🎧

Listen to this song while following the score in your anthology. The song tells the story of a sick boy and his father, who are riding through a stormy night on horseback. The son hears the calls of the Erlking (a mythic creature associated with darkness and doom), who eventually woos the boy to his death. The passages we will analyze are sung by the Erlking.

(1) Analyze the chords in measures 65 to 72 (downbeat) (track 27). Write in the Roman numerals and figures in your score and circle and label all embellishing tones, then copy the Roman numeral analysis into the chart below. Provide a contextual analysis (T, PD, and D) beneath.

	m. 65	66	67	68
Roman numerals:				
Key: _____				

	69	70	71	72	
Roman numerals:					

(2) Compare the progression in these measures with the progression in measures 58–65 (the first portion of this verse). Where do secondary dominants or seventh chords appear? What words do they emphasize?

(3) Now make a chordal reduction of measures 86–96 (in the piano) on your own staff paper (track 29). Write the Roman numerals and figures for each chord underneath your reduction. Above the staff, number each of the secondary dominants or leading-tone chords. Mark the resolution of any tendency tones, and comment beneath the staff if any of them resolve irregularly.

(4) What is the mood of this verse (mm. 86–96)? Write a paragraph discussing how the accompaniment pattern, melodic embellishment, and harmonic choices correspond to the mood of the text. What interpretive choices by the performers would help bring out the mood? Turn in your analyzed reduction of this passage with your paragraph.

B. Wolfgang Amadeus Mozart, Variations on "Ah, vous dirai-je, Maman" (p. 165)   **2.86** 🎧

Follow your anthology as you listen to this piece, paying particular attention to Variation X (track 93). Then review our analysis of measures 244b–248 in Chapter 21 of the text. In your anthology, write in the Roman numerals and figures for measures 249–256. Circle any secondary dominants or leading-tone chords. Examine each of these chords, and mark the resolution of the tendency tones.

(1) On staff paper, make a chordal reduction of measures 249–256. Copy out the Roman numerals and figures for these measures and the tendency-tone resolution markings from your score. Above the staff, number each of the secondary dominants or leading-tone chords.

(2) Beneath the staff, answer the following questions for each of the chords you numbered.

- Is the chord approached as you would expect?

- Is it resolved as expected?

- If it is not resolved as you would expect, what about the resolution makes it "work"?

(3) One special feature of this variation is the use of descending chromatic scales as voice-leading strands. Which voice-leading strands have chromatic scale segments? How do these segments fit into the chord progression that Mozart has chosen? Write your answer beneath your chordal reduction to turn in.

Modulation to Closely Related Keys

CHAPTER 22

Basic Elements

I. Pivot chords

A. Identifying multiple functions of triads

In the charts below, four triads are given in the top row. For each Roman numeral in the left-hand column, fill in the key in which the triad at the top would take that Roman numeral. Each chart has been started for you.

(1)

	C-Major triad	E-Major triad	G-Major triad	A♭-Major triad
I	C Major			
III	A minor			
IV	G Major			
V				
VI				
VII				

(2)

	A-minor triad	D-minor triad	F-minor triad	B-minor triad
i	A minor			
ii	G Major			
iii	F Major			
iv				
v				
vi				

B. Identifying pivots between key pairs

Following are pairs of keys. On your own staff paper, write out the diatonic triads for each degree of the scale in the first key. Then write the diatonic triads for the second key, positioned so that potential pivot chords are aligned vertically. Label all chords with Roman numerals. Put a box around each of the possible pivot-chord pairs.

(1) G Major, D Major

(2) D minor, F Major

(3) E Major, B Major

(4) G minor, B♭ Major

(5) A♭ Major, F minor

II. Modulating phrases with pivot chords

On staff paper, part-write the brief pivot-chord progressions in the specified keys below, using SATB voicing. Remember to include the accidentals needed for the cadence in the new key and to resolve all leading tones and sevenths. These progressions correspond to the key pairs in exercise I/B; select an appropriate pivot chord to place in the box provided. The first progression (and pivot) has been provided for you. After you have checked your part-writing, select one of these progressions to arrange into an Alberti bass accompaniment pattern.

   (Note: These phrase progressions have been lifted out of context; assume that the initial key is well established in previous phrases, and that the new key continues in a subsequent phrase.)

A. Modulation from G Major to D Major

Establish first key:

G:	I	V$^6_5$	I	vi
				=
Second key (V):		D:	ii	V^7	I

B. Modulation from D minor to F Major

Establish first key:

d:	i	vii°⁶	i⁶	
				=
Second key (III):		F:		V^7	I

C. Modulation from E Major to B Major

Establish first key:

E: I   V$\frac{4}{3}$ I^6

=

Second key (V):   B: V^7 I

D. Modulation from G minor to B♭ Major

Establish first key:

g: i   V$\frac{6}{5}$ i

=

Second key (III):   B♭:   V^7 I

E. Modulation from A♭ Major to F minor

Establish first key:

A♭:   I   vii^{o6} I^6

=

Second key (vi):   f: V^7 i

III. Melody harmonization

Each of the one-measure melodic fragments below, taken from the end of a chorale phrase, may be harmonized in at least two different keys. Set each fragment twice: once in the major or minor key associated with the key signature and once in another, closely related key. Use SATB voicing, label the key, and write an analysis with Roman numerals and figures under each cadence. You may write accidentals in the lower voices, but don't change the given pitches. The key signature (one sharp) applies to all four fragments.

Key: Key: Key: Key:

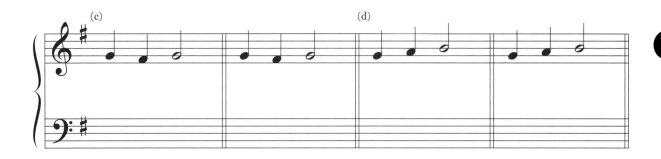

(c)   (d)

Key: _____   Key: _____   Key: _____   Key: _____

Writing Exercises

I. Part-writing

On staff paper, part-write the two-phrase progressions in the keys indicated below, using keyboard spacing.

A. D Major, $\frac{4}{4}$: ‖: I | vi | V⁷ | I ‖ I | [vi] =
A: [ii] | V⁷ | I :‖
(V)

B. G minor, $\frac{3}{4}$: ‖: i VI | iv ii^{ø6}₃ | V$^{8-7}_{4-3}$ | i ‖ i | [VI | iv] =
B♭ Major: [IV | ii] ii$^6_5$ | V$^{8-7}_{4-3}$ | I :‖
(III)

C. Write a keyboard elaboration of one of the progressions above. (Hint: Exercise A works well with a Classical-style Alberti bass; exercise B works well with a Baroque dance rhythmic pattern, such as a Minuet.)

II. Melody harmonization

Follow the instructions below to harmonize each melody. Provide a Roman numeral analysis of your harmonization, and indicate cadence types.

A. Wolfgang Amadeus Mozart, Menuetto I, from Piano Sonata in C Major, K. 6, mm. 1–8

Write a keyboard accompaniment for this solo instrumental melody. There are several chromatic tones in the melody. Which are embellishing? Which indicate a change of key? The first phrase (mm. 1–4) should confirm the initial key; the second (mm. 5–8) should modulate to the key indicated by the melodic shape. First sketch out your keyboard accompaniment in block chords with correct voice-leading, then arrange the chords in an appropriate accompaniment pattern for a Classical-period dance.

Andante grazioso

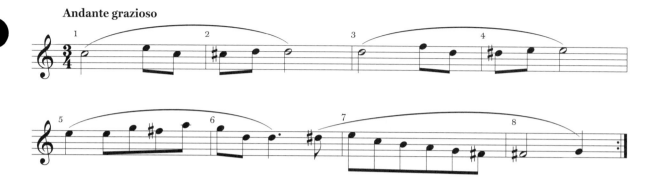

B. Franz Schubert, Waltz in B minor (D. 145, No. 6), mm. 1–16

Consider this melody as the right-hand part of a keyboard piece, and write a waltz-style accompaniment for the left hand. The melody divides into four phrases (four measures each), with a harmonic rhythm of one chord per measure. Examine the melody carefully to determine where and how to modulate. (Hint: The first and third phrases are identical, and end with a half cadence.)

On staff paper, sketch out your accompaniment in four-part block chords with correct voice-leading. Since all four voice-leading strands will be in the left hand part, voice them in keyboard spacing, with the upper three parts in close position in the upper bass-clef range and the lowest part in the lower bass-clef range. After you have checked your voice-leading, arrange the chords in an appropriate accompaniment pattern for a Romantic-period waltz (the first measure has been provided for you).

III. Figured-bass realization

Realize the following figured basses in four voices.

A. Johann Sebastian Bach, "Erhalt uns, bei deinem Wort" ("Keep Us in Thy Word," Chorale No. 72)

This figured bass has been adapted from a Bach chorale setting by retaining the bass and soprano lines, but representing the inner voices with figures. Of this chorale's four phrases, one establishes the tonic, one modulates to the relative major, one returns to the original tonic by means of a phrase modulation, and one tonicizes (but does not modulate to) the relative major. Realize the figured bass, using SATB spacing, with one chord on each beat in the given meter. Identify which phrase has each function as you prepare your realization. Then write in a Roman numeral analysis underneath the bass staff. Be sure to mark any pivot chords and key changes clearly.

When you have completed and checked your voice-leading, you may add in embellishing tones in chorale style to complete your setting. Try to arrange for a performance in class. Then compare your setting with those of your classmates and with Bach's; you should have chosen the same chords and progressions, but the embellishments will likely be different.

B. Jean Baptiste Loeillet, Sonata in B minor for Flute, Oboe or Violin, and Continuo, Op. 3, No. 10, fourth movement (Allegro), mm. 1–8

Realize this figured bass to accompany the flute melody. Use keyboard spacing (bass only in the left hand, three parts in the right), with one chord per bass note. If possible, arrange for a performance of your realization. Provide a Roman numeral analysis under the bass staff.

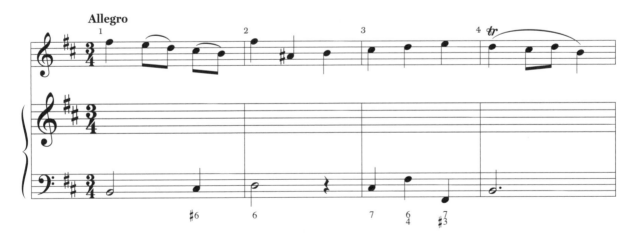

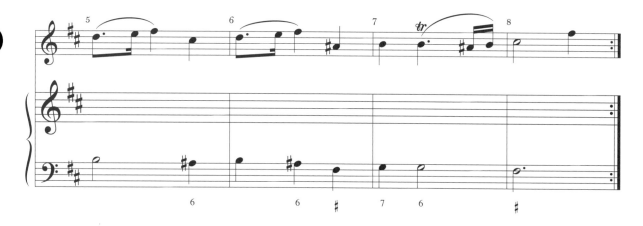

Is there a modulation in measures 5–8? If so, to what key, and how is it accomplished? If not, what is the progression, and why is it not a modulation?

C. Loeillet, Sonata in B minor, Op. 3, No. 10, third movement (Largo), mm. 1–8

Prepare a keyboard realization of the figured bass below to accompany the flute melody. Use keyboard spacing (bass only in the left hand, three parts in the right). With one exception (m. 7, beat 1), write no more than one chord per half-note beat in the $\frac{3}{2}$ meter; in some measures, a half-note chord followed by a whole-note chord or a dotted-whole-note chord will be more appropriate. Provide a Roman numeral analysis underneath the bass staff.

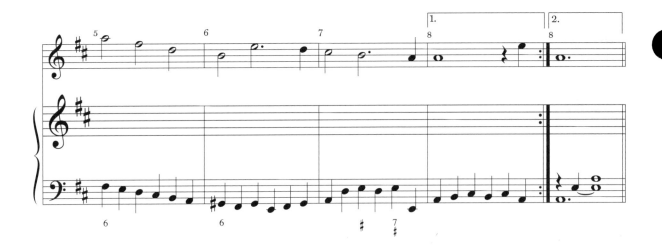

(1) What type of cadence is found in measures 3–4?

(2) What is the goal of the modulation in the first section? How is the modulation accomplished?

If possible, arrange a performance of your realization. Remember that continuo includes the keyboard part and an instrumentalist to reinforce the bass line. Bassoon works well with a flute or oboe soloist, and cello with a violin soloist; both are historically accurate. But take advantage of the instrumentation available in your class: the bass line could also be reinforced by a bass clarinet, trombone, or baritone. The melody may also be transposed for a trumpet, clarinet, saxophone, or other treble instrument as soloist—use your imagination and willing players!

Analysis

I. Brief analysis

A. Scott Joplin, "Pine Apple Rag" (p. 127)   **2.28** 🎧

Look at measures 53–60a of this piece in the anthology, while listening to the passage on your CD (track 30). Write in a Roman numeral and figures analysis in your score, labeling all embellishing tones. Adopt a harmonic rhythm of one or two chords per measure. Use your Roman numeral analysis to answer the following questions.

(1) If the harmonic rhythm is one or two chords per measure, how do you label the syncopated eighth-note "chord" in measures 53, 54, and 57? How else could it be labeled? If considered an actual chord, does it resolve as expected?

(2) What type of cadence do you find in measures 55–56? Is this the type you would expect at the end of a first phrase in a new section?

(3) What type of cadence appears in measures 59–60? Is this modulation to a key you would expect?

(4) Where is the pivot chord? Which pivot is used?

(5) How is the new key established? Does the music continue in that key? If so, for how long? If not, what happens next?

B. Archangelo Corelli, Allemanda, from Trio Sonata in A minor, Op. 4, No. 5 (p. 78)   **1.78**

Realize the figured-bass continuo part on the blank staff in your anthology. Then write the Roman numerals and figures below the bass staff. Copy your Roman numerals and figures into the chart below, then answer the following questions. You may listen to one possible realization on your CD.

	m. 1	2	3	4	
Roman numerals:					
Key: _____					

Roman numerals:

Key: _____

(1) Where is the pivot chord in this progression?

(2) How and where is the new key established?

C. Richard Rodgers and Lorenz Hart, "My Funny Valentine," mm. 29–36

This entire song is in C minor, except for the final four measures. The excerpt below shows the end of the song, with the cadence in measures 30–31 setting up the old key of C minor. Analyze the passage from measure 30b to 35 by placing Roman numerals beneath the example, then answer the following questions.

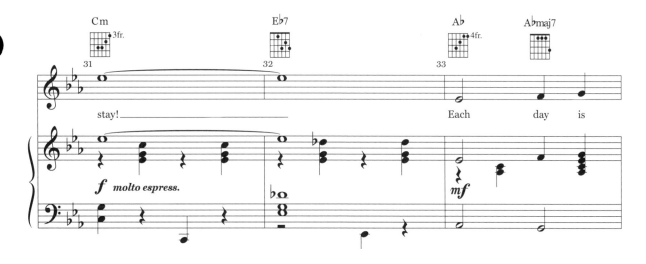

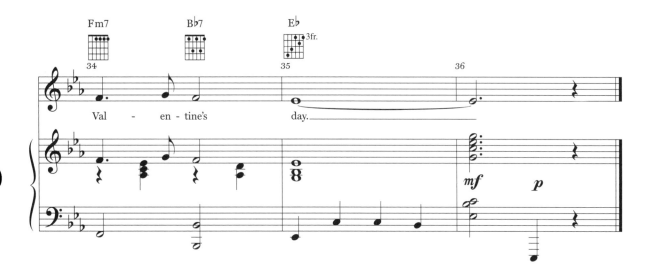

(1) What is the pivot chord? How does this pivot differ from others we have considered in this chapter?

(2) Is there something in the text that might motivate this modulation?

II. Extended analysis

A. Corelli, Allemanda, from Trio Sonata in A minor, Op. 4, No. 5 (p. 78)   **1.78** 🎧

Realize the figured-bass continuo part on the blank staff in your anthology. Then write the Roman numerals and figures for measures 13–21 below the bass staff. (Hint: You may want to first review measures 1–6 in "Brief analysis"/B. Begin in the key of C Major.) There are four short changes of key in this passage, each similar in harmonic structure to the progression in measures 1–6.

To hear a realization, listen to your CD.

(1) List the four key changes in the chart below.

	OLD KEY	NEW KEY	MEASURE NUMBER OF PIVOT CHORD	PIVOT ROMAN NUMERAL IN OLD KEY	PIVOT ROMAN NUMERAL IN NEW KEY	HARMONIES THAT ESTABLISH NEW KEY
1.	_____	_____	_____	_____	_____	_____
2.	_____	_____	_____	_____	_____	_____
3.	_____	_____	_____	_____	_____	_____
4.	_____	_____	_____	_____	_____	_____

(2) What is unusual about the cadence into measure 21?

B. Bach, Prelude in E♭ Major, from *The Well-Tempered Clavier*, Book II, mm. 1–12a

Listen carefully to this prelude on a recording in your library, or play through it at the keyboard. Then circle all the embellishing tones in the score that follows, and label chords with Roman numerals and figures. This excerpt includes both a tonicization and a modulation. Label each.

How do you distinguish between the tonicization and modulation in this passage?

C. Schubert, "Erlkönig" (p. 203)   **3.25** 🎧

Listen to the piano introduction and first verse of this song, while following the score in your anthology. Write a Roman numeral analysis for measures 1–32 in your anthology, and copy a portion of it into the chart below. Label the key changes as modulations, and indicate the pivot chords. Then answer the questions that follow.

	m. 12	13	14	15	
Roman numerals:					
Key: _____					

16   17   18   19

Roman numerals: | | | | |

Key: _____

20   21   22   23

Roman numerals: | | | | |

Key: _____

24   25   26   27

Roman numerals: | | | | |

Key: _____

28   29   30   31   32

Roman numerals: | | | | | |

Key: _____

(1) This verse begins and ends in the same key, but modulates twice in the middle. What are the pivot chords for each modulation? How are these prepared?

(2) Can you imagine any justification for the key change that is motivated by the text?

(3) Write a paragraph describing ways Schubert sets the scene for the story of this poem in the first verse. Include the piano figuration, key scheme, harmonic choices, motives, and so on, citing specific measures.

Binary and Ternary Forms

CHAPTER 23

Basic Elements

Writing binary forms: The second section

On staff paper, part-write the following four-measure chord progressions in the keys indicated, using SATB voicing. Remember to include any accidentals needed for the specified chord qualities and to resolve all leading tones and sevenths correctly. (These phrase progressions are designed to give you practice with Riepel's *ponte*, *monte*, and *fonte* models. They have been lifted out of context; in a complete binary form second section, they would be followed by a concluding phrase.) After you write the progression in block chords, write an elaborated version in keyboard texture for each.

A. *Ponte*: F: V | V | V$^{8-7}$ | I |

B. *Monte*: E♭: V^7/IV | IV | V^7/V | V |

C. *Fonte*: G: V^7/ii | ii | V^7 | I

Writing Exercises

I. Part-writing

In the workbook exercises for Chapter 22, we wrote two-phrase progressions that could serve as the first section (**A**) of a binary form. Here, we write the second section (**B**) to complete a small binary composition. On staff paper, part-write the progressions below in the keys indicated, using keyboard spacing.

A. D Major, $\frac{4}{4}$: ‖: V^7/IV | IV | V^7/V | V ‖ I | ii | V^7 | I :‖

B. B♭ Major, $\frac{3}{4}$: ‖: I I^6 ii^6 | V | G minor: i i^6 ii^{o6} | V ‖ i VI | iv ii$^{ø6}_{5}$ | V$^{6-5}_{4-3}$ | i :‖

C. Copy out your elaboration from Chapter 22, "Writing Exercises" I/C (in either D Major, $\frac{4}{4}$, or G minor, $\frac{3}{4}$). Write in the repeat signs at the beginning and end of the section, as is customary in the **A** section of a binary composition. You may write a first and second ending if you like, to make the connection between measure 8 and the beginning (when the section is repeated) and the continuation from measure 8 into the **B** section smoother. Then write a keyboard elaboration of the corresponding progression (in D major or G minor) above. If possible, arrange for a performance in class.

II. Melody harmonization

Harmonize the melodies below, following the instructions for each.

A. Wolfgang Amadeus Mozart, Menuetto I, from Piano Sonata in C Major, K. 6, mm. 9–16

Write a keyboard accompaniment for this solo instrumental melody. This is the second half of a binary form; we harmonized the first half in Chapter 22. The first phrase should include a sequence. The second may either continue the sequence one more iteration before cadencing in the main key, or be harmonized completely in the main key. First sketch out your keyboard accompaniment in block chords with correct voice-leading, then arrange them in an appropriate accompaniment pattern for a Classical-period dance.

If possible, perform your completed binary form for your classmates. How are the settings by classmates similar? How are they different? Compare your setting with Mozart's as well.

B. Franz Schubert, Waltz in B minor (D. 145, No. 6), mm. 17–32

As in Chapter 22, consider this melody as the right-hand part of a keyboard piece, and write a waltz-style accompaniment for the left hand. The melody divides into four phrases (four measures each), with a harmonic rhythm of one chord per measure. Examine the melody carefully, thinking about the harmonic patterns associated with the second half of a binary form. (Hint: The first and second phrases are identical except for their ending, as are the third and fourth.) Which of the common harmonic plans is followed in measures 17–24? What happens in measures 25–32? There are quite a few accidentals there! (Hint: Compare these measures to mm. 1–8 in Chapter 22.)

Sketch out your accompaniment in four-part block chords with correct voice-leading. Since all four voice-leading strands will be in the left-hand part, voice them in keyboard spacing, with the upper three parts in close position in the upper bass-clef range and the lowest part in the lower bass-clef range. After you have checked your voice-leading, arrange the chords in an appropriate accompaniment pattern for a Romantic-period waltz.

Combine your harmonization here with the setting of measures 1–16 from Chapter 22 to make a complete binary-form waltz. Perform (or ask one of your classmates to perform) your setting in class. Compare your setting with Schubert's.

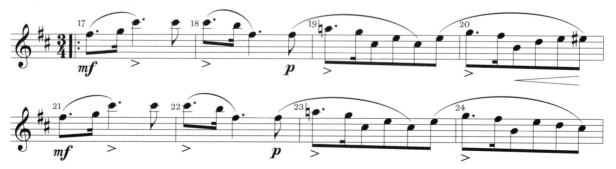

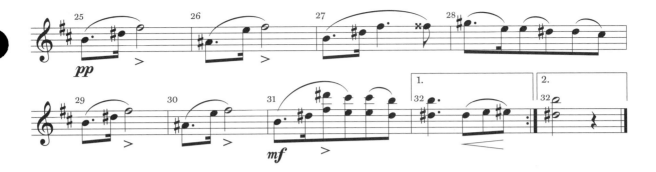

III. Figured-bass realization

Realize the figured basses below, following specific instructions for each.

A. Jean Baptiste Loeillet, Sonata in B minor for Flute, Oboe or Violin, and Continuo, Op. 3, No. 10, third movement (Largo), mm. 9–16

Realize this figured bass to accompany the flute melody. Use keyboard spacing (bass only in the left hand, three parts in the right). To choose an appropriate harmonic rhythm, carefully examine the bass line and figures before you begin. Write in a Roman numeral analysis under the bass staff. How often do the chords actually change? Use that durational value in the right-hand part to make a simple accompaniment.

We completed the first section of this movement in Chapter 22 of the workbook. If possible, arrange for a performance of both in class. Consider both that assignment and this one to answer the questions below.

(1)   Look back at the first half of this movement (which you analyzed in Chapter 22, p. 245). What type of cadence is found in measure 8? Which of the harmonic plans for binary-form first sections does this piece correspond to?

(2)   Compare the second section of this binary form to the harmonic plan charts in Chapter 23 of the text. How does this piece correspond to expectations for a second section?

B.   Archangelo Corelli, Sarabanda, from Sonata in E minor, Op. 5, No. 8, for violin and continuo

Realize this figured bass to accompany the violin melody. Use keyboard spacing (bass only in the left hand, three parts in the right). Write one chord per beat. (The ♩ in mm. 9, 11, 17, and 19 indicate that the bass note on beat 3 is a passing tone. The bass note on the "and" of beat 3 is the chord tone.)

Provide a Roman numeral analysis under the bass staff. After completing your realization, answer the following questions.

(1) What type of cadence is found in measure 8? Which of the harmonic plans for binary-form first sections does this section correspond to? What does the use of this cadence type reveal about the date of composition and style of this Sarabanda?

(2) Compare the second section with the harmonic plan charts in Chapter 23 of the text. How does it correspond to expectations for a second section? Which of Riepel's formulas is at work here: *ponte, monte,* or *fonte?*

(3) What type of binary form is this—simple or rounded? What elements of the music did you investigate to make your decision?

C. Corelli, Allemanda, from Trio Sonata in A minor, Op. 4, No. 5 (p. 78)   **1.78**

On the blank staff in your anthology, realize the figured-bass continuo part for any measures you have not completed in previous exercises. Listen to the movement on your CD, then consider its overall form. Make a graph below showing the tonal plan and large sections. You need not do an entire chord-to-chord analysis, but do include any substantial tonicization or modulation.

(1) What is the name for this formal design?

(2) Compare the phrase structure in this piece with the phrase structure of the Classical-era pieces we have considered—what is different?

(3) How is the custom of having a sequence or "harmonic instability" at the beginning of the second section handled in this movement?

(4) How does each key area touched on relate to the main key of the piece? What is the plan behind the ordering of keys?

Analysis

I. Brief analysis

In each of the exercises below, begin by listening to or playing through the piece (the score to A is in your anthology; for C, you may want to read the oboe and contrabassoon lines). Next play through each section individually, locate and analyze the cadences, then write in the Roman numerals and figures beneath the score. After you have completed your analysis, determine which type of binary or ternary form the piece represents, then answer the questions that follow.

A. Franz Joseph Haydn, Scherzo, from Sonata No. 9 in F Major (p. 117)   **2.17** 🎧

(1) What is the phrase structure of the first section?

(2) What is the relationship of measures 1–8 and 17–24?

(3) Is this a rounded or simple binary? Continuous or sectional binary? Are the sections balanced? What criteria help you decide?

(4) Above the staff, label the phrases with lowercase letters, and label the main sections with uppercase letters.

(5) This piece doesn't stray far from the tonic key, but does move briefly away. Where? How does this move fit into the harmonic plan for binary form?

B. Mozart, Minuet in F Major, K. 2

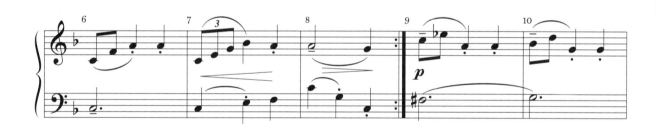

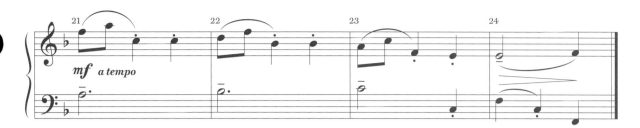

(1) How is the **A** section structured? What types of cadences do you find? How are motives organized within each of the two phrases (mm. 1–4 and 5–8)?

(2) What is the harmonic relationship between the third and fourth phrases (mm. 9–12 and 13–16)? What device is used to structure the melody in measures 9–11 and 13–15?

(3) What is the relationship between the last two phrases (mm. 17–20 and 21–24)?

(4) Is this a rounded or simple binary? What criteria help you decide? Are the sections balanced?

(5) Above the staff, label the phrases with lowercase letters, and label the main sections with uppercase letters.

(6) Choose one prominent motive from the first phrase, and write an essay explaining how this motive is transformed throughout the piece.

C. Johannes Brahms, *Variations on a Theme by Haydn*, mm. 1–29 (theme)

Find a recording of this work in your library, and listen to the theme while following the score below.

(1) What is the phrase structure of the first section?

(2) What is the relationship of measures 1–10 and 19–29? How are they alike? How are they different? What label is appropriate for this relationship?

(3) Is this a rounded or simple binary? Is it continuous or sectional? What criteria help you decide?

(4) Above the staff, label the phrases with lowercase letters, and label the main sections with uppercase letters.

(5) This theme doesn't stray far from the tonic key, but does move briefly away. Where? And how does this move fit into the harmonic plan for binary form?

(6) How does the orchestration of measures 11–18 support the function of that passage? How about measures 19–29?

II. Extended analysis

Here we primarily consider the phrase structure, tonal structure, and overall form of a piece. You do not need to prepare a complete chordal analysis. For each piece:

- Listen carefully to locate each phrase and cadence. Label the phrases and cadences in your score. Observe where there are tonicizations or changes of key.

- Make a chart showing your phrase analysis and cadence labels. Be sure to indicate the measures included in each phrase and any changes of key.

- Listen again for the overall formal plan. Look at the score for clues, such as repeat signs. Determine whether the piece is a binary or ternary design. Assign uppercase letters to designate the large sections, and write those letters in the chart.

A. Mozart, String Quartet in D minor, K. 421, third movement (Menuetto) (p. 157)   **2.74** 🎧

Begin by listening to the Menuetto on your CD, while following the score in your anthology.

Chart of form:

This Menuetto's form is: _____.

(1) What is unusual about the phrase structure in measures 1–10?

(2) We will examine measures 10b–29 in more detail in a later chapter. For now, simply indicate the cadence type in measure 29, and describe what you hear in those measures. What is their function, and where do they fit in the formal design?

(3) Identify any distinctive motives, and discuss how they are developed over the course of the movement.

B. Mozart, String Quartet in D minor, K. 421, third movement (Trio) (p. 157)   2.79 🎧

Listen to the Trio on your CD, while following the score.

Chart of form:

This Trio's form is _____.

In this movement, the Menuetto and Trio together make a _____ form.

(1) Compare the texture of the Menuetto with that of the Trio. How do they differ? How are they similar?

(2) What is the key relationship between the Menuetto and Trio?

(3) If you were making a chart of the form from the beginning of this movement (from the Menuetto), what capital letters would you assign to the sections in the Trio?

Make a chart below showing the overall form of the movement (Menuetto and Trio).

C. Scott Joplin, "Pine Apple Rag" (p. 127)   **2.28** 🎧

The composite form of this piece is different from those examined in Chapter 23 of the text. Use your form chart to determine which smaller forms make up the larger composite structure. (Note: If you do a chordal analysis, you will find one harmony that is new to you in measures 69–70 and 77–78. It is called ♭VI, and substitutes for the normal submediant here. We will learn more about harmonies of this type in Chapter 24.)

(1) Write a detailed form chart here including tonal structure, thematic design, measure numbers, and alphabet letters.

(2) Composite form:

Measures 5–52 are in _____ form.

Measures 53–84 are in _____ form.

Measures 5–52:   **2.29** 🎧

(3) Compare the phrase structure of this section with the phrase structure of "Solace," measures 53–84 (discussed in Chapter 21 of the text). How are the two pieces alike in phrase structure?

(4) We have seen how a sequence or some sort of "harmonic instability" may appear in the **B** section of binary forms. What happens in that location here?

Measures 53–84:   **2.30** 🎧

(5) Is there a modulation in the first section of this passage? If so, where, and to what key?

(6) At the beginning of the **B** section, do we find harmonic instability? How would you characterize the section?

(7) What is the overall tonal plan for the work?

D. John Philip Sousa, "The Washington Post March"

Play through the piano score of this march, or listen to a recording in your library. Like many Sousa
marches, this one begins with an introduction (mm. 1–8). Where are the other formal divisions?
(Hint: Reread the discussion in Chapter 23 of "The Stars and Stripes Forever," listen carefully, and
look for visual clues in the score.) Identify the main sections, and make a chart below, showing only
the main sections and keys (you don't need to identify all the phrases and cadences).

Part IV Further Expansion of the Harmonic Vocabulary

Chart of form:

(1) Which smaller forms make up the overall design of this march? Where are they? Which part would be considered the Trio?

(2) What is the relationship of the different key areas?

(3) The texture is markedly different in measures 57–63. How does that passage fit into the overall scheme of that portion of the march?

(4) How do the melodic ideas of the chromatic introduction return in the following strains?

(5) At the time it was composed (1889), this march was frequently performed at dances, to accompany the two-step, a wildly popular dance of the day. What rhythmic elements contribute to its dance-like character?

(6) If possible, listen to several recordings of this march. In some performances, it sounds quite dramatic; in others, dance-like; and in still others, like a routine march (meant for actual marching). How are the repeated sections treated in the various performances? Do all of them follow the notated dynamic markings? Would you make the repeats distinctive if you were conducting this march, or would you play them the same? What would the dramatic character be for each section in your ideal performance?

Color and Drama in Composition:

Modal Mixture and Chromatic Mediants and Submediants

Basic Elements

I. Spelling exercises

On the staves below, spell each mixture chord in the key and clef specified. First provide the correct key signature, then supply any necessary accidentals.

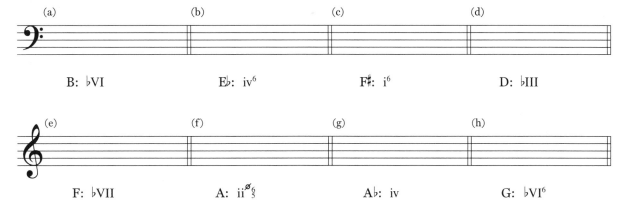

(a)   B: ♭VI   (b)   E♭: iv^6 (c)   F♯: i^6 (d)   D: ♭III

(e)   F: ♭VII   (f)   A: ii$^{\varnothing 6}_{5}$ (g)   A♭: iv   (h)   G: ♭VI^6

II. Two-chord pairs with mixture

Part-write the chord pairs in the keys specified below, using SATB voicing and following common-practice voice-leading guidelines. Pay careful attention to accidentals when spelling mixture chords, and watch for parallels when writing V to ♭VI.

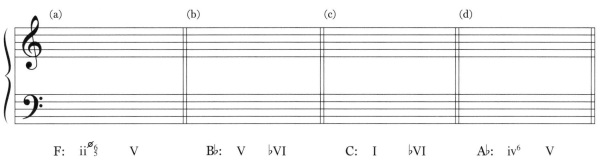

(a)   F: ii$^{\varnothing 6}_{5}$ V   (b)   B♭: V   ♭VI   (c)   C: I   ♭VI   (d)   A♭: iv^6 V

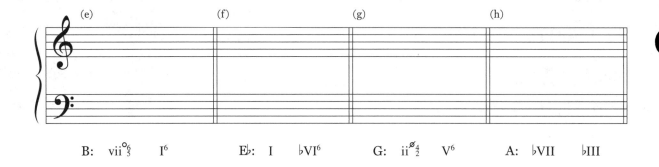

B: vii°⁶₅   I⁶   E♭: I   ♭VI⁶   G: ii°⁴₂   V⁶   A: ♭VII   ♭III

Writing Exercises

I. Part-writing

On staff paper, part-write the progressions in the keys below, using SATB spacing. Choose one progression to elaborate into a freer keyboard texture.

A. A Major, ³₄: I vii°⁷ I | ♭VI iv | ii°⁶₅ vii°⁷/V V⁷ | I ‖

B. F Major, ⁴₄: I V⁴₃ I⁶ V⁶₅/IV | iv V⁶₅/♭III ♭III | i⁶ ii°⁶₅ V♭⁶⁸₋⁷₅₋₃ | I ‖

II. Figured-bass realization

Figured bass is a technique rooted in Baroque and early Classical style. Mixture, on the other hand, is associated with Romantic-era composition. In the exercises below, Bach chorale figured basses have been altered slightly to include mixture chords, allowing them a more Romantic "interpretation." For each, melody and bass are given.

- Use keyboard spacing: three voices in the right hand, the given bass in the left.

- Place one chord on each beat in the given meter, revoicing the upper parts as needed to cooperate with the arpeggiations in the bass line.

- Write a Roman numeral analysis underneath the bass staff.

For additional figured-bass practice, a good source is *Bach Riemenschneider 371 Harmonized Chorales and 69 Chorale Melodies with Figured Bass* (New York: Schirmer, 1941).

A. Johann Sebastian Bach, "Eins ist Not! ach Herr, dies Eine" ("One Thing Alone, Lord, I Covet," Chorale No. 7 from *69 Chorale Melodies . . .*), mm. 1–4 (altered version)

B. Bach, "Jesu, meines Glaubens Zier" ("Jesus, Ornament of My Faith," Chorale No. 8 from *69 Chorale Melodies . . .*), mm. 1–4 and 13–14 (altered)

III. Melody harmonization

The melody that follows is adapted (considerably shortened) from Franz Schubert's 1815 setting of Johann Wolfgang von Goethe's "Kennst du das Land?" ("Lied der Mignon"). Set this melody for voice and piano (on your own staff paper) in an idiomatic keyboard style, and include mixture chords where appropriate. Provide a Roman numeral analysis underneath. (You might enjoy listening to Schubert's extensive setting once you have finished your composition!)

Kennst du das Land,	Do you know the land
Wo die Zitronen blühn,	Where the lemon trees bloom,
Im dunklen Laub	Where, in dark foliage,
Die Gold-Orangen glühn,	Golden oranges glow,
Ein sanfter Wind vom	Where a gentle breeze blows
Blauen Himmel weht,...	From the blue sky,...
Kennst du es wohl?...	Do you know it?...
Kennst du das Land,	Do you know the land
Wo die Zitronen blühn?	Where the lemon trees bloom?

blau - en___ Him - mel weht, O kennst___ du es wohl?

Kennst du das Land,___ wo die Zi - tro - nen blühn?

Analysis

I. Brief analysis

A. Fanny Mendelssohn Hensel, "Nachtwanderer" (p. 118)   **2.19** 🎧

Listen to measures 14–17 of this song on your CD (track 20), while following the anthology score. Write a harmonic analysis beneath the staves, and circle any modal scale degrees. Use your analysis to answer the questions that follow.

(1) What type of embellishing role does the modal scale degree in measure 15 play?

(2) The translation of this passage is "Then everything is gray again, everything is gray and quiet." How does Hensel color the second statement of "grau" (gray) musically? What harmony does she use? Is this a mixture chord?

B. Wolfgang Amadeus Mozart, Piano Sonata in D Major, K. 284, third movement (p. 139)   **2.48** 🎧

Listen to Variation XII on your CD while following the score in your anthology (track 56), then write in a Roman numeral analysis for measures 25–28a. Expect a fast harmonic rhythm in measures 26 and 27.

(1) Copy your analysis into the following chart (just to the downbeat of measure 28). Circle any mixture chords.

m. 25   26   27   28

Roman numerals:

Key: _____

(2) How does Mozart set up a strong tonal expectation so that the mixture chord surprises the listener?

C. Leonard Bernstein and Stephen Sondheim, "One Hand, One Heart," from *West Side Story*, mm. 1–17

This love song between Maria and Tony, the two main characters in Bernstein and Sondheim's updating of the *Romeo and Juliet* story, includes numerous mixture chords. Write a Roman numeral analysis beneath the staves, and circle the mixture chords.

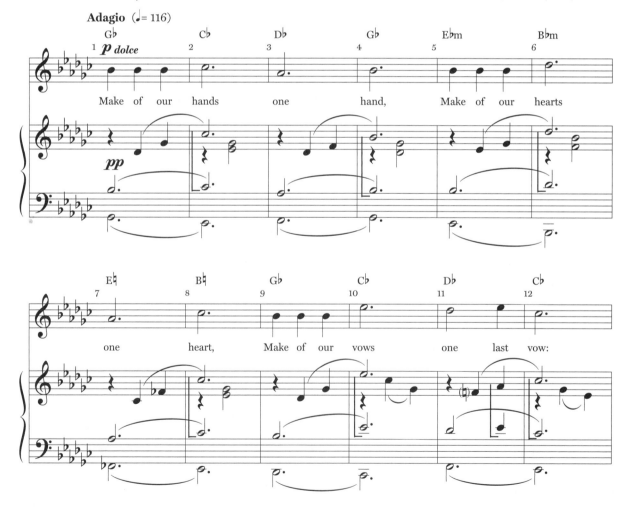

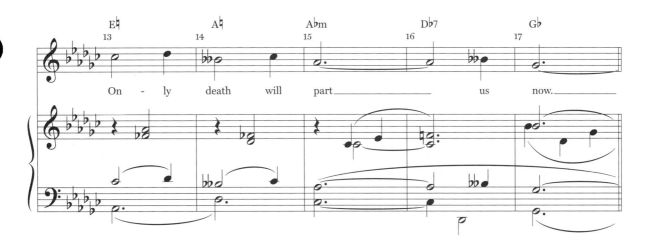

(1) Bernstein uses only two of the three modal scale degrees. Which are they? Where are they?

(2) In what way are the popular-music symbols misleading when compared with your Roman numeral analysis?

(3) With which phrase of text does the most mixture appear? Why might the composer have chosen this line to set apart for special harmonic treatment?

D. Scott Joplin, "Pine Apple Rag" (p. 127)   **2.28** 🎧

Follow your anthology score for this rag as you listen to the concluding strain on your CD (mm. 69–84; track 31). Analyze measures 77–84 in the anthology, then copy your analysis into the chart below. Circle the mixture chords.

   Hint: There are many embellishing tones; ignore them, and focus on finding the chord tones for your harmonic analysis. The harmonic rhythm moves slowly, with one chord per one or two measures for most of the excerpt. Write dashes to show a harmony that continues for more than one measure. To decide on the inversion in an arpeggiated bass line like this, take the lowest pitch of the measure, whether it appears on beat 1 or not; don't change the inversion in your analysis of the other beats in that measure.

Chapter 24   Color and Drama in Composition: Modal Mixture and Chromatic Mediants and Submediants

	m. 77	78	79	80	
Roman numerals:					
Key: _____					

	81	82	83	84	
Roman numerals:					

(1) Sometimes composers prepare listeners for the harmonic surprise of mixture by introducing a chromatic pitch—such as an embellishing tone or the seventh of a seventh chord—that will later become crucial to the mixture harmony. And sometimes this "foreshadowing" pitch appears in an enharmonic respelling. Can you find an example of this technique in measures 69–84?

(2) What voice-leading pattern stands out to your ears as Joplin resolves the mixture chord in measure 79? (Hint: Check the soprano and bass voices.)

(3) What is the function of the $^6_4$ chord in measure 79?

(4) Look back now at measures 69–76; compare them with the measures you just analyzed. What is the phrase organization of this section?

II. Extended analysis

A. Hensel, "Neue Liebe, neues Leben" (p. 122)   **2.22** 🎧

Start by listening to the entire song on your CD while following the score in your anthology. Copy our analyses from text Chapters 18 and 21 (Examples 18.16, 18.24, and 21.13) into the score, then write in the Roman numerals and figures for the remaining measures of the final verse (mm. 56–77; track 24). Circle the mixture chords, and think about their function in relation to the text. Then, on your own paper, write an essay that covers the following.

(1) The first eight measures begin as though they are antecedent and consequent phrases. Summarize the harmonic language of the first eight measures, including any sequences, cadence types, distinctive embellishing tones, and mixture chords you analyzed. How does Hensel vary the consequent portion, in comparison with the antecedent? Conclude by describing what surprising harmonic event occurs in measure 64 and how this might relate to the text.

(2) Hensel draws out the last line of text through repetition, building to a climactic high G5 in the vocal part in measure 71. Again, she uses parallel phrase structure as her model, but modifies the second phrase harmonically to achieve the climax. Discuss how you would divide measures 64b–73 into phrase units and specifically how the second phrase differs from the first. Include a detailed analysis of the harmony leading up to the climax, including any secondary dominants and mixture chords you find.

(3) Discuss Hensel's use of dissonance from measure 64b to the end. Identify any of the following that you find: accented dissonance, chromatic passing tones, chromatic pitches that foreshadow mixture chords heard later, augmented triads, suspensions, or diminished seventh chords. Which of these dissonances might you single out for special treatment in performance? What interpretive decisions would you make? Give specific measure numbers in your answer.

B. Ludwig van Beethoven, Piano Sonata in C Major, Op. 53 (*Waldstein*), first movement (p. 37)   **1.51** 🎧

Listen to this movement on your CD while following your anthology score. Listen for melodies and motives that return throughout the movement. We will study this piece in detail in Chapter 28; for now, we focus on the opening phrase and some of its variants: measures 1–13, 156–174, and 295–302.

(1) Write in the Roman numerals and figures for measures 1–13 in your anthology, then copy them into the chart below. Circle any mixture chords.

	m. 1	2	3	4	5	6	7
Roman numerals:							
Key: _____							

Chapter 24   Color and Drama in Composition: Modal Mixture and Chromatic Mediants and Submediants

	8	9	10	11	12	13
Roman numerals:							

(2) When this passage returns in measures 156 and following (track 57), how is it different? Discuss the role of mixture chords in creating the sensation of surprise. How were these harmonies prepared in measures 1–13?

(3) Provide Roman numerals for measures 167–174 (track 58), and circle any mixture chords.

	m. 167	168	169	170	171	172	173	174
Roman numerals:									

Key: _____

(4) Compare the final presentation of this material (mm. 295-302; track 59) with the previous two. Write a paragraph summarizing how Beethoven has varied this musical material in each of its appearances.

C. Johannes Brahms, "Die Mainacht" (p. 54)   **1.63** 🎧

Listen to this piece on your CD while following the score in your anthology, then answer the following questions.

(1) Describe the story of the poem. One of the ways Brahms depicts the restlessness of the main character is by avoiding the root-position tonic triad on the downbeat. Where is the first of these? Examine the phrase structure in light of this root-position tonic avoidance. Where are there true phrase divisions, as defined by cadences? What implications does this have for performance?

(2) Discuss the use of mixture in measures 9–14 (track 64). How does this harmonic language prepare us for the key change at measure 15? The key at measures 15 and following can be heard as a large-scale tonicization of a mixture chord. Explain.

(3) Comment on text painting for the words listed below. Consider their harmonic setting, texture, contour, register, and so on.

"traurig" (sadly; m. 11)

"Taubenpaar" (pair of doves; m. 17)

"wende mich" (turn away; m. 22)

"suche dunklere Schatten" (seeking darker shadows; m. 23–26)

"einsame Träne" (lonely tear; mm. 28–30, 40–42)

(4) What is the harmonic function of the piano postlude? Where is the final authentic cadence? What modal scale degrees play a role here? How might these observations influence your performance decisions?

Chromatic Approaches to V:
The Neapolitan Sixth and Augmented Sixths

CHAPTER 25

Basic Elements

I. Spelling the Neapolitan sixth and augmented-sixth chords

Practice spelling chords in the specified keys below, in close position. Remember to place the ♭$\hat{2}$ of the N⁶ in an upper voice and the ♭$\hat{6}$ of augmented-sixth chords in the lowest part.

A. G minor

     N⁶   It⁶   Fr⁶   Gr⁶

B. E minor

     N⁶   It⁶   Fr⁶   Gr⁶

C. F Major

     N⁶   It⁶   Fr⁶   Gr⁶

D. A Major

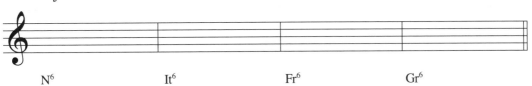

     N⁶   It⁶   Fr⁶   Gr⁶

II. Neapolitan sixth

Practice spelling and resolving Neapolitan sixth chords by part-writing the following three- and four-chord progressions on your own staff paper. Use SATB voicing in the specified key. No rhythmic or metric context is necessary. Draw arrows to show the resolution of $\flat\hat{2}$ and $(\flat)\hat{6}$ downward.

A. d: iv – N^6 – V

B. f♯: N^6 – vii°^{7}/V – V

C. b: N^6 – V$^{6-5}_{4-3}$

D. c: iv^6 – III^6 – N^6 – V

E. G: I – $\flat$VI – N^6 – V

F. A: I^6 – N^6 – vii°^{7}/V – V

G. d: iv^6 – V^7/N – N – V$^{6-5}_{4-3}$

H. B$\flat$: I – $\flat$VI – V^7/N – N – N^6 – V

III. Augmented sixths

Practice spelling and resolving augmented-sixth chords by part-writing the following three- and four-chord progressions on your own staff paper. Use SATB voicing in the specified key. No rhythmic or metric context is necessary. Draw arrows to show the resolution of $\flat\hat{6}$ downward and $\sharp\hat{4}$ upward.

A. g: iv^6 – It^6 – V

B. c♯: VI – Fr^6 – V

C. a: i – Gr^6 – V$^{6-5}_{4-3}$

D. f: i – iv^6 – Fr^6 – V

E. E$\flat$: $\flat$VI – Gr^6 – V$^{6-5}_{4-3}$

F. B: I – iv^6 – It^6 – V

IV. Figured-bass progressions featuring N^6 and A^6

Realize the following short figured-bass progressions in the keys indicated, using SATB voicing. Analyze each progression with Roman numerals, and mark the resolution of tendency tones with arrows.

Writing Exercises

I. Part-writing

On staff paper, part-write the two progressions below, both adapted from Mozart piano sonatas. Use SATB spacing in the keys indicated. Choose one progression to elaborate into a freer, Mozart-style keyboard texture.

A. G minor, $\frac{4}{4}$: i vii°⁶ i⁶ V⁶ | VI⁶ V⁶ VI⁶ vii°⁶/iv | iv⁶ III⁶ N⁶ vii°⁷/V | V⁶⁻⁵₄⁻₃ i

B. D Major, $\frac{3}{4}$: I vii°⁷/ii ii | vii°⁴₃ I⁶ V⁶₅/IV | iv iv⁶ Gr⁶ | V⁶⁻⁵₄⁻₃ (HC)

II. Figured-bass realization

Realize the figured basses below. For each:

- Use keyboard spacing: three voices in the right hand, the given bass in the left.
- Write a Roman numeral analysis underneath the bass staff.
- Follow any instructions included with the individual exercises.

A. Jean Baptiste Loeillet, Sonata in F Major for Flute, Oboe or Violin, and Continuo, Op. 1, No. 2, fourth movement (Giga), mm. 1–21

In addition to harmonies studied in this chapter, this piece provides a review of sequences, modulation, and binary form.

Place a chord on each beat, except

- in measures 1–7, where a rest occupies the second beat of each measure;
- in measure 12, where the figures indicate a faster harmonic rhythm; and
- in measure 14 (a cadential extension).

(1) Where do you find a N⁶? Is it resolved as you would expect?

(2) What type of sequence is found in measures 1–8?

(3) This excerpt is the opening (**A**) section of a movement in binary form. What is the expected modulation for a piece in D minor? Where does the modulation take place? Is it a pivot-chord modulation? Is the ending sectional or continuous?

(4) This Baroque Giga is a dance movement—but the gigue is a dance that features continuous lively motion, with pauses only at the end of main sections. Where are the phrase endings? How do the progressions and phrase endings contribute to a sense of forward motion?

B. Johann Sebastian Bach, "Nicht so traurig, nicht so sehr" ("Why So Troubled, [O My Heart]?," Chorale No. 41 from *69 Chorale Melodies . . .*), mm. 1–4, 9–12 (altered)

As in Chapter 24, this Bach chorale figured bass has been altered slightly for practice in the harmonies we are studying.

III. Melody harmonization

On staff paper, harmonize the melodies below with SATB voicing. When you have finished your setting, compare it against the composer's original.

A. Adapted from Franz Schubert, "Die Krähe" ("The Crow"), from *Winterreise*, mm. 1–5a

Write a Neapolitan chord where specified by the asterisk, and at least one secondary dominant of your choice. The harmonic rhythm is three to four chords per measure. Optional: Set for solo line with piano accompaniment.

B. Adapted from Franz Joseph Haydn, String Quartet in D minor, Op. 76, No. 2, first movement, mm. 1–4

This short excerpt ends with a half cadence. Set with a harmonic rhythm of one or two chords per measure, and place an augmented-sixth chord in a harmonically appropriate spot. Optional: Arrange your harmonization for string quartet.

Analysis

I. Brief analysis

A. Wolfgang Amadeus Mozart, Piano Sonata in C Major, K. 545, third movement (p. 155)   2.71 🎧

Follow your anthology score as you listen to this piece on your CD, then write in the Roman numerals and figures for measures 41–48a. Although the movement is in C Major, this portion is in the relative minor. Because of the exchange of motives between right and left hands, the excerpt begins with a ⁶₄ chord, and harmonies change before the downbeat. Mark your analysis with a harmonic rhythm that is primarily one chord per measure, notating the change of harmony on the downbeat.

(1) Copy your Roman numerals and figures into the chart below.

	m. 41	42	43	44
Roman numerals:				

Key: _____

	45	46	47	48
Roman numerals:				

(2) How is the Neapolitan approached and left? Is this normal voice-leading?

B. Schubert, "Erlkönig" (p. 203)   **3.25**

Follow your anthology score as you listen once more to this song on your CD. We have already ana-lyzed several passages in earlier chapters. Here, we focus on the concluding stanza, in which the child—snatched from life by the Erlking—arrives home dead in his father's arms. Write the Roman numerals and figures for measures 137–148 (track 32), then answer the questions below.

(1) Copy your Roman numerals and figures into the chart below.

	m. 137	138	139	140
Roman numerals:				

	141	142	143	44
Roman numerals:				

	145	146	147	148
Roman numerals:				

(2) How is the Neapolitan approached and left? Is this normal voice-leading? How is the Neapolitan emphasized musically?

(3) The song is pervaded with a left-hand scalewise motive (see measures 132 and 134) that helps depict the frantic ride through the night. How does this motive help shape the large structure of the vocal line in measures 135 to the end?

C. Ludwig van Beethoven, Piano Sonata in C minor, Op. 13 (*Pathétique*), third movement, mm. 41–51a   **1.46**

(1) Listen to this movement on your CD. Then provide Roman numerals on the score below, to turn in (track 48). Although the sonata is in C minor, this passage is in the relative major throughout. Draw arrows to mark the resolution of any tendency tones.

(2) Where is the augmented-sixth chord? Which type is it? How is it approached and resolved? Is this normal voice-leading?

(3) Examine the approach to C5 and C6 in measures 49–50. Is this an augmented-sixth chord? If so, what type? If not, why not?

II. *Extended analysis*

A. Beethoven, Variations on "God Save the King," Variation V

Begin by playing through the score excerpt that follows.

(1) Write a Roman numeral analysis into the score to turn in.

(2) This excerpt has two Neapolitan chords. Where are they? Discuss their harmonic preparation and voice-leading.

(3) The theme of this variation set is known in the United States as "My Country, 'Tis of Thee" (anthology, p. 173; CD 2, track 97). Consider the relationship of this variation to the original theme. What is the same? What is different? Write a paragraph explaining your findings.

B. Mozart, Piano Concerto in A Major, K. 488, second movement, mm. 1–12

(1) Listen to (on a library recording), or play through, this beautiful Adagio passage, paying particular attention to the striking setting of the Neapolitan harmony. Provide Roman numerals beneath the score excerpt. Circle and label all embellishing tones. (Be prepared to turn in your score analysis.)

(2) Consider how you might draw a phrase diagram for these measures, including alphabet letters to show similar or contrasting phrases, as well as the cadence types. You may find this challenging for a number of reasons. Write a paragraph discussing these challenges. What factors argue for and against calling these phrases parallel or contrasting? What factors make the second phrase key area and cadence difficult to determine? Which Roman numerals were ambiguous—might more than one analysis be correct?

(3) Write a second paragraph that addresses performance issues. Identify embellishing tones that, in your opinion, require special attention in performance. How might you interpret the harmonic surprises of measures 8–10?

C. Johannes Brahms, "Die Mainacht" (p. 54) **1.63** 🎧

In Chapter 24, we examined the use of mixture in this song. We now look at the harmonic and formal devices in the final stanza. Listen to the entire song on your CD while following the score in your anthology. Provide Roman numerals in the anthology for the third stanza (mm. 33–51; track 65). Use your analysis to write a short essay (one or two pages) about this final stanza. Be sure to answer each of the following questions in your essay.

(1) Where is the song's climax? How is it colored harmonically? Has this harmony been foreshadowed (or prepared tonally) earlier in the song? What embellishing tones intensify the moment?

(2) We have already learned that this song has few root-position tonic triads on downbeats. Where is the first in this passage? How might that observation inform your performance?

(3) Although singers sometimes interpret textual phrases as musical phrases, the two do not always coincide. It is absolutely necessary for performers to determine from the accompaniment where true phrases occur. Discuss measures 33–38 in this respect—does the word "Morgenrot" coincide with a phrase ending? How might you interpret this spot in performance? Is measure 44 a phrase ending? How might you perform this spot?

(4) How is the piano postlude structured harmonically? What formal role does it play in the song? What "emotional" role does it seem to play? How might you bring these factors out in performance?

Musical Form
and Interpretation

CHAPTER 26

Popular Song and Art Song

Basic Elements

I. Reading chord symbols

In the space below, notate the chords indicated by the chord symbols above the staff.

A. A^{add6} **B.** $C\sharp dim$ **C.** $B\flat^9$ **D.** D^7 **E.** Fm^9 **F.** $E\flat^{add6}$

G. $A\flat aug$ **H.** $D^{7\flat 9}$ **I.** $G\sharp m^7$ **J.** $C\sharp^9$ **K.** $G^{7\flat 5}$ **L.** F^+

II. Writing blues scales

On the staves below, write blues scales beginning on the pitches indicated.

A. Begin on E4:

B. Begin on B♭2:

C. Begin on G2:

Analysis

I. Brief analysis

A. Stephen Foster, "Jeanie with the Light Brown Hair"

Perform this song, either with a friend or by singing the melody line while accompanying yourself. Listen to identify phrase structure, key changes, and formal design.

(1)   Label each phrase with a lowercase alphabet letter and identify each cadence and key change, then summarize your observations in a form chart in the space below. What is the form of this song?

(2)   Analyze the harmonies from measure 13 to the end. What new harmony, discussed in this chapter, is present in this passage?

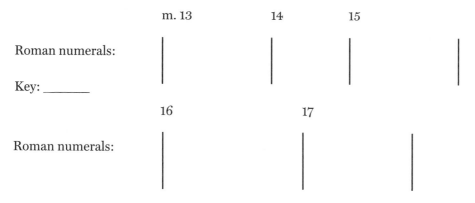

(3)   How does Foster create contrast in the bridge section?

B.   Fanny Mendelssohn Hensel, "Bitte" (poem by Nikolaus Lenau)

Play slowly through this song, and listen carefully to the harmonies. Write a harmonic analysis for measures 9 through 16, and consider ways that the harmonies complement the text.

Weil' auf mir, du dunkles Auge,	Linger on me, dark eyes,
übe deine ganze Macht,	exert your entire power,
ernste milde träumereiche,	somber, mild, dream-like,
unergründlich süße Nacht.	unfathomably sweet night.
Nimm mit deinem Zauberdunkel	With your magic darkness
diese Welt von hinnen mir,	take from me this world,
daß du über meinem Leben	so that above my life
einsam schwebest für und für.	you alone will float for ever and ever.

Translated by Emily Ezust

(1) Copy your harmonic analysis in the chart below. Circle any chord whose quality results from mixture.

	m. 9	10	11	12
Roman numerals:					
Key: _____					

	13	14	15	16
Roman numerals:					

(2) Look at the phrase endings in measures 5, 9, 13, and 16. What types of cadences are represented? How do the harmonic choices in measures 9 and 13 propel the song forward and correspond with repetitions in the text? How might these observations affect your performance?

(3) Examine the words and music for text painting that might help explain Hensel's heavy use of mixture in this song. Write a paragraph that describes this use, citing specific measures, words, and harmonies.

(4) What is the form of this song? Compare the form of the text with the form of the song.

II. Extended analysis

A. Franz Schubert, "Der Lindenbaum," from *Winterreise* (p. 194)   **3.16**

Before listening to the song in its entirety, read the poem by Wilhelm Müller and its translation as given in your anthology. Think about imagery in the poem that might be reflected in the song setting; think also about its formal design. Then listen to the song while following the score to see how Schubert's musical realization does or does not match what you anticipated.

(1) Write a paragraph about the structure of the poem. Into how many strophes is it divided? Does it have a consistent rhyme scheme? What poetic images are evoked by the text, and what story does it tell? Is there an objective-subjective duality in the lines, couplets, or strophes? What shifts in the story might suggest a musical departure from a strict strophic setting?

(2) How is the poem realized musically? Within each strophe, is there correspondence between the rhyme scheme and the musical rhyme of phrases? How do poetic strophes align with musical sections? Explain any irregularities.

(3) Trace the progression of keys, and relate any key change to the poem. The setting of strophe 5 prolongs a mixture chord—which one? How has this element of mixture been prepared musically by the prominent neighbor-tone motive in the introduction and elsewhere?

(4) Discuss text painting in this song. Relate images in the poem to Schubert's musical depiction, citing specific measure numbers and supporting your discussion with harmonic and motivic analysis.

B. George and Ira Gershwin, "'S Wonderful!" (p. 94)   1.91 🎧

(1) Listen to the song while following the score in your anthology. Write two or three sentences that identify the song's form. Specify the subsections with measure numbers. What musical features characterize each section?

(2) Contrast the overall harmonic structure of the song's two large sections. Which of the two is more stable harmonically? What musical factors create the stability/instability?

(3) What linear process underlies the vocal melody and bass in the opening section (mm. 5-20)? (Hint: Think in two-bar units.)

(4) Find three different examples of nondiatonic harmonies or added-sixth chords after measure 29. List them below, citing measure numbers. For each, discuss how the harmony functions within the phrase and how it contributes to the dramatic effect of the song.

(5) The highpoint of the song in measure 47 draws attention to the word "glamorous." How does Gershwin harmonize this E♮5 in the context of an E♭-Major song?

C. Hensel, "Neue Liebe, neues Leben" (p. 122) **2.22**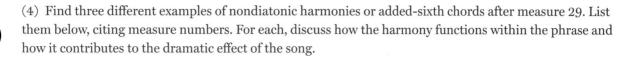
Clara Schumann, "Liebst du um Schönheit" (p. 210) **3.34**

Choose one of these songs as the topic of an analytical paper (three to five pages long). Begin by reading the translation in your anthology. Think about the structure and meaning of the text, as well as the ways you might interpret them musically if you were the composer. Next, listen to the song on your CD while following the score. Use all the skills you have developed so far to analyze form, harmony, phrase structure, modulatory schemes, motivic analysis, and text painting. Support each point you make by giving measure numbers, reproducing musical examples with analytical markings, or creating diagrams. Your essay should include the following:

- A description of the form of the song and its relation to the form of the text, including rhyme scheme and musical rhyme, strophe and verse structure, objective vs. subjective lines of text and their interpretation, characteristics of contrasting sections, and all changes of key.

- A detailed harmonic analysis of at least two sections of your choice, with a discussion of the dramatic and musical function of any mixture or chromaticism and its possible relation to the text.

- Analysis of motives, text painting, and/or embellishment of repeated motives.

- A discussion of the relationship between the vocal line and piano accompaniment, including changes in the relationship between the two as the song progresses and changes of texture that correspond with form.

- A discussion of the dramatic structure and interpretation, including comments on how your analysis of this song may have enriched your ideas about its interpretation and how you would shape the large-scale structure of your performance.

Variation and Rondo

CHAPTER 27

Writing Exercises

I. Continuous variations

Compose a set of continuous variations using the bass line given below. Begin by harmonizing the bass line with a simple progression, then prepare three variations—one with eighth notes, one with triplet eighth notes, and one with sixteenth notes. Keep the bass line identical in each variation, altering only the upper voices. Arrange your settings from the simplest to the most complex, and write a lead-in to connect each variation to the next.

II. Sectional variations

Choose a familiar children's song, patriotic song, or holiday song to serve as the basis for a set of sectional variations. The variations may be written for keyboard or for any small ensemble that is available in your class. If you like, you may work on this assignment as a group or class project, with each person writing a few variations and then arranging the results into a satisfying musical whole.

A. Begin by harmonizing the song to make the theme. Keep your harmonization simple—in a four-part chordal style. Check the harmonization and voice-leading carefully before proceeding. This setting will be the opening for your set of variations.

B. Prepare four or more variations of the theme you have chosen. One variation should have a contrast of mode. One should be a figural variation, with melodic embellishment. One should be a "character variation," with rhythms, meter, and figuration characteristic of a specific genre—a march, waltz, minuet, rock setting, and so on. And one should substitute more complex harmonies or add embellishing secondary dominant or seventh chords.

C. Arrange your variations in a logical order to make a set. Add a coda if you wish.

D. Prepare a performance for your class.

Analysis

I. Analysis of variation movements

A. Henry Purcell, "Ah, Belinda, I am prest," from *Dido and Aeneas*

Perform this song in class, or read through it at the keyboard. Alternatively, find a recording of the opera in your library, and listen to this aria.

(1) Underlying this expressive Baroque aria is a set of variations. What type of variation set is it? How many statements of the theme do you hear (including transpositions)? Number them in the score.

(2) Provide a Roman numeral analysis of measures 1–4, then compare them with measures 53–56.

	m. 1	2	3	4

Roman numerals:

Key: _____

	53	54	55	56

Roman numerals:

Key: _____

(3) On your own paper, write an analysis of this song. Your essay should include answers to the following questions:

(a) How does Purcell create a large-scale form in tandem with the variation form? Discuss changes in key, mood, text, or other musical elements to support your answer, giving specific examples and measure numbers.

(b) Does the variation "theme" ever change? Does it migrate into other voices? How does the phrase length of the theme interact with the phrase length of the vocal lines? Give examples where the two do and do not coincide.

(c) How does Purcell portray the torment of the text with embellishing tones, harmonic choices, or other musical features?

B. George Frideric Handel, Chaconne in G Major, from *Trois Leçons* (p. 100)   2.1

Listen to this piece while following the score in your anthology.

(1) Rhythmic patterns and organization: Begin by examining the prevalent durations in each variation. Do they get smaller or larger as the set progresses? Write a paragraph on your own paper discussing the rhythmic patterns in this set. Cite specific variations and durational values in your discussion, noting when variations group into pairs, threes, or fours. What specific musical features group these variations together? Are patterns exchanged between the two hands?

(2) Harmonic organization: These variations also have an overall organization in regard to the complexity and types of harmonies used.

(a) Begin by filling in the chords for the theme in the chart below.

	m. 1	2	3	4
Roman numerals:				
Key: _____				

	5	6	7	8
Roman numerals:				

Now compare the harmonies in variations 1–8. Are the same chords used in each variation? How does the texture of the variations change as the prevalent durations become shorter?

(b) Examine the harmonies in the minor variations. How is the descending bass line (first four measures of each variation) set in Variations 9, 10, 14, and 16? What about 11, 12, 13, and 15? Where do you find chromaticism? Write in Roman numerals and figures for these progressions in your anthology. Find at least two examples of each of the chords below, and list their measure numbers.

Neapolitans: _____

Secondary dominants: _____

Secondary leading-tone chords: _____

Minor v: _____

Are these types of progressions evident in the major-key variations? What would the overall form of the piece be if the decision were based solely on mode and harmonic complexity?

(3) Variation type: This set of variations contains elements of both continuous and sectional variations. Write a paragraph that summarizes aspects of continuous variation technique and sectional variation technique that may be found.

C. Wolfgang Amadeus Mozart, Variations on "Ah, vous dirai-je, Maman" (p. 165)   **2.86**

(1) Listen to this composition while following the score in your anthology. On your own paper, make a chart like the one below (which has been started for you). For the figural variations in the set, describe the figure (or insert music notation), and indicate whether it appears in both hands or only one.

VARIATION	ELEMENTS VARIED	ELEMENTS NOT VARIED	FIGURE?
I	Right-hand quarter notes change to 16ths, with neighbor tone patterns.	Left hand mostly the same, with some rhythmic variants.	Yes, ♩♩♩♩ in rh.

(2) Overall organization: Now consider the set as a whole. Are there variations that share techniques and make pairs? Which ones? How is the whole set shaped? Are there places it seems to lose momentum or build momentum? How does the final variation bring the set to a close? On your own paper, beneath the chart, write a paragraph that answers these questions.

D. John Barnes Chance, Variations on a Korean Folk Song (p. 59)   **1.66**

Begin your study of this piece by listening while examining the score excerpts in your anthology. The score includes all of the theme (mm. 1–37) and parts of several variations. On your own paper, write a short essay that addresses the questions below.

(1) Variation procedures: What musical features help delineate the variations? Describe the theme (mm. 1–37) and each variation given in the anthology. Include information about the meter, tempo, articulation, prominent rhythmic patterns, mood, instruments, range, and any other features that you notice are varied.

(2) Overall organization: In other variation sets we have considered, there has been an evident strategy for the overall organization—for example, a rhythmic acceleration. What seems to be the strategy here?

(3) The concluding portion (m. 211 to the end) brings together thematic and motivic elements introduced earlier in the piece, in overlapping statements. Discuss which elements are featured and how themes are altered rhythmically or melodically to create a rousing finale.

II. Analysis of rondo forms

A. Jeremiah Clarke, *Trumpet Voluntary* (*Prince of Denmark's March*) (p. 69)   **1.69** 🎧

Lisen to this rondo movement while following the score in your anthology.

(1) Close analysis: Review your previous harmonic analysis of this piece (from workbook Chapter 19), and complete the analysis on your score with Roman numerals and figures. (You don't need to recopy the analysis for sections that are repeated.) Use this information to assist you in answering questions 2 and 3.

(2) Form analysis: Label the phrases, sections, and key areas on your score. Then, on your own paper, make a chart showing the location of each of these features. (A sample chart has been started for you.) Use the sectional repetitions to help you identify the overall rondo design, and name the rondo type.

SECTION	PHRASES	MEASURES	KEY/MODE	COMMENTS
A (with		1–8	D Major	
trumpet)	**a**	1–4		Ends with a HC.
	a´	5–8		Ends with a PAC.
A repeated		9–16		
(without				
trumpet)				

(3) Style: This rondo was composed in the late seventeenth century, over a hundred years before the other rondo movements we have examined. Beneath your form chart, write a paragraph that describes how this rondo differs from others we have studied. Discuss the interaction between organ and trumpet, as well as the features that define the movement's large-scale form.

B. Ludwig van Beethoven, Piano Sonata in C minor, Op. 13 (*Pathétique*), third movement (p. 30)   **1.46** 🎧

Begin by listening carefully to the movement several times while following the score in your anthology. Watch for sections that seem transitional or developmental in nature, and comment on them in the chart below. We will learn terminology to go with these sections in Chapter 28, in our study of sonata form.

(1) Analyze the phrase and motivic structure of the rondo theme (mm. 1–17). Does Beethoven's theme fit the antecedent-consequent mold, with four-bar hypermeasures, or does it depart from this norm in some ways? Identify key motives in the theme (by alphabet letter or descriptive name), and give measure numbers for each. On your own paper, provide a diagram that summarizes your phrase analysis.

(2) Beneath your phrase diagram, diagram the form of the movement taking the incomplete chart below as your model. List any important elements of phrase structure and phrase rhythm (cadence types, parallel or contrasting phrases, elisions, prefixes or suffixes, etc.) in the "Comments" section.

SECTION	PHRASE	MEASURES	KEY/MODE	COMMENTS
A		1–17	C minor	
	a	1–4		HC
	b	5–8		PAC; contrasting period.
	b´			Begins as a varied repetition of **b**, includes an extension and a strong PAC cadence.
	suffix	12–17		Suffix, elided to **b´**; strong PAC cadence.

(3) Finally, write a paragraph or two about the movement. Identify the form, and comment on the arrangement of tonal areas. What musical material is included in the coda? Identify the sources earlier in the movement of as many of the coda's motives and themes as you can. List specific measures in the coda and specific phrase letters (from your chart) to which they correspond.

C. Beethoven, Sonatina in F Major, Op. Posth., second movement (p. 52)   **1.60** 🎧

Listen to this brief rondo movement while following the score in your anthology.

(1) Close analysis: Write a complete harmonic analysis of this piece, with Roman numerals and figures. Since the texture is only two to three voices, you may have to consider carefully some ambiguous chords and use your knowledge of progressions to make an appropriate analysis. You needn't recopy analysis for sections that are repeated without changes. Use this analysis to answer the questions that follow.

(2) Form diagram: Label the phrases, sections, and key areas. In the space on page 324, make a chart showing the location of each of these features. Use the key areas to help you identify the overall rondo design.

(3) Analytical essay: On your own paper, write a two- or three-page essay that answers questions (a) through (d) below.

(a) This movement has a hybrid form: what aspects of five-part rondo do you see? seven-part rondo? composite ternary? Discuss the elements that belong to each of these possible designs.

(b) If you were analyzing measures 1–36 alone, what form label would you give them? Do they conform in every way to that form? How does the form fit within the rondo plan? What is the function of measures 27–28 in the rondo design? Are measures of that sort typical in the form you identified for measures 1–36?

(c) If you were analyzing measures 37–66 alone, what form label would you give them? Do they conform in every way to that form? How does the form fit within the rondo plan? What about measures 67–74? What function do they have in the rondo design?

(d) Examine the phrase rhythm in this little piece. What observations can you make regarding the phrase rhythm in the **A** sections as compared with the contrasting sections?

Sonata-Form Movements

CHAPTER 28

Analysis

Any of the analyses in this chapter may be represented by either (1) analytical charts listing measure numbers and events, as shown in some of the exercises; (2) phrase-arc graphs as in Chapter 20; or (3) other alternatives suggested by your teacher.

A. Muzio Clementi, Sonatina in C Major, Op. 36, No. 1, first movement (p. 76)   1.74

Listen to this little sonatina movement while examining the score in your anthology.

(1) Close analysis: Provide a complete harmonic analysis with Roman numerals and figures in the score. Since the texture is only two to three voices, you may have to consider carefully some ambiguous chords and draw on your knowledge of progressions to make an appropriate analysis. Label each phrase and cadence.

(2) Form analysis:

(a) Label each large section in this piece, as well as the key areas.

(b) Based on your phrase analysis, where are the first and second theme groups? Is there a transition between them? Draw a diagram that shows these formal areas, citing specific measure numbers and keys.

(c) What themes or motives are explored in the development section? What type of harmonic motion is featured in this section?

(d) What changes when the themes return in the recapitulation? Are the themes all in the tonic key? If so, discuss changes to the passage between the first and second themes when compared with the exposition.

(e) A sonatina is typically a shortened sonata-form movement, which may have an abbreviated development section or none at all. How does this sonatina compare in scope with the Mozart sonata-form movement we studied in the text chapter? What elements are shortened or left out?

B. Wolfgang Amadeus Mozart, Piano Sonata in C Major, K. 545, first movement (p. 149)   2.57

Listen to this movement in its entirety while following the score in your anthology. Think about the overall formal organization, and mark in your score where you hear sections beginning or ending. Label any familiar themes or motives that return later in the movement, and write in measure numbers to show where you first heard them.

(1) Form analysis: For this analysis, you don't have to label every chord, but do examine the harmony closely. Label each section as well as themes, phrases, and key areas in your score. On your own paper, continue this chart to the end of the movement, then answer the questions below.

ELEMENT	MEASURES	KEY/MODE	COMMENTS
Exposition	1–28		
First theme	1–	C Major	Ends with an IAC.

(2) What is developed in the development section? What type of harmonic motion is featured in this section?

(3) What changes when the themes return in the recapitulation? Are the themes all in the tonic key? If so, discuss changes to the passage between the first and second themes when compared with the exposition.

(4) Choose one motive that is important in this piece, and briefly describe it. Write a paragraph explaining where the motive appears, and how it is developed.

C. Mozart, String Quartet in D minor, K. 421, first movement, mm. 1–41

Find a recording of this quartet in your library, and listen to the opening forty-one measures as you follow the score below. In the next three exercises, we will examine extended passages from this movement in detail.

(1) Form analysis: In this exposition, locate the first theme, transition, and second theme group, including any closing theme or codetta. (Hint: Look for a strong cadence in the new key to locate the beginning of the second theme group.) Within each theme, label the phrase structure and cadences. On your own paper, make a chart listing the location of each element (one has been started for you). Then answer the questions below in a short essay.

ELEMENT	MEASURES	KEY/MODE	COMMENTS
Exposition	1–41		
First theme	1–	D minor	
phrase **a**	1–4	D minor	Ends with an IAC.

(2) This movement is in D minor—what is the expected second key area? Where does the modulation occur?

(3) Do the first and second themes contrast in ways other than key? In what ways? What is the character of each? How would you perform these themes to bring out their emotional content?

(4) Is the closing material better labeled a codetta or a closing theme? Defend your choice.

(5) Scoring: Give measure numbers for passages with the following typical string quartet textures:

- One instrument plays a solo part while the others accompany.

- The first violin and cello play a duet, with accompaniment in the second violin and viola.

- A motive is passed through the quartet, with each instrument playing it in turn.

D. Mozart, String Quartet in D minor, K. 421, first movement, mm. 70–117

Listen to this movement again, paying particular attention to measures 1–41 and 70–117.

(1) Form analysis: Begin by locating the recapitulation. Then identify the first theme, transition, second theme, and closing theme or codetta. On your own paper, complete the chart below, listing the location of each element. Then answer the questions that follow in a brief essay.

ELEMENT	MEASURES	KEY/MODE	COMMENTS
Recapitulation	70–		
First theme	70–	D minor	
phrase **a**	70–73	D minor	Identical to mm. 1–4.

(2) Is the entire recapitulation in the tonic key (D minor)? If so, how is the transition between the first and second themes altered to stay in D minor?

(3) What is unusual about the location of the entry of the second theme as compared with the exposition? What is added to place this entry where it is, and how is the shifted location compensated for later in the recapitulation? What does the location of this entry reveal about metrical practices in the Classical era?

(4) In this movement, the second large section is intended to be repeated. How is the end of the recapitulation designed to facilitate the repetition? And how does the movement end?

E. Mozart, String Quartet in D minor, K. 421, first movement, mm. 42–70

Listen to this movement again in its entirety, now focusing on measures 42–70.

(1) Form analysis: On your own paper, make a chart listing the location and source of each element that is developed (the chart has been started for you). Then answer the questions below in a brief essay.

ELEMENT	MEASURES	KEY/MODE	COMMENTS
Development	42–70		

(2) In which key does the development begin? What material is developed there?

(3) Which three motives are developed the most in this section? Identify the origin of each, giving measure numbers.

(4) Where does the retransition begin? What element identifies it as a retransition? What motive appears here?

(5) Scoring: Give measure numbers for passages with the following typical string quartet textures:

- One instrument plays a solo part while the others accompany.

- The first violin and cello play a duet, with accompaniment in the second violin and viola.

- A motive is passed through the quartet, with each instrument playing it in turn.

- The first and second violins play a duet.

(6) Large essay (optional): Write an analytical paper of three to four pages that synthesizes your answers to Exercises C, D, and E. Use musical examples, charts, or diagrams to illustrate your analysis. Conclude with a discussion of how this analysis might assist a quartet in shaping their interpretation. Include at least two specific examples (with measure numbers) to support your points.

F. Felix Mendelssohn, Violin Concerto in E minor, first movement, mm. 1–72a

This excerpt is the first portion of a movement that spans 528 measures. In this passage, the violin and orchestra introduce the first theme of the movement. Find a recording of this movement in your library, or listen to the movement together in class. Then consider the following questions.

(1)   In Classical concertos, the first theme is usually presented one time by the full orchestra and one time by the soloist with orchestral accompaniment. In Romantic-era compositions, the order may vary, or the "double exposition" may be absent altogether. How is the first theme introduced here? Is it stated more than once?

(2)   Write in a harmonic analysis with Roman numerals and figures for measures 1–25. What types of progressions do you find?

(3) Locate the phrases and cadences in the first presentation of the theme. Are the phrase lengths regular? If not, what accounts for the irregularity? Give specific measure numbers in your answer.

(4) Beginning in measure 24b, the violin soloist is featured, with only occasional punctuating chords in the orchestra. Compare the solo violin part in measures 24b–34 with the theme—how are the two related?

(5) What is the function of measures 25–47? What is the function of measure 47 to the end of the excerpt?

Chromaticism

CHAPTER 29

Basic Elements

I. Writing chromatic sequences

For each of the diatonic sequence frameworks below, write embellished versions as indicated.

A. Falling-fifth sequence with seventh chords, root position

(1) With secondary dominants alternating with triads:

(2) With each chord made into a secondary dominant:

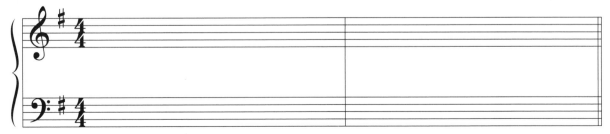

(3) With chromatic passing tones filling in any whole-step voice-leading:

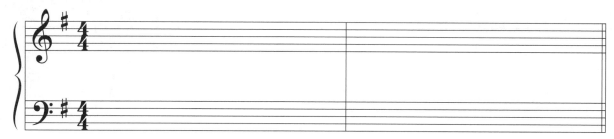

B. 5–6 ascending sequence

With chromatic passing tones:

C. Falling thirds with stepwise bass

With chromatic passing tones:

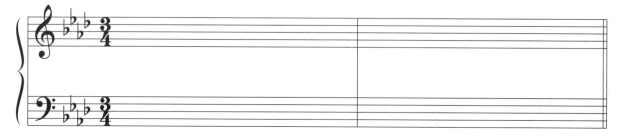

D. 7–6 descending (parallel sixths)

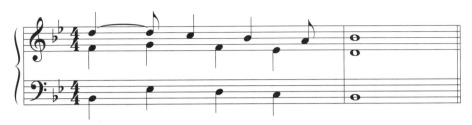

With added chromaticism:

E. Falling fifths

With a descending chromatic bass line:

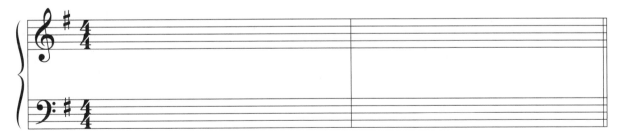

II. Writing chromatic elaborations of voice exchanges

For each of the voice exchange frameworks below, write chromaticized versions as indicated. You may sketch in the voice-leading using note heads without rhythmic values.

A. Fill in the outer voice exchange with chromatic passing tones (see Example 29.3 in the text).

B. Fill in chromatically with rhythmically staggered chromaticism (see Example 29.4f).

C. Make a harmonized segment of the chromatic scale based on this voice exchange (use segments of the chromatic scale in the soprano and bass in contrary motion).

III. *Writing other chromatic embellishments*

Decorate each of the following chords or progressions with the requested embellishment.

A. Common-tone diminished seventh chords (see Examples 29.8b and c):

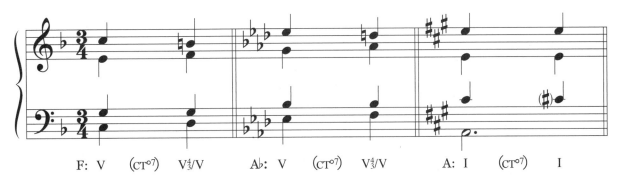

F: V (CT°7) V$^4_3$/V   A♭: V (CT°7) V$^4_3$/V   A: I (CT°7) I

B. Common-tone augmented-sixth chord (see Example 29.8d):

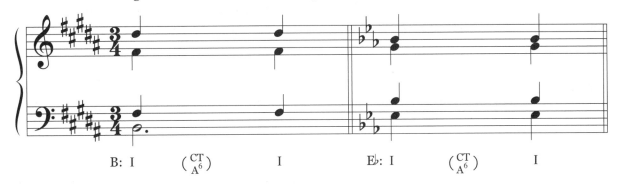

B: I $\begin{pmatrix} \text{CT} \\ \text{A}^6 \end{pmatrix}$ I   E♭: I $\begin{pmatrix} \text{CT} \\ \text{A}^6 \end{pmatrix}$ I

C. Chromatic passing embellishments:

E♭:

(1) Set progression C with rhythmic patterns appropriate for $^4_4$.

E♭:

(2) Set progression C with rhythmic patterns appropriate for $\frac{12}{8}$.

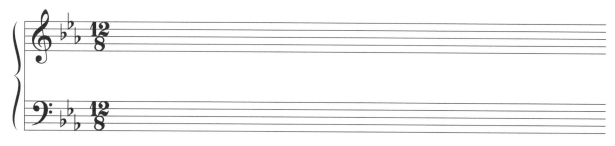

E♭:

Writing Exercises

I. Writing a chromatic introduction

Write a four-measure chromatic introduction in G Major modeled after Joplin's introduction to "Pine Apple Rag," given in your anthology (p. 127). Use chromaticism in parallel motion.

II. Chromatic modulations

Write four-measure progressions for keyboard that modulate from the first specified key to the second, using the technique indicated. Begin by firmly establishing the first key, then complete each progression with a strong cadence in the new key.

A. Begin in E Major and modulate to C Major (♭VI) using mixture.

B. Begin in A♭ Major and modulate to C♭ Major (♭III) using a pivot pitch or dyad.

C. Begin in E♭ Major and modulate to G Major (III) using chromatic inflection.

D. Begin in E♭ Major and modulate to A minor (♯iv) using an enharmonic reinterpretation of V⁷ as a German A⁶ chord.

E. Begin in G Major and modulate to A♭ minor using one or more fully diminished seventh chords.

Analysis

I. Brief analysis

A. Jerry Gray and Eddie de Lange, "A String of Pearls"

We first examined the harmonies and the chromatic passing inner voice of this song in Chapter 13 of the workbook; we now return to consider some chromatic details. As you play through the excerpts below, listen to the chromatic voice-leading.

(1) Look at the connection between the first and second phrases (mm. 11–13), shown below. Label the quality for each chord, and explain how each chord is connected to the next. Are there harmonies that do not resolve functionally?

(2) The tag ending, shown below, is a typical one at the time this song was written. How are the last two chords connected? Explain.

Wool - worth.

B. Ludwig van Beethoven, Piano Sonata in C Major, Op. 53 (*Waldstein*), first movement, mm. 74–92 (p. 40)   **1.55**

This passage ends the exposition, connecting from the E Major context of the codetta back to C Major for the repetition of the exposition. Listen to the first half of the movement to put this passage in context. The end of the passage also facilitates a modulation from E Major to D minor to begin the development. Let's examine how Beethoven accomplishes this dual transition.

(1) Begin by considering the quality of each chord in these measures, then examine the melodic pattern in measures 80b–89. Write Roman numerals showing the function underneath each chord in your anthology score, then copy the Roman numerals for measures 79–90 here:

m. 79   80   81   82   83

Roman numerals: | | | | | |

Key: _____

(1st ending)

84   85   86   87

Roman numerals: | | | | |

Key: _____

(2nd ending)

86   87   88   89   90

Roman numerals: | | | | | |

Key: _____

(2) Now identify the sequences in this passage. You should find a two-beat-long melodic sequence, but underlying the melodic sequence is a longer sequential pattern involving the entire texture. Mark the longer pattern and its sequential repetitions on the chart above with a bracket and arrows. Label the interval of transposition for each.

(3) How do the longer full-texture sequences and the shorter melodic sequences interact in this passage? What harmonic device connects the end of one longer sequence with the next? On your own paper, write a brief essay explaining how the sequences of this passage make a smooth connection from the E Major end of the exposition back to the C Major of the first ending and also connect to the D minor of the development in measure 90.

II. Extended analysis

A. Wolfgang Amadeus Mozart, String Quartet in D minor, K. 421, third movement (p. 157)   2.74 ⓧ

We considered the form of this movement in the workbook exercises for Chapter 23; we now look at the harmonic progressions in detail. Begin by listening to the movement while following the score in your anthology.

(1) Examine the first section, measures 1–10. What harmonies are employed with this chromatic descending bass line? Write the Roman numerals and figures in the chart below.

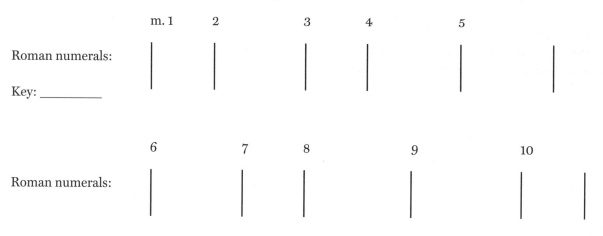

(2) Analyze measures 11–20 (track 76), and answer the following questions. What is the name for the device used in the cello part in measures 14–19a? What harmony is prolonged throughout these measures?

(3) Analyze the harmonic progression in measures 22–29 (track 77). Begin by making a primarily three-voice reduction of this passage on your own staff paper (eliminating octave doublings). Identify the quality and function of each chord. With arrows, mark the resolution of each chordal seventh and leading tone (including temporary leading tones).

(4) Compare the violin 1 and violin 2 lines in measures 22–29 with the passages we analyzed in (1) and (2)—what similarities are there? With arrows, identify the resolution of the tendency tones of measures 28–29 on your reduction. What is this progression?

(5) Now consider measures 30–39 (track 78). It will not be necessary to prepare a harmonic analysis of this passage to complete your analysis of this movement—why not?

B. Frédéric Chopin, Mazurka in F minor, Op. 68, No. 4

This little Mazurka displays an extraordinary range of chromatic harmonic techniques. After you have finished the step-by-step analysis below, complete the summary chart given at the end of this exercise.

(1) Measures 1–8:

(a) Circle and label the embellishing tones of the melody on the score, then examine the harmonies. Do you think that harmonic analysis is appropriate in this chromatic language?

(b) Try some Roman numerals: think of a harmonic rhythm of one chord per measure. Which chords may be identified with Roman numerals and figures? Which may not? Is there a sequence involved in this progression?

(c) What underlying counterpoint do you see unifying most of this passage?

(d) What chords participate in the cadence in measures 7–8?

(2) Measures 9–15:
(a) What is the relationship of measures 9–15 to the music analyzed above? What is similar? What is changed? Start by comparing the right-hand melodic lines of the two phrases. Circle and label the melodic ornamentations in the melody in measures 9–15.

(b) Examine the harmonies. What is different about the cadence?

(c) Explain the chord progressions in measures 14–15. What type of chromatic modulation technique is used? What is the relationship of the goal of that modulation to the original key?

(3) Measures 15–23:
(a) Circle and label the embellishing tones in the score, considering the harmonic context carefully, then write in Roman numerals. Compared with the previous measures, how chromatic are the harmonic progressions? What is the function of the A2 in the left-hand part?

(b) Compare the melodic line in measures 19–20 with 21–22. What are the harmonies underlying this melody? Explain.

(4) Measures 24–32: What harmony is tonicized at the beginning of the passage? Which key is established in this passage? How is that key related to the main key of the Mazurka?

(5) Measures 32–40:
(a) What type of sequence is found in measures 32–37a?

(b) Examine measures 37–39. How are the chord connections organized?

(c) Find several beats in these measures in which there are two different chromatic notes with the same letter name (for example, E♯ and E♭ on beat 2 in measure 38). Explain the functional meaning of each.

(6) What is the meaning of "dal segno senza fine"? How might you perform the Mazurka following this instruction?

(7) Summary chart: Indicate which measures illustrate each of the following techniques or features.

   Chromaticized falling-fifth sequence: _____

   Enharmonic reinterpretation of a Gr⁶ as V⁷: _____

   Modulation to a chromatic-mediant-related key: _____

   Chromatic passing tones embellishing a melody: _____

C. Robert Schumann, "Widmung" ("Dedication"), from *Myrten*, Op. 25

Read through the text of the poem by Friedrich Rückert (translated by Emily Ezust).

Du meine Seele, du mein Herz,	You my soul, you my heart,
Du meine Wonn', o du mein Schmerz,	You my bliss, O you my pain,
Du meine Welt, in der ich lebe,	You the world in which I live;
Mein Himmel du, darein ich schwebe,	You my heaven, in which I float,
O du mein Grab, in das hinab	O you my grave, into which
Ich ewig meinen Kummer gab.	I eternally cast my grief.
Du bist die Ruh, du bist der Frieden,	You are rest, you are peace,
Du bist vom Himmel mir beschieden.	You are bestowed upon me from heaven.
Dass du mich liebst, macht mich mir wert,	That you love me makes me worthy of you;
Dein Blick hat mich vor mir verklärt,	Your gaze transfigures me before you;
Du hebst mich liebend über mich,	You raise me lovingly above myself,
Mein guter Geist, mein bessres Ich!	My good spirit, my better self!

Find a recording in your library, or listen to this song together as a class. Write an analytical paper (two to four pages) that includes answers to the following questions, but don't limit yourself to just these questions if other aspects of the song interest you.

schwe - be, mein gut - er Geist, mein bess' - res Ich!

(1) Discuss the meaning of the poem. Are there objective lines and subjective lines? Are certain lines set apart from the rest by their structure or meaning? What musical aspects of the song do you believe are suggested by the poem's structure? What aspects are suggested by its meaning? What is the large-scale form of the song?

(2) Discuss the striking modulation that takes place in measures 13–14. What type of modulation is it? How are the keys related? What other musical and textural factors play into the change of mood here? How are these musical features consonant (or dissonant) with the meaning of the text?

(3) Identify important elements of chromaticism in the song (for example, the local climax in mm. 8–9 on G♭5). Provide harmonic analyses of these measures, and name any chromatic technique at work.

(4) Discuss possible performance implications of your analysis. Include phrase or hypermetric analysis, important harmonic events, suggestions for tempo and *rubato*, tone color, and so on. Be sure to provide suggestions that include both the vocal and piano parts.

PART VI

Into the Twentieth Century

CHAPTER 30 Modes, Scales, and Sets

Basic Elements

I. Mode and scale identification

Each of the excerpts below is drawn from Bartók's *Mikrokosmos*, a multi-volume set of piano pieces. *Mikrokosmos* provides both a systematic introduction to piano performance and technique, and a survey of Bartók's compositional style and method.

Play through each excerpt, then: (1) write out a list of the pcs; (2) identify the pc center, if applicable; (3) name the diatonic mode or other scale type; (4) write a few sentences that explain how the pc center is established (repetition, register, etc.). If a particular subset of the scale is featured, specify it (e.g., C Phrygian tetrachord). Finally, if the passage is polytonal (polymodal), identify the modes or scales used and which hand plays each.

A. Béla Bartók, *Mikrokosmos*, No. 37, mm. 1–8

(1) Pc list: _____

(2) Pc center(s): _____

(3) Mode(s) or scale(s): _____

(4) How is the pc center established? _____

_____

B. Bartók, *Mikrokosmos*, No. 41, mm. 1–4

(1) Pc list: _____

(2) Pc center(s): _____

(3) Mode(s) or scale(s): _____

(4) How is the pc center established? _____

_____

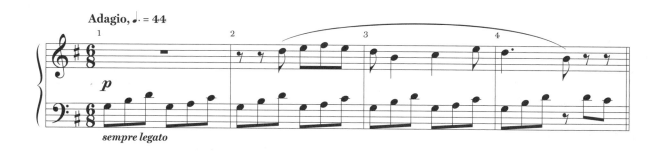

C. Bartók, *Mikrokosmos*, No. 59, mm. 1–6

(1) Pc list: _____

(2) Pc center(s): _____

(3) Mode(s) or scale(s): _____

(4) How is the pc center established? _____

_____

D. Bartók, *Mikrokosmos*, No. 101, mm. 1–5

(1) Pc list: _____

(2) Pc center(s): _____

(3) Mode(s) or scale(s): _____

(4) How is the pc center established? _____

_____

II. Pitch-class integer notation

Fill in the missing information below. In the "Chord #1" and "Chord #2" columns, either name the chord given in integer notation or provide integers for the given chord type. Then combine the two chords to form a scale or mode, taking the root of chord #1 as tonic pitch. In the last column, list the pcs in the mode or scale you have created, and give the correct name. The first exercise has been completed for you.

A.

	Chord #1	Chord #2	Combine to form what scale?
Integer notation:	2 6 9 0	4 7 e	2 4 6 7 9 e 0 (2)
Chord/scale type:	D Mm7	E-minor triad	D Mixolydian

B.

	Chord #1	Chord #2	Combine to form what scale?
Integer notation:	_____	_____	0 1 3 5 7 8 t (0)
Chord/scale type:	C mm7	D♭-Major triad	_____

C.

	Chord #1	Chord #2	Combine to form what scale?
Integer notation:	4 8 0	6 t 2	_____
Chord/scale type:	_____	_____	_____

D. | Chord #1 | Chord #2 | Combine to form what scale?

Integer notation: _____ 0 4 7   t 0 2 4 5 7 8 (t)

Chord/scale type: B♭ Mm7 _____ _____

E. | Chord #1 | Chord #2 | Combine to form what scale?

Integer notation: 2 6 9 0 _____ _____

Chord/scale type: _____ F^{ø7} _____

Writing Exercises

I. Writing modal melodies

Refer to the Bartók melodies in "Basic Elements" I as you write melodies in the modes or scales specified below. Melodies should be six to eight measures in length. Include expressive markings (for dynamics, articulation, tempo, etc.) to help achieve the aesthetic effect desired.

A. A lyrical, folk-inspired melody in $\frac{5}{8}$ time; G Dorian mode, treble clef.

B. A syncopated, aggressive melody in $\frac{2}{4}$ time; C Lydian mode, bass clef.

C. An ethereal whole-tone melody in $\frac{6}{4}$ time; treble clef.

D. An octatonic melody; mood, meter, and clef of your choice.

II. Writing accompaniments to modal melodies

Arrange two of your melodies for performance. Score one arrangement for solo instrument with piano accompaniment, the other for piano solo. Maintain the mode, meter, and mood of your melodies in these arrangements. Choose expressive markings to convey your musical intent precisely. Begin by studying the examples from Chapter 30 of the text to see how modal melodies are harmonized. Experiment at the keyboard, creating harmonies from the pcs of the mode you have chosen. Use your ear as your guide.

Experiment with different textures: your accompaniment might feature a melodic line in counterpoint with the melody instead of chords. Adapt familiar keyboard textures (such as Alberti-bass patterns or jump-bass accompaniments) to this style; try an ostinato or pedal point in the accompaniment. Find classmates who will play your arrangements in class (be sure to prepare a transposed score, if necessary, for the solo instrument).

● Analysis

I. Brief analysis

A. Benjamin Britten, "In Freezing Winter Night," from *Ceremony of Carols*, mm. 1–6

This composition is scored for treble chorus and harp. Listen to a recording from the library, or sing through the excerpt with your class.

(1) What is the tonic or centric pitch of the excerpt? What musical cues support your conclusion?

(2) Which diatonic mode is used in this passage? How does Britten emphasize the distinctive scale degree that differentiates this mode from natural minor?

(3) What are the relationship(s) between the melodies in treble voices 1 and 2? between 1 and 3?

B. Bartók, *Mikrokosmos*, No. 136, mm. 1–19

(1) Play through this passage at the piano. Make a list of the pitch classes in measures 1–6. Of which collection is this a subset? Is there a pitch or pc center? If so, what is it, and how is it established? What aspects of this phrase separate it from the next, which begins in measure 7?

(2) In measures 7–12, we can consider each hand a separate layer. How do they relate to each other and to the opening phrase? Make a list of the pitch classes in each hand part. Of which collections are these subsets? Are there focal pitches or pitch classes? If so, what are they, and how are they established?

(3) Measures 13–19 make up the third phrase of this work. What is the relationship between this phrase and the second, in terms of the pc sets in each hand? How are the two hands in this phrase similar to those of the second phrase? What motivic similarities and differences do you find in comparing the two phrases?

II. Extended analysis

A. Bartók, *Mikrokosmos*, No. 109 ("From the Isle of Bali")

(1) Play through this piece at the piano. What is the primary mode or scale of this composition? Where does Bartók depart from this pc collection? Speculate on reasons why Bartók may have made those departures.

(2) Comment on motivic development in this piece and the relationship between the two hands. How are measures 5–10 related to 1–4? How is the *Risoluto* passage (mm. 12–30) related to the opening, and how does Bartók develop motives through this section as a whole?

(3) In measures 31 to the end, how do the two hands relate to each other? (Both are notated in the treble clef in mm. 31–35 over a dyad sustained in the pedal in the bass clef.) Discuss the role of pitch symmetry in measures 31–39 and 40–43.

B. Claude Debussy, "La cathédrale engloutie" ("The Engulfed Cathedral"), from *Préludes*, mm. 1–43

Peu à peu sortant de la brume

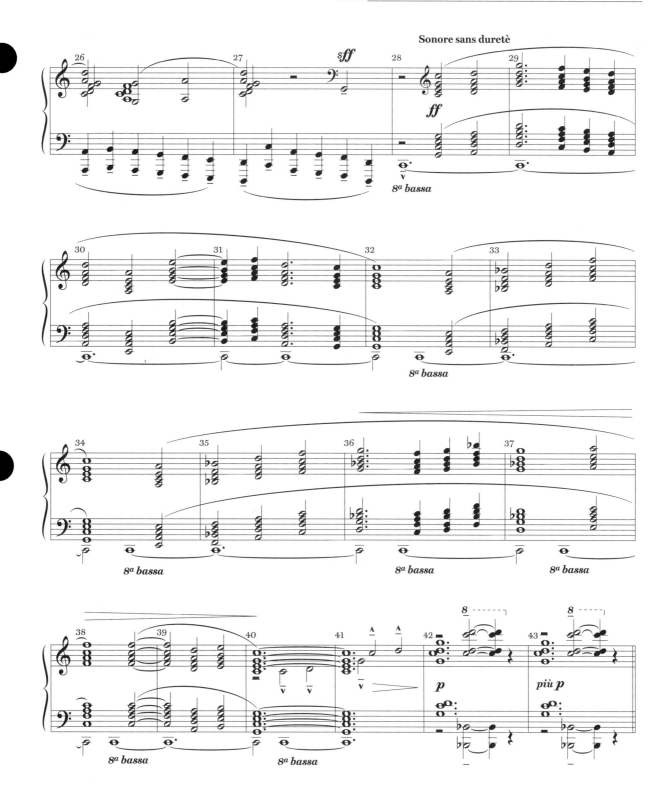

(1) Find a recording of this prelude in your library and listen to it, keeping in mind its programmatic and evocative title. What musical elements do you hear that paint the image of a Gothic cathedral shrouded perhaps in fog, or rising out of a mist? What stylistic elements does the piece share with the excerpt from Debussy's "Voiles" discussed in Chapter 30 of the text?

(2) One difficulty that arises in analyzing a work like this is how best to divide it into sections. The prelude does not easily fit into any established formal design. One possible division of this opening section (mm. 1–43) is shown below; fill in the missing elements. Write N/A on a "Mode/scale" blank if the pc center is too ambiguous to determine the mode.

	Theme group 1			"Transition"			Closing theme		
	a¹	b	a²	c¹		c²	c³	trans...
mm.	1–6	7–13	14–15	16–22		22–27	28–42	42–43
Pc center	_____	_____	_____	_____	_____	_____	_____	_____
Mode/scale	_____	_____	_____	_____	_____	_____	_____	_____

(3) Discuss how you made your decisions about pc center and mode (it may be helpful to list pitch collections for the various modes/scales), citing specific measures. If the pc center was too ambiguous to determine the mode, discuss what musical elements created the ambiguity.

(4) Follow the long sustained bass line as far as you can. This line is expressed by dotted whole notes, pedal points, or the lowest pitch of each bar, and extends through much of this passage. What role does it play in helping to establish formal units, stability, and mode? Do you see or hear long-range linear motion in the bass? Where?

(5) Trace reappearances of the opening D-E-B motive. How is this motive developed?

C. Samuel Barber, "Sea-Snatch," from *Hermit Songs*

Listen to a recording of this song. Familiarize yourself with the melodic line and accompaniment by singing and playing portions of the song at your own tempo. Then write an essay that discusses the role of the pentatonic and diatonic collections in this song. Be sure to address the following issues (but you need not structure the essay simply as answers to these questions).

- What is the form of the song? How is this form defined by text, mode or scale, tessitura, and accompaniment?

- How is the pentatonic scale hinted at in the opening? What pcs are missing from the diatonic collection? How are these missing pcs specially treated later in the song?

- Where are the diatonic sections? Are they written in major or minor or some other mode? (Give specific measure numbers.) Does the harmonization support a modal interpretation or a tonal one?

- Discuss Barber's use of text painting. How does the piano accompaniment depict the words of the poetry? What motivic and harmonic materials shape the accompaniment?

CHAPTER 31

Music Analysis with Sets

Basic Elements

I. Transposing pitch sets

Transpose the following melodic segments as indicated. Since these are pitch transpositions, they should maintain the pitch intervals of the original segment. Duplicate the rhythm and articulation of the original exactly.

Segment a:

A. Transpose segment a down seven semitones to make segment b.

B. Transpose segment a up eight semitones to make segment c.

Segment d:

C. Transpose segment d down seven semitones to make segment e.

D. Transpose segment e down twenty-nine semitones (two octaves and five semitones) to make segment f.

E. Now listen to the fourth movement of Anton Webern's String Quartet, Op. 5, while following the score in your anthology (p. 244). **3.57** 🎧 Locate these segments in the music.

Segment a is in measure(s) _____

Segment b is in measure(s) _____

Segment c is in measure(s) _____

Segment d is in measure(s) _____

Segment e is in measure(s) _____

Segment f is in measure(s) _____

II. Transposing and inverting pitch-class sets

Explore each of the following tetrachords by writing out its twelve transpositions. Then invert the tetrachord, reorder it so that the integers are in ascending order, and write out each of the inverted set's twelve transpositions. The first one has been started for you. Does each pcset have twelve distinct transpositions? twelve distinct inversions? Circle any sets that duplicate pc content. Finally, calculate the interval-class vector for each pcset.

A. {0 1 4 6}

    Transposed: {1 2 5 7}, {2 3 6 8},

    Inverted: {6 8 e 0}, {7 9 0 1},

Interval-class vector:

B. {0 1 3 7}

Transposed:

Inverted:

Interval-class vector:

C. {0 1 4 5}

Transposed:

Inverted:

Interval-class vector:

D. {0 1 6 7}

Transposed:

Inverted:

Interval-class vector:

III. Interval-class vectors

For each melody excerpted below, write out the pc integers. Calculate the ic vector for the pentachord from these pcs. Then answer the following questions.

- Which two pentachords share the same ic vector? _____

- Which one has the most ic 3? _____

- Which one has the fewest ic 1? _____

- Which two have the fewest ic 5? _____

A. Joseph Schwantner, "Sparrows," m. 11 (vocal part)

pc integers: _____   ic vector: _____

B. Béla Bartók, "Bulgarian Rhythm," m. 1

pc integers: _____   ic vector: _____

C. Bartók, *Music for Strings, Percussion, and Celesta*, m. 1

pc integers: _____   ic vector: _____

D. Webern, "Dies ist ein Lied," Op. 3, No. 1, m. 4 (vocal part)

pc integers: _____   ic vector: _____

E. Olivier Messiaen, *Méditations sur le mystère de la Sainte Trinité* (*Meditations on the Mystery of the Holy Trinity*), for organ, fourth movement, m. 76

pc integers: _____   ic vector: _____

F. Webern, String Quartet, Op. 5, third movement, mm. 18–19

pc integers: _____   ic vector: _____

IV. T_n/T_nI relationships

Each pcset identified in the string quartet excerpts below is related by T_n or T_nI. In the blank, specify the relationship between the two sets (for example: B = T_7 A means that if you transpose set A by 7, the result is set B).

A. Webern, String Quartet, Op. 5, fourth movement, mm. 3–5a (p. 244)   **3.58**

Begin by listening to this movement.

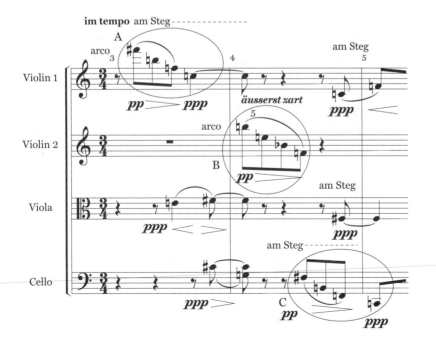

B. Webern, String Quartet, Op. 5, fourth movement, mm. 6, 10   3.59 🎧   3.61 🎧

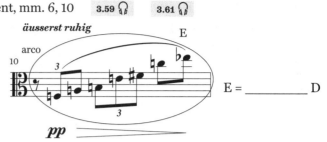

E = _____ D

C. Igor Stravinsky, *Three Pieces for String Quartet*, third movement, mm. 10–11

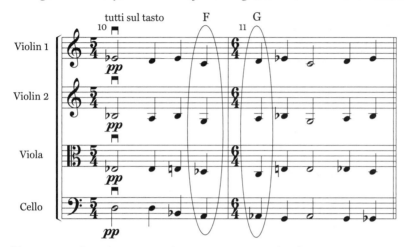

G = _____ F

D. Stravinsky, *Three Pieces for String Quartet*, third movement, mm. 15–18

J = _____ H   K = _____ J   K = _____ H

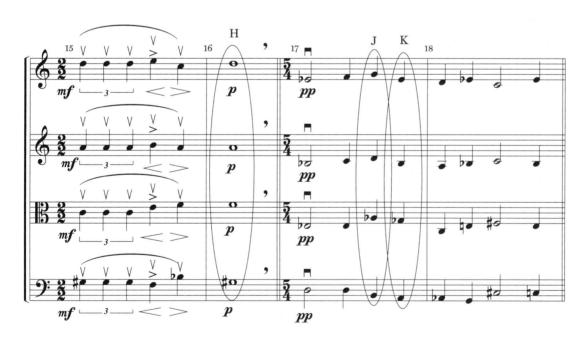

Writing Exercises

I. Melody writing

A. On your own staff paper, write a phrase in $\frac{5}{8}$ meter, in a dance-like folk style, using the unordered pcset {0 1 3 4 6 7 9}. Then write a second phrase whose unordered pcset content is related by T_5. (Don't simply transpose the ordered set, but transpose and reorder.) As always when composing, include expressive and tempo markings, dynamics, etc.

B. Write a lyrical phrase in $\frac{3}{4}$ meter, featuring the unordered pcset {0 1 4 5 8 9}. Then write a second phrase whose unordered pcset content is related by T_6I.

C. Musical challenge!

Choose one of the melodies you have written, and score it for a solo instrument plus piano accompaniment. Create the accompaniment from different voicings and spacings of the pcs in the melody line.

II. Harmonic writing

A. On your own staff paper, compose a progression of eight chords made from sets {0 1 4 5} and {0 1 6 7} and their transpositionally or inversionally related sets; you listed these in "Basic Exercises"/II above. Connect the chords so that you retain some common tones, and move at least some voice parts by step. Remember, these are pitch-class sets, and each pitch class can be realized in any octave.

B. Compose a progression of ten chords made from sets {0 1 3 7} and {0 1 4 6} and their transpositionally or inversionally related sets; you also listed these in "Basic Exercises"/II. Connect the chords so that you retain two pitches between each pair of chords as common tones—for example, C and C♯ could connect {0 1 3 7} and {0 1 4 6}, or C♯ and E♭ could connect {0 1 3 6} and {9 t 1 3}.

Analysis

I. Brief analysis

A. Bartók, *Bagatelle*, Op. 6, No. 2, mm. 8–11a (p. 21)   **1.26** 🎧

(1) Listen to this piece while looking at the score in the anthology, then consider the following melodic motives from measure 10 (track 29). For each segment, first write out the pitch-class integers in the order they appear in the motive. Fill in the appropriate blanks to show the T_n relation between segments.

Right-hand part

segment a pcs: _____   segment b pcs: _____   segment c pcs: _____

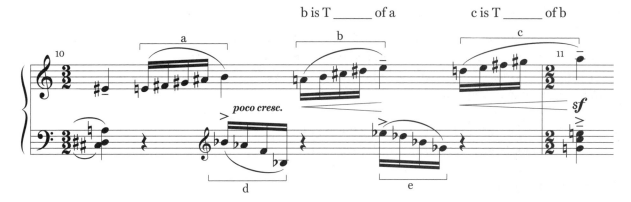

b is T _____ of a   c is T _____ of b

Left-hand part

segment d pcs: _____   segment e pcs: _____

Which pc in segment e does not match an exact transposition between segments d and e? _____

(2) Now consider segment f below, from measure 8 (track 28). Write out the pitch-class integers in the order they appear in the motive.

segment f pcs: _____

Segments a, b, c, and f are segments of diatonic scales. Use the pattern of whole and half steps between adjacent pcs to determine which major scale each motive belongs to.

segment a: _____   segment c: _____

segment b: _____   segment f: _____

B. Bartók, *Bagatelle*, Op. 6, No. 2, mm. 7–8 and 14–16 (p. 21)   1.26 🎧

Listen to this piece while looking at the score in the anthology, then consider the melodic motives from measures 7–8 and 14–16. Most of the seven-note motives of measures 14–16 begin or end with a transformation of trichord x or y, both of which are introduced in measures 7–8.

The pcs in sets x and y have been identified for you, and listed in ascending order and most compact form. For each of the seven-element sets a–d in measures 14–16, compare the first three pcs to set x and the last three pcs to set y. Write each set's pcs in ascending order and most compact form (as around a clock face), for ease of comparison. Determine the precise relationships using T_n notation. If the trichords are not related, write NE for "not equivalent." Exercise (1) has been completed for you.

Measures 7b–8a   **1.28**

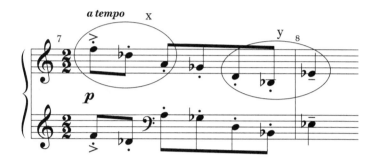

x trichord: {1 5 9}

y trichord: {t 2 3 }

Measures 14b–16   **1.30**

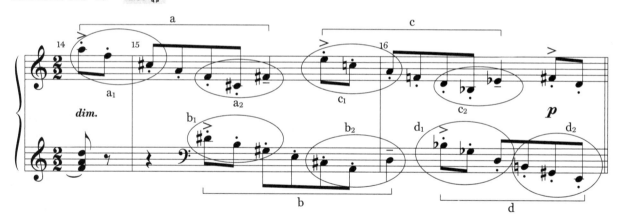

(1) Measures 14–15 right hand (set a)

pcs in a_1: { _____ 1 5 9 _____ }   pcs in a_2: { _____ 1 5 6 _____ }

Relationship between set a_1 and x trichord (m. 7): $a_1 = \underline{T_0\ x}$ between set a_2 and y trichord: $a_2 = \underline{T_3\ y}$

(2) Measures 15–16 left hand (set b)

pcs in b_1: { _____ }   pcs in b_2: { _____ }

Relationship between set b_1 and x trichord: $b_1 = T$ _____ x between set b_2 and y trichord: $b_2 = T$ _____ y

(3) Measures 15–16 right hand (set c)

pcs in c_1: { _____ }   pcs in c_2: { _____ }

Relationship between set c_1 and x trichord: $c_1 = T$ _____ x   between set c_2 and y trichord: $c_2 = T$ _____ y

(4) Measure 16 left hand (set d)

pcs in d_1: { _____ }   pcs in d_2: { _____ }

Relationship between set d_1 and x trichord: $d_1 = T$ _____ x   between set d_2 and y trichord: $d_2 = T$ _____ y

(5) Motive d is only six pcs long, rather than seven. What pc would best complete the motive? _____

(6) What aspects of these motives make audible links between them even though the motives are not, in their entirety, exact transpositions of each other?

(7) How is the effect here different than it would be if the entire seven-note segments were exact transpositions?

II. Extended analysis

Alban Berg, "Sahst du nach dem Gewitterregen" ("Did You See, After the Summer Rain"), from *Fünf Orchester-Lieder* (*Five Orchestral Songs*), Op. 4 (piano reduction)

Find a recording of this song in your library, or listen to it in class. Play through the vocal line at the piano while thinking about the text translation. Where possible, play portions of the accompaniment as well, to get the pcsets "in your ears."

Translation:
> Did you see, after the summer rain, the forest?
> All is quiet, sparkling, and more beautiful than before.
> See, woman, you too need summer rainstorms!

Write an extended essay that analyzes this song, using the following questions as springboards for your thoughts. Organize the essay as you see fit (don't simply answer the questions in a list). Support your ideas with specific examples from the piece, citing measure numbers. If you'd like, turn in an annotated copy of the score with your essay.

A. As always when dealing with text, look carefully at the poetry and the relationship of its form and content to the music. Does the song draw on elements of any standard formal schemes, or is it "through-composed"? Support your answer by discussing pcsets used as melodies and harmonies in the song. If appropriate, cite instances of imitation or other contrapuntal procedures.

B. Much of the material for this song is presented in the opening vocal phrase (the first two and a half measures). Divide the phrase into distinct motives, and identify the pcsets for each motive. How do these motives return later in the song? How are they developed? If the pcsets return transposed or inverted, give the T_n and T_nI relationships.

C. This song is filled with thirds, which often occur in the context of the split-third chord: a major-minor triad, such as {0 3 4 7}. It also features transpositions and inversions of {0 1 4}. Find as many examples of these sonorities as possible, including transposed or inverted forms.

D. Is this music centric? Is there a predominant focal pitch class? Support your answer, pro or con, with examples from the music.

Sets and Set Classes

CHAPTER 32

Basic Elements

I. Trichord identification

In each excerpt below, identify the two specified trichords. Circle as many statements of each trichord as possible, even if the musical segments overlap by one or two pcs. Remember to look for differing transpositions or inversions of the trichords (not just the prime form!).

Circle the first specified trichord with a solid line; circle the second with a dotted line.

A. Béla Bartók, *Music for Strings, Percussion, and Celesta*, mm. 1–4a

Find SC 3-1 [0 1 2] and SC 3-3 [0 1 4].

B. Olivier Messiaen, *Méditations sur le mystère de la Sainte Trinité* (*Meditations on the Mystery of the Holy Trinity*), for organ, fourth movement, mm. 72–76

Find SC 3-4 [0 1 5] and SC 3-5 [0 1 6].

C. Alban Berg, "Sahst du nach dem Gewitterregen" ("Did You See, After the Summer Rain"), from *Fünf Orchester-Lieder* (*Five Orchestral Songs*), Op. 4 (piano reduction), mm. 1–4

Find SC 3-3 [0 1 4] and SC 3-5 [0 1 6].

Translation: Did you see, after the summer rain, the forest? All is quiet, sparkling, and is [more beautiful than before].

D. Anton Webern, String Quartet, Op. 5, third movement, mm. 1–8 (p. 242)   **3.54** 🎧

Listen to this passage on your CD. Then find SC 3-3 [0 1 4] and SC 3-4 [0 1 5].

II. Prime form

Below are the six pentachords featured in Chapter 31, "Basic Elements"/III. For each, calculate the prime form and look up the Forte number in Appendix 5 of the text.

A. Joseph Schwantner, "Sparrows," m. 11 (vocal part)

prime form: _____

Forte number: _____

B. Bartók, "Bulgarian Rhythm," m. 1

prime form: _____

Forte number: _____

C. Bartók, *Music for Strings, Percussion, and Celesta*, m. 1

prime form: _____

Forte number: _____

D. Webern, "Dies ist ein Lied," m. 4 (vocal part)

prime form: _____

Forte number: _____

E. Messiaen, *Méditations sur le mystère de la Sainte Trinité*, fourth movement, mm. 76

prime form: _____

Forte number: _____

F. Webern, String Quartet, Op. 5, third movement, mm. 18–19a

prime form: _____

Forte number: _____

● Writing Exercises

Melody writing

A. On your own staff paper, write a phrase in $\frac{6}{8}$ meter that includes two transpositionally related statements of set-class [0 1 6 7]. Then write a second phrase using the pcs of its complement; repeat pcs as needed. (Analyze the set classes in your melody with brackets.)

B. Write a phrase in $\frac{2}{4}$ meter that includes two transpositionally related and two inversionally related forms of set-class [0 1 4 6]. Then write a second phrase with two transpositionally related and two inversionally related forms of set-class [0 1 3 7]. Design your phrases with similar rhythms, contours, and articulation to make them go together. Repeat pcs as needed; you may also feature interval classes between melodic pitches to make the phrases similar.

Analysis

I. Brief analysis

A. Arnold Schoenberg, *Drei Klavierstücke* (*Three Pieces for Piano*), Op. 11, No. 1, mm. 1–5

Play through this passage at the piano, then complete the exercises that follow.

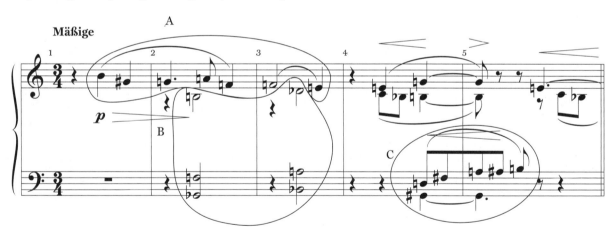

(1) Identify the prime form for each of the three hexachords circled in the example.

A = _____

B = _____

C = _____

● (2) Calculate their ic vectors, and write them to the right of each prime form in #1.

(3) What can you say about two of the ic vectors?

(4) Look up the Forte numbers for each hexachord in Appendix 5 of the main text.

A = _____

B = _____

C = _____

(5) How do the Forte numbers reflect the relation you discovered in question #3?

B. Igor Stravinsky, Kyrie, from *Mass*, mm. 1–5

With your class, sing through the opening measures of Stravinsky's *Mass*, then answer the following questions.

Translation: Lord have mercy upon us.

(1) To what set class does the entire piano accompaniment belong? _____

Additional statements of this SC are sung by the basses. Find them and circle them in your score. What is the transpositional relationship between these statements?

(2) The SC sung by the tenors in their initial "Kyrie eleison" is repeated by the sopranos in their second "Kyrie eleison." To what set class do these melodies belong, and what is the relationship between the two?

(3) The altos' two statements of "Kyrie eleison" belong to the same set class. What is the relationship between them?

(4) If all the pitches of the choral parts in measures 4–5 were considered together as a collection, to what set class would this collection belong?

SC _____ Prime form: _____ Normal order: _____

(5) If we consider the single B♭ in measure 5 (tenors) to function as a passing tone (and therefore eliminate it from our set), to what set class would the pitches of the entire excerpt (voices and piano reduction) belong?

SC _____ Prime form: _____ Normal order: _____

This SC is a subset of what scale or mode? _____

By what criteria could we consider the B♭ a passing tone in this nontonal context?

C. Benjamin Britten, "That yongë child," from *Ceremony of Carols*, mm. 1–8

Sing the melody of this excerpt while accompanying yourself at the piano, until the song's sonorities become familiar. As you will hear, Britten features sonorities made up of a triad plus a half step, which create several different types of tetrachords. First identify the tetrachords circled in the score, then answer the questions that follow.

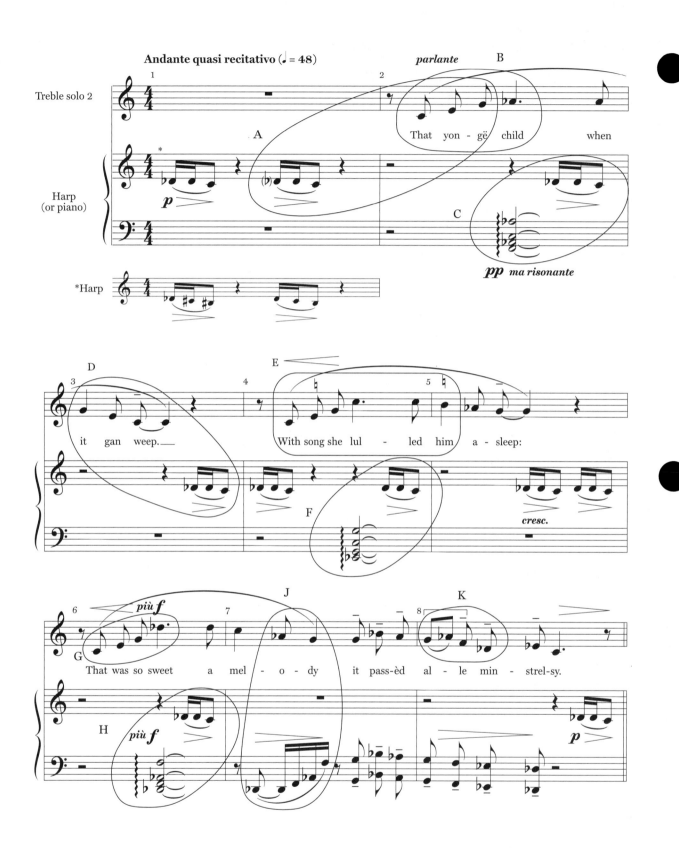

(1) After identifying the tetrachords in the score, copy the SC information into this chart for easy comparison.

(A) Normal order: _____ Prime form: _____ Forte number: _____

(B) Normal order: _____ Prime form: _____ Forte number: _____

(C) Normal order: _____ Prime form: _____ Forte number: _____

(D) Normal order: _____ Prime form: _____ Forte number: _____

(E) Normal order: _____ Prime form: _____ Forte number: _____

(F) Normal order: _____ Prime form: _____ Forte number: _____

(G) Normal order: _____ Prime form: _____ Forte number: _____

(H) Normal order: _____ Prime form: _____ Forte number: _____

(J) Normal order: _____ Prime form: _____ Forte number: _____

(K) Normal order: _____ Prime form: _____ Forte number: _____

(2) How many different set classes did you find that result from a triad plus a half step? What can you discover about their location in Forte's table of sets? How does this location reflect their intervallic structure? (Hint: Check the ic vector.)

(3) Identify the T_n and T_nI relations between the sets in the chart below. Use the normal order of each set (the pcs that appear in the score) to determine these relationships. The first one is completed for you.

D = T_0 A

E = _____ C

H = _____ E

J = _____ F

G = _____ D

(4) What can you say about the "progression" from SC A to D to G? from C to E to H? Comment on the pcs held as common tones from one transposition to another.

II. Extended analysis

Webern, String Quartet, Op. 5, third movement (p. 242)   **3.54** 🎧

Write an extended essay analyzing this movement, using the following questions as guidelines. Organize the essay as you see fit. Support your ideas with specific examples, citing measure numbers. You may turn in an annotated copy of the score with your essay if you wish.

A. Listen to the movement a few times without a score. What makes the work "hang together," and what elements help you divide it into formal sections? What type of mood does this music convey to you? What musical elements contribute to the mood?

B. If we take the presence of ostinatos in the bass as a means to divide the composition into sections, we find three parts: measures 1–6 (C♯ ostinato), 9–14, and 15–21 (B–G–A♯ ostinato). How would you characterize these sections? What elements are different (or the same) between sections? How would you characterize measures 7–8 and 22–23?

C. We have already identified the use of SCs 3-3 and 3-4 in the opening section (in "Basic Elements"/I, exercise D). Do these set classes continue to play a prominent role in the remainder of the movement? Discuss.

D. There are a few places in the movement where whole-tone collection subsets may be found. Identify these by measure number and set-class type.

E. Find at least three canonic passages (including canon by inversion). Cite measure numbers and instruments.

Ordered Segments and Serialism

CHAPTER 33

Basic Elements

I. Identifying ordered pitch segments related by serial operations

The ordered pitch segments A and B below are related to the segments (1), (2), and (3) by transposition, inversion, retrograde, or retrograde inversion. To identify how the segments are related, first write in the ordered pitch intervals underneath each segment (using + and − signs), then compare the segments. Write T, I, R, or RI in the spaces provided to indicate the type of serial operation used to transform segments A and B into (1), (2), and (3). (Note: These are pitch segments, *not* pitch-class segments.)

A.

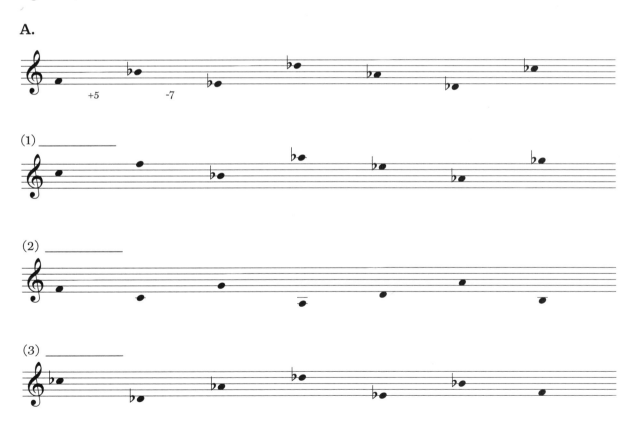

(1) _____

(2) _____

(3) _____

B.

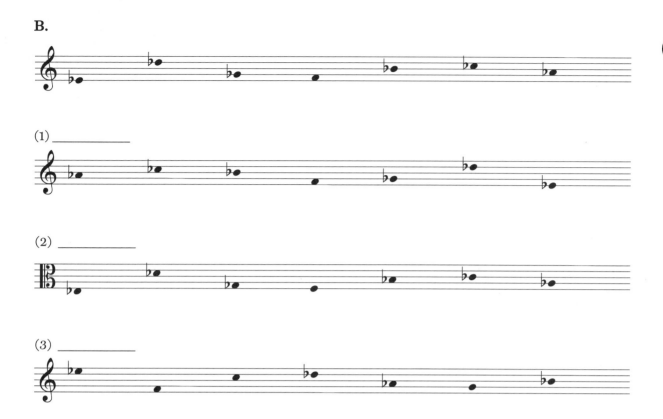

(1) _____

(2) _____

(3) _____

II. Identifying ordered pitch-class segments related by serial operations

The ordered pitch-class segments A and B below are related to the segments (1), (2), and (3) by transposition, inversion, retrograde, or retrograde inversion. To identify how the segments are related, first write in the ordered pitch-class intervals (clockwise around the clock face) underneath each segment, then compare the segments. Write T, I, R, or RI in the spaces provided to indicate the type of serial operation used to transform segments A and B into (1), (2), and (3). (Note: These are pitch-class segments, *not* pitch segments.)

A.

(1) _____

(2) _____

(3) _____

B.

(1) _____

(2) _____

(3) _____

III. Serial operations on ordered pitch segments

Taking the pitch segment below as a starting point, transform the segment in the following ways. (Reminder: We are working with pitches, not pitch classes, in this exercise.)

A. Transpose up ten semitones.

B. Invert with the same starting pitch as the original.

C. Retrograde the original series of pitches.

D. Retrograde and transpose the original down three semitones.

IV. Serial operations on ordered pitch-class segments

Write in the pitch-class integers under the melodic segment below, then provide the pc series for segments transformed in the following ways. For each, indicate how many pcs are invariant with the original segment by circling the integer(s) your transformed segment does not share with the original. Which row has the fewest invariant pcs?

A. P_0:

B. P_8:

C. I_8:

D. R_t:

E. R_1:

Writing Exercise

Serial composition

Write a melody that features six pitch classes without repetitions. Taking this melody as the prime form of a segment, write out the retrograde, inversion, and retrograde-inversion forms. You may transpose any of these forms if you wish.

Use these row forms to make a short composition in $\frac{3}{4}$ meter. Score your piece for two to four instruments in your class, or for instrumental solo. Label each segment in the score. Prepare your composition to perform in class, with appropriate dynamics, tempo, markings, and articulation.

Analysis

I. Brief analysis

A. Igor Stravinsky, "Full Fadom Five," m. 1

(1) What is the name of the collection found in the vocal melody? (Hint: Write it out as a scale below, beginning on the last pitch class, then name it.)

Collection type: _____

(2) Now consider the construction of the vocal melody. Write out the melody, without rhythm, on the blank staff below. Then label the intervals between the adjacent pitches: label tonal pitch intervals (e.g., M6, P4), integers (e.g., 9, 5), and interval classes. Write + or - to show ascending or descending direction (except for interval classes). What observations can you make about the construction of this melody? (Hint: Look for symmetries and repetitions of interval patterns.) The exercise has been started for you.

Tonal pitch intervals: + P4   - P5

Integers: + 5   - 7

Interval classes: 5   5

Observations about melodic construction:

(3) What is the name of the collection found in the viola part? (Hint: Write it out as a scale, then name it.) What is this line's relationship to the vocal melody? Is this melody a pitch or pitch-class transformation of the vocal line?

Collection type: _____

(4) What is the relationship of the flute line to the clarinet line? Why do you think Stravinsky combined these instruments in this way? What is the relationship of the flute and clarinet parts to the vocal line? Why might Stravinsky have chosen this transformation? Write a paragraph that answers these questions.

(5) What chords are created by the counterpoint? Write out the pitches of the melodies on the staff below so that you can examine the simultaneities (the first ones are provided), then label the intervals. Which pitch intervals are featured? Which interval classes?

(6) Write a paragraph explaining how this short passage of music achieves coherence in the absense of functional tonality. Use details from the analysis above to support your points.

B. John Tavener, "The Lamb" (p. 233)   **3.49** 🎧

Listen again to this piece while following the score in your anthology. Identify another serial passage in the work (different from the measures discussed in the text chapter). Find one example of the work's prime segment in each of its four forms (P, I, R, and RI). On the staves below, write the segment, and give its location (measure number and voice part) and its label (for example, I_7).

SEGMENT	MEASURE NUMBER	S, A, T, OR B	LABEL
P:	_____	_____	_____
I:	_____	_____	_____
R:	_____	_____	_____
RI:	_____	_____	_____

II. Extended analysis

A. Stravinsky, "Full Fadom Five," mm. 2–14

This portion of the piece is based on a seven-tone row, first presented in the vocal melody in measures 2–3, and its serial transformations.

(1) Supply the following information.

  (a) pitch classes of the prime row (P_3): _____

  (b) ordered pc intervals of P: _____

  (c) retrograde of above (R_3): _____

  (d) ordered pc intervals of R: _____

  (e) inversion of the prime row, beginning with its first pitch class (I_3): _____

  (f) ordered pc intervals of I: _____

  (g) inversion of the retrograde, beginning with its first pitch class (IR_3): _____

  (h) ordered pc intervals of IR: _____

Is the inversion of the retrograde (IR_3) the same as the retrograde inversion (RI_3) of the prime row? (Hint: List the pitch classes of line e in retrograde order and compare them with line g.)

(2) Write in P_3 at the beginning of the vocal melody in measure 2, then identify the row forms of the viola and clarinet lines. Some rows may be completed in a different line from the one in which they began. (Hint: How do the first two pitches of the flute line fit in?) When a row is completed, first check the next series of pitch classes to see if it matches one of these rows. If not, back up and check to see if rows are elided. Label as many complete rows P_3, I_3, IR_3, and R_3 in measures 2–14 as you can; not all of the rows are these three transformations, however, so there will be some pitch classes unlabeled when you finish.

(3) Using the ordered pc intervals for each row form listed above, identify the remaining row forms in measures 4–14.

B. Milton Babbitt, "Play on Notes"

This composition, written for a children's music textbook, was intended for performance by children's voices and bells. Consider the first two measures of the voice part to be the segment P_0. The remaining segments are also two measures each.

Part I

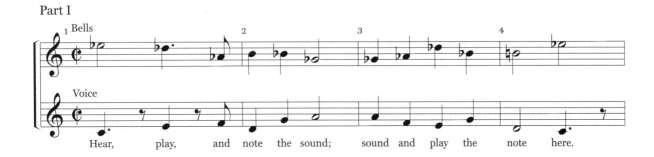

Hear, play, and note the sound; sound and play the note here.

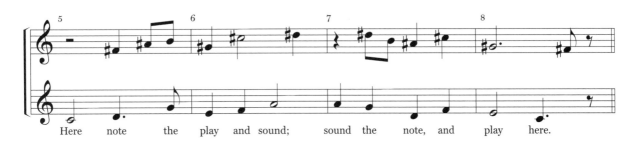

Here note the play and sound; sound the note, and play here.

Part II

Hear, play, and note the sound; sound and play the note here.

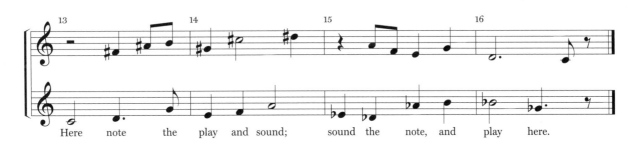

Here note the play and sound; sound the note, and play here.

(1) Complete the chart below, labeling each segment. The first two have been completed for you.

Part I	mm. 1–2	3–4	5–6	7–8
Bells:	R_6	_____	_____	_____
Voice:	P_0	_____	_____	_____

Part II	mm. 9–10	11–12	13–14	15–16
Bells:	_____	_____	_____	_____
Voice:	_____	_____	_____	_____

(2) What is the unordered pcset of each part in measures 1–2? List each as pcs, then consider to what scale type each part belongs.

Bells: { _____ }   Scale type: _____

Voice: { _____ }   Scale type: _____

(3) When the pcs of measures 1–2 (both parts) are combined, what type of collection results? Can this combination be found elsewhere in the piece?

(4) Babbitt divides the piece into two parts, as marked in the score. What musical features support this division? Consider phrase structure, rhythms, and patterns of repeated segments.

(5) Associate each word of the text with its particular pitch class from measure 1 ("Hear" = pc 0, "play" = pc 4, and so on). Now use these pitch classes to describe the structure of the song's lyrics.

Twelve-Tone Rows and the Row Matrix

CHAPTER 34

Basic Elements

I. Making a row matrix

Following the instructions given in the text chapter, make a row matrix for each of the twelve-tone rows below on the grids provided, using integers to represent the pitch classes. Begin by writing in the pitch classes below the staff for each pitch of the row, then transpose the row to begin with 0. Finally, write the integer representation of the series on the top row, and complete the rest of the matrix.

A. Anton Webern, "Wie bin ich froh!" ("How Happy I Am!"), Op. 25, mm. 2–4a

This row is P_7.

Wie bin ich froh!   noch ein - mal   wird mir   al – les grün

Translation: How happy I am! Once more everything around me grows green.

0											
	0										
		0									
			0								
				0							
					0						
						0					
							0				
								0			
									0		
										0	
											0

B. Webern, *Symphonie*, Op. 21, second movement, mm. 12–17

This cello part is P_t.

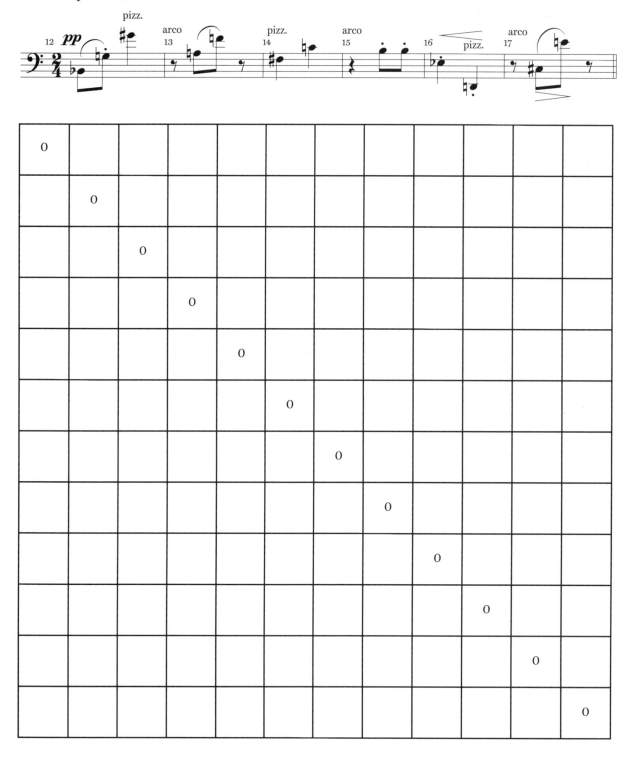

C. Webern, "Das dunkle Herz" ("The Dark Heart"), Op. 23, No. 1, mm. 2–6a

This vocal melody is P_5.

Das dunk - le Herz,   das   in   sich lauscht,   er - schaut den Früh - [ling]

For translation, see page 433.

O											
	O										
		O									
			O								
				O							
					O						
						O					
							O				
								O			
									O		
										O	
											O

II. *Finding combinatorial row pairs*

A. A row matrix for Arnold Schoenberg's Violin Concerto is given below. Circle hexachords on the matrix to answer the following questions.

(1) P_0 is combinatorial with which I row? _____

(2) R_9 is combinatorial with which RI row? _____

(3) P_7 is combinatorial with which R row? _____

0	1	6	2	7	9	3	4	t	e	5	8
e	0	5	1	6	8	2	3	9	t	4	7
6	7	0	8	1	3	9	t	4	5	e	2
t	e	4	0	5	7	1	2	8	9	3	6
5	6	e	7	0	2	8	9	3	4	t	1
3	4	9	5	t	0	6	7	1	2	8	e
9	t	3	e	4	6	0	1	7	8	2	5
8	9	2	t	3	5	e	0	6	7	1	4
2	3	8	4	9	e	5	6	0	1	7	t
1	2	7	3	8	t	4	5	e	0	6	9
7	8	1	9	2	4	t	e	5	6	0	3
4	5	t	6	e	1	7	8	2	3	9	0

B. Refer to the matrix you constructed for Webern's *Symphonie*, Op. 21 (in exercise I/B), to answer the following questions.

(1) P_0 is combinatorial with which I row? _____

(2) P_0 is combinatorial with which P row? _____

(3) P_0 is combinatorial with which R row? _____

(4) P_0 is combinatorial with which RI row? _____

(5) What do the answers to the previous questions suggest about this type of row?

Writing Exercises

Serial composition

Write a short twelve-tone composition (at least sixteen measures) featuring one of the three Webern rows for which you constructed a matrix in "Basic Elements"/I. Score your piece for an instrument you play, or for a duo of instruments in your class. Remember that the row need not be a melody; you may stack up pitch classes from the row to form harmonies or distribute the row between instruments.

Think about musical factors as you compose your piece: draw on contrasts in texture, dynamics, tempo, articulation, timbral effects, phrase climax and closure, set classes as harmonic design factors, and so on, as appropriate to your musical ideas. You may want to choose a composition we studied in Chapters 31–34 as a model. Pick several different row forms, and mark all rows analytically in your score. Prepare your composition for performance in class.

Analysis

I. Brief analysis

A. Webern, *Symphonie*, Op. 21, second movement, mm. 1–11 (theme, winds and harp)

(1) Begin by listening to a recording of the opening measures of this movement. Then label the row forms. The clarinet melody has one row, the accompaniment has another. The row matrix for this piece was one you constructed in "Basic Elements"/I, exercise B. Because of special properties of this row, some of the retrograde forms are identical to the P and I forms. When labeling in this excerpt, write P and I forms instead of R or RI. Write in the name of the row just before the first pitch of the row in the score, then label row members with order numbers (1 to 12).

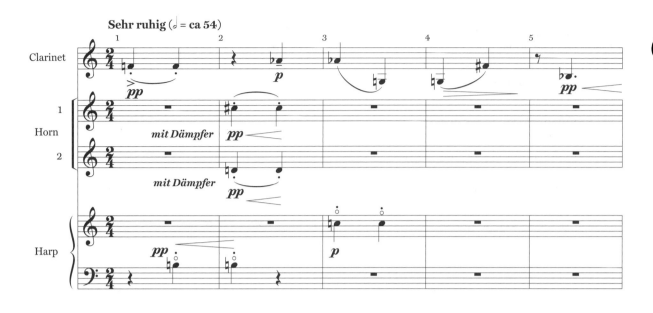

(2) When you have labeled the rows, take a close look at the ways the pcs are realized. What technique discussed in the text chapter motivates the choice of registers? Consider the pitches in measures 5–7: what is the pattern of these pitches between the melody and accompaniment? (Hint: Check the order.) Listen to the recording again to see if you can hear this relationship.

(3) Look at the two hexachords of this row. How are the hexachords related? How does this relationship facilitate the technique you identified in question #2?

B. Webern, *Symphonie*, Op. 21, second movement, mm. 11–23 (Variation I, string parts)

Begin by listening to a recording of these measures. Then label the row forms in the string parts. Each string part has its own row form. (The matrix for this piece is given in "Basic Elements"/I, exercise B.) Write in the name of the row form just before the first pitch of the row in the score, then label row members with order numbers (1 to 12).

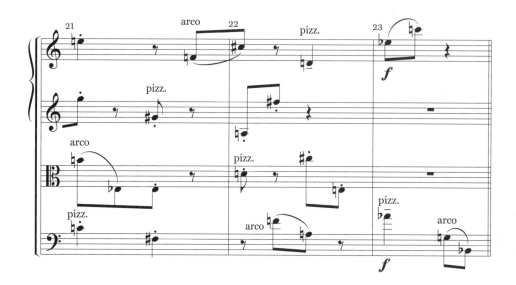

(1) What happens when a part gets to the end of its row?

(2) Look closely at the pitch intervals, rhythms, and articulation in each string part. These rows are written in pairs, making a double canon. Which rows pair with which other rows? Are the canons exact?

(3) Listen carefully to this excerpt again. Can you hear the "turning points" in each line? Listen for the first violin's high pitches and repeated F♯4 to get your bearings, then listen for each line to hear the "turns." How does Webern's realization of the row forms make the turns audible?

C. Webern, *Symphonie*, Op. 21, second movement, mm. 89–99 (coda, harp and strings)

Begin by listening to a recording of the end of this movement. Then label the row forms. (The matrix for this piece is given in "Basic Elements"/I, exercise B.) Write in the name of the row form just before the first pitch of the row in the score, then label row members with order numbers (1 to 12).

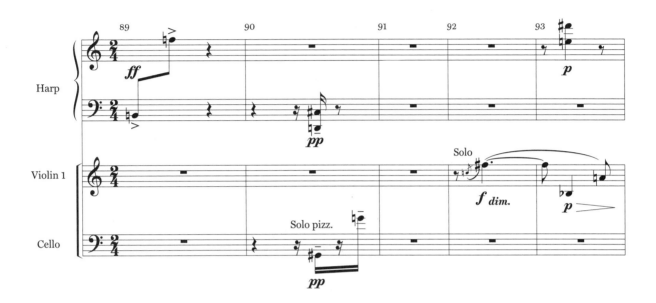

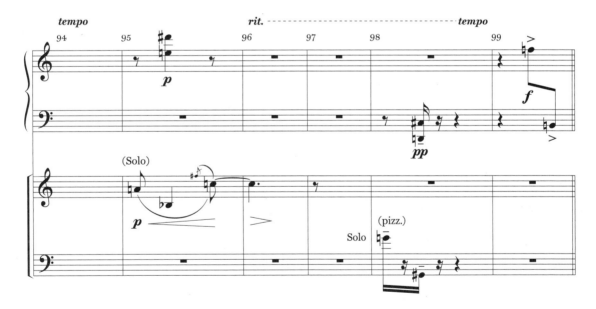

(1) Compare these measures with the opening of this movement (exercise A in this section, p. 426). How are they similar? How do they differ?

(2) Which part(s) here take(s) the role of the opening clarinet melody? Which take(s) the role of the accompaniment?

(3) Do you find registral invariance? Is there a mirroring here, as in the previous sections we have analyzed from this movement?

(4) Write a paragraph that summarizes the links you have identified between measures 1–11 and this coda.

II. Extended analysis

A. Schoenberg, *Klavierstück*, Op. 33a (p. 189)   **3.12** 🎧

Listen to the entire work while following the score in your anthology. Mark the "sonata form" formal divisions in your score, as discussed in Chapter 34 of the text.

(1) On your own paper, write a paragraph that supports or refutes the idea that this movement is in sonata form. Cite specific measure numbers, row forms, and such other musical features as texture, harmonic rhythm, tempo, and articulation.

(2) Circle the appropriate hexachords in the row matrix below to find the combinatorial row pairs specified.

P_t is combinatorial with what I form? _____

P_5 is combinatorial with what I form? _____

P_0 is combinatorial with what I form? _____

0	7	2	1	e	8	3	5	9	t	4	6
5	0	7	6	4	1	8	t	2	3	9	e
t	5	0	e	9	6	1	3	7	8	2	4
e	6	1	0	t	7	2	4	8	9	3	5
1	8	3	2	0	9	4	6	t	e	5	7
4	e	6	5	3	0	7	9	1	2	8	t
9	4	e	t	8	5	0	2	6	7	1	3
7	2	9	8	6	3	t	0	4	5	e	1
3	t	5	4	2	e	6	8	0	1	7	9
2	9	4	3	1	t	5	7	e	0	6	8
8	3	t	9	7	4	e	1	5	6	0	2
6	1	8	7	5	2	9	e	3	4	t	0

(3) Discuss combinatoriality at the end of the "development" section, measures 28b–32a. Identify the row forms used. (Hint: Refer back to question #2.)

B. Webern, "Das dunkle Herz," Op. 23, No 1, mm. 1–11

Find a recording of this piece in your library. Listen to it twice—once without the score, and once while looking at the score below. You completed the matrix for this piece in "Basic Elements"/I, exercise C.

Translation: The dark heart, which listens to itself, recognizes spring not only by the breeze and scent that bloom through its glow; it feels spring in the dark realm of roots that reach down to the dead.

(1) Label the row forms on the score, beginning with the vocal line. Write in the row's name (e.g., P$_6$ or RI$_4$) at the beginning of its pitches, then label row members with order numbers (1 to 12). Analyzing the keyboard part, which has chords, may take some detective work to deduce which row forms are used. As you identify the row forms and trace them through, write in the order numbers to show the correspondence of the row ordering to the chord pitches. There are several row elisions.

(2) Now consider the harmonic dimension. Are particular intervals or harmonies featured? Name them with set-class or pitch-class interval names.

(3) Is there text painting in this piece? Look at words like "dunkle Herz" (dark heart), "Frühling" (spring), and "Toten" (dead)—how are they set?

C. Webern, "Herr Jesus Mein" ("My Jesus"), Op. 23, No. 3, mm. 1–8

Find a recording of this song in your library. Listen to it twice—once without the score, and once while following the score below.

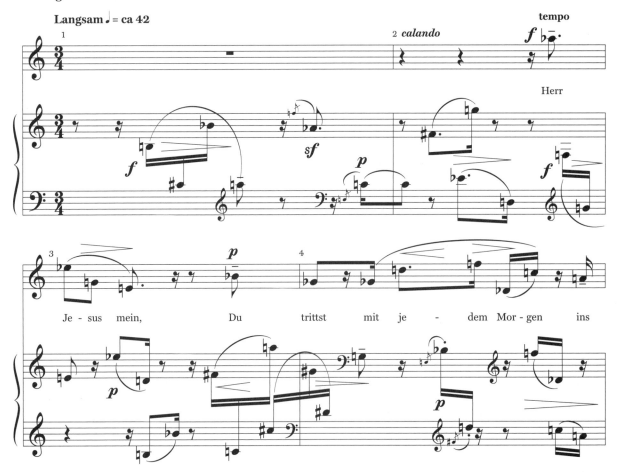

Translation: Lord Jesus mine, every morning you enter the house where hearts are beating and bestow on each sorrow your hand of mercy.

(1) This song uses the same row as "Das dunkle Herz." We built a row matrix for it in "Basic Elements" /I, exercise C. Label the row forms, beginning with the vocal line. Write in the row's name (e.g., P_6 or RI_4) at the beginning of its pitches, then label row members with order numbers (1 to 12).

Analyzing the keyboard part, which has chords, may take some detective work to deduce the row forms. As you identify the row forms and trace them through, write in the order numbers to show the correspondence of the row ordering to the chord pitches. There are several row elisions; other than these, and two pitch classes missing at the end of this excerpt (which are in the following measure of the piece), all of the rows are complete, with their pitch classes in row order.

(2) Now consider the harmonic dimension. Are particular intervals or harmonies featured? Name them with set-class or pitch-class interval names.

(3) Examine the relationship between the keyboard part and the vocal line. Are there places where the keyboard part helps the singer locate his or her pitches? If so, mark these places. What aspects of the row structure make possible pitch repetitions between the voice and accompaniment?

(4) Are there examples of text painting? The last vocal row ends at the fourth pitch class of the series; where does this row continue? What might be the relationship of that closing gesture to the text?

(5) If you analyzed both Webern songs ("Extended Analysis"/B and C), write a paragraph comparing the two. What characteristics distinguish these songs from each other, despite the fact that they share the same row? What characteristics, other than the row, do they share?

New Ways to Organize Rhythm, Meter, and Duration

CHAPTER 35

Basic Elements

I. Identifying changing meter, asymmetrical meter, ostinato, and polymeter

Identify the rhythmic or metric technique in each of the examples below. Write a few sentences to explain your choice. Be sure to answer the following questions:

- If the excerpt features polymeter, which type is it?

- If the excerpt features asymmetrical meter, how is the measure divided into beat units?

- If the excerpt features ostinato, mark the content and length of the pattern on your score.

A. Béla Bartók, *Bagatelle*, Op. 6, No. 2, mm. 16–18 (p. 21)   **1.26**

Listen to this work while following the score in your anthology.

Technique: _____

Discussion:

B. Igor Stravinsky, "Triumphant March of the Devil," from *L'histoire du soldat*, mm. 7–15

Technique: _____

Discussion:

C. Stravinsky, *The Rite of Spring*, rehearsal number 31 (mm. 216–223) (two-piano score)

Technique: _____

Discussion:

D. Modest Mussorgsky, "Promenade," from *Pictures at an Exhibition*, mm. 1–8

Allegro giusto, nel modo russico; senza allegrezza, ma poco sostenuto.

Technique: _____

Discussion:

II. Metric modulation, additive rhythm, and time-line notation

Identify the rhythmic or metric technique in each of the examples below. Write a few sentences to explain your choice. Be sure to answer the following questions:

- If the excerpt features metric modulation, how is the tempo change made?
- If the excerpt features additive rhythm, what is the basic additive unit?
- If the excerpt features time-line notation, what is the length of time in each unit of measurement?
- What other techniques that we have studied can you find in each example?

A. Pierre Boulez, *Structures Ia*, mm. 73–81 (piano 2, left hand)

Hint: Start by identifying the duration of each pitch combined with the rest that follows.

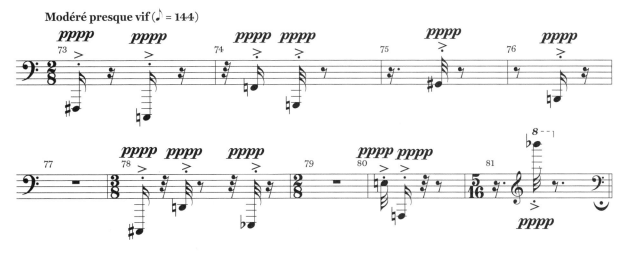

Technique: _____

Discussion:

B. Elliott Carter, String Quartet No. 2, first movement, mm. 54–60

Technique: _____

Discussion:

C. Krzysztof Penderecki, *Threnody for the Victims of Hiroshima*, rehearsal numbers 64–66

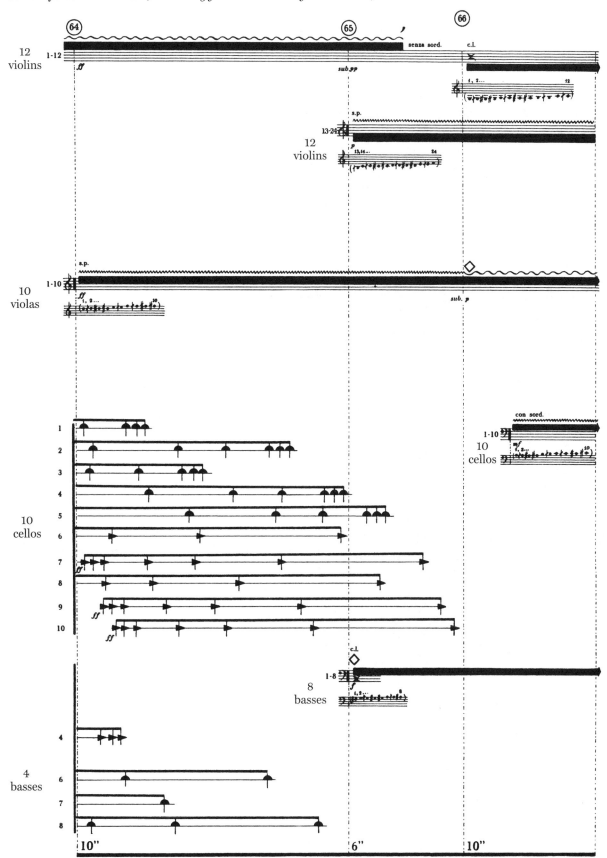

Technique: _____

Discussion:

D. Carter, "Canaries," from *Eight Pieces for Four Timpani*, mm. 1–16

Technique: _____

Discussion:

E. John Tavener, "The Lamb," mm. 1–2 (p. 233)   **3.49** 🎧

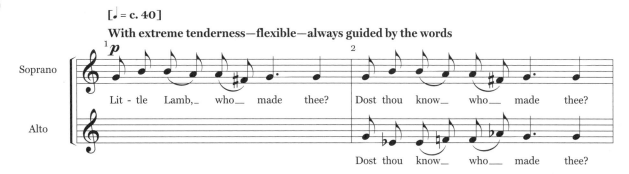

Technique: _____

Discussion:

Writing Exercises

I. Short rhythmic exercises

On your own paper, write a short rhythmic composition in one part for each exercise below. Before beginning the exercise, carefully study the relevant examples in the chapter. You need write only the meter signature(s), measure lines, and durations (no pitches). If you'd like, add dynamic and tempo markings. Be prepared to perform your rhythmic patterns in class and explain how each fits the specified criteria.

A. Ametric

Write a four-measure rhythmic composition that is notated with a meter signature but sounds ametric. Above your example, mark where all the beats fall, and circle rhythmic patterns that work against the perception of those beats.

B. Changing meter

Write an eight-measure rhythmic composition that features changing meter. Each measure should include rhythmic patterns characteristic of that measure's notated meter.

C. Perceived meter vs. notated meter

Write a rhythmic pattern that is notated in one meter but sounds like it is in another meter. When you perform this rhythm in class, ask your classmates to conduct along, first in the meter that they hear, then in the notated meter.

II. Two-part rhythmic exercises

On your own paper, write the following rhythmic compositions in two parts. Before beginning each exercise, carefully study the relevant examples in the chapter. You need write only the meter signature(s), measure lines, and durations (no pitches). Write one part aligned above the other, using stems up to designate one part and stems down for the other. If you'd like, add dynamic and tempo markings. Choose a partner and perform one or more of your duets in class. Afterward, ask your classmates to name the combination you were performing.

A. Polymeter with one part in $\frac{3}{4}$ and the other in $\frac{2}{4}$. Each part should have rhythmic patterns that strongly imply its notated meter, while combining well with the other part.

B. Ostinato in one part, changing meter in the other. You may notate both parts in the same meter or notate each in its own metrical framework.

C. Polymeter with one part in $\frac{3}{4}$ and the other in $\frac{9}{8}$. Each part should have rhythmic patterns that strongly imply its notated meter, while combining well with the other part.

D. To your ametric rhythmic composition from exercise I/A, add a second part that emphasizes the beats of the notated meter. Does your example sound syncopated? Or polymetric?

E. To the rhythmic pattern you wrote for exercise I/C, add a second part that implies the notated meter. Does your example sound syncopated? Or polymetric?

III. Writing phrases

On your own staff paper, compose a four-measure melodic phrase for each of the pitch and rhythmic descriptions that follow.

A. Use subsets of one of the octatonic collections and changing meter.

B. Use the whole-tone collection and additive rhythms.

C. Use a twelve-tone row, short durations, and lots of rests, in $\frac{3}{2}$; create a rhythm that strongly implies the $\frac{3}{2}$ meter.

IV. Writing two-part counterpoint

Draw on our study of Bartók's "Song of the Harvest" and *Mikrokosmos* pieces to write short phrases (four to eight measures) in two parts (for two monophonic instruments or two melodies played together on the piano) for each exercise below. Each part should make a good melodic line on its own, while combining well with the other part.

A. Use imitation, an octatonic collection divided between the hands, and an asymmetrical meter.

B. Use the chromatic collection, exact mirror inversion between the parts, and changing meter.

C. Use the F Lydian mode and an ostinato.

Analysis

I. Brief analysis

A. Stravinsky, "Four Duos," from *Agon*, mm. 1–7a

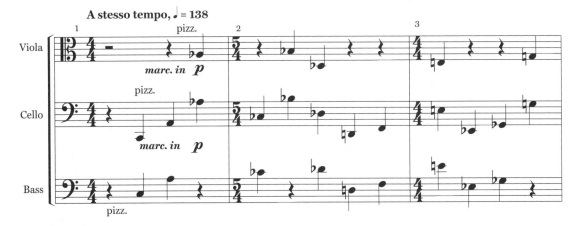

(1) Which rhythmic and metrical practices that we have studied in this chapter are illustrated in this example? Why is it notated as it is?

(2) How are the pitches organized? To consider this question, examine the relationship between the three parts, and write the pcs in the order that they sound below.

(3) What is the relationship of the pitches in measures 1–3 to those of 4–7a?

B. Luciano Berio, *Sequenza I*, for solo flute, first two staves

Try to perform the excerpt below at the keyboard or on your own instrument, then answer the questions that follow.

(1) The tempo is indicated as quarter note = 70. At that rate, about how long does this passage last? How did you compute the duration?

(2) Is there a strong sense of beat or meter in this passage? Explain.

(3) Are there any repeated rhythmic patterns in this passage? What effect does the lack of repetition of patterns have on the sound of the passage?

II. Extended analysis

A. Bartók, "Song of the Harvest" (p. 25)   1.37 🎧

We considered the pitch content and overall form of this piece in Chapter 30 of the text. Listen to it again, while following your anthology score, then answer the following questions.

(1) Where are there examples of changing meter? Explain. Will the notated changing meters be audible to the listener? Why or why not?

(2) Where are there examples of polymeter? What type(s) of polymeter are used? Are these audible to the listener? Why or why not?

(3) Each of the sections in this duet constitutes a phrase. In earlier chapters, a phrase was defined as a unit of music ending with a cadence. This piece does not have functional tonality; how, then, are the cadences made? Write a sentence or two explaining how rhythmic and metrical aspects contribute to the perception of cadences.

(4) Do you think the rhythmic structure (polymeter and changing meter) will create ensemble problems between the two players? What rehearsal strategies might help you stay together?

B. George Crumb, "Los muertos llevan alas de musgo," from *Madrigals*, Book I, mm. 1–7

Find a recording of this work in your library, or listen to it as a class.

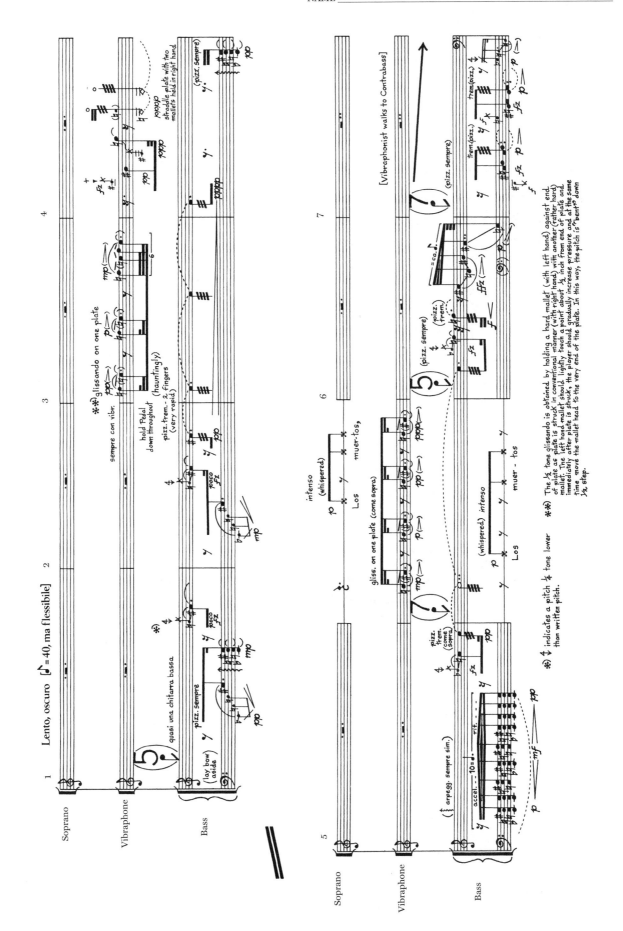

(1) Where are there examples of changing meter? Will the notated changing meters be audible to the listener? Why or why not?

(2) Based on the tempo, notated rhythms, and performance instructions, will any sort of regular beat be perceptible in a performance following those instructions? If so, where, and what element creates the sense of a pulse? Explain.

(3) What types of pitch intervals are featured in the bass part? in the vibraphone part? Where are pitches, intervals, or chords repeated?

(4) Look back at the notation of pitch, durations, articulations, and timbres in these measures. List as many elements as possible that indicate that this score was composed after 1945, and be prepared to discuss your findings in class. How do these elements contribute to the overall aural effect of the piece?

C. Cathy Berberian, *Stripsody*, pages 10–11

Examine the score below. Page 10 includes two scenes (we could informally call them "sounds" and "baby"). Page 11 includes one continuous scene that begins with barnyard sounds and ends with a baby crying. After studying the score, answer the questions that follow.

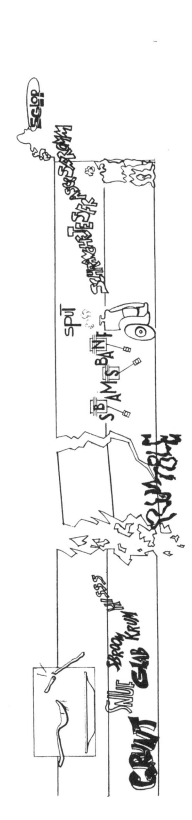

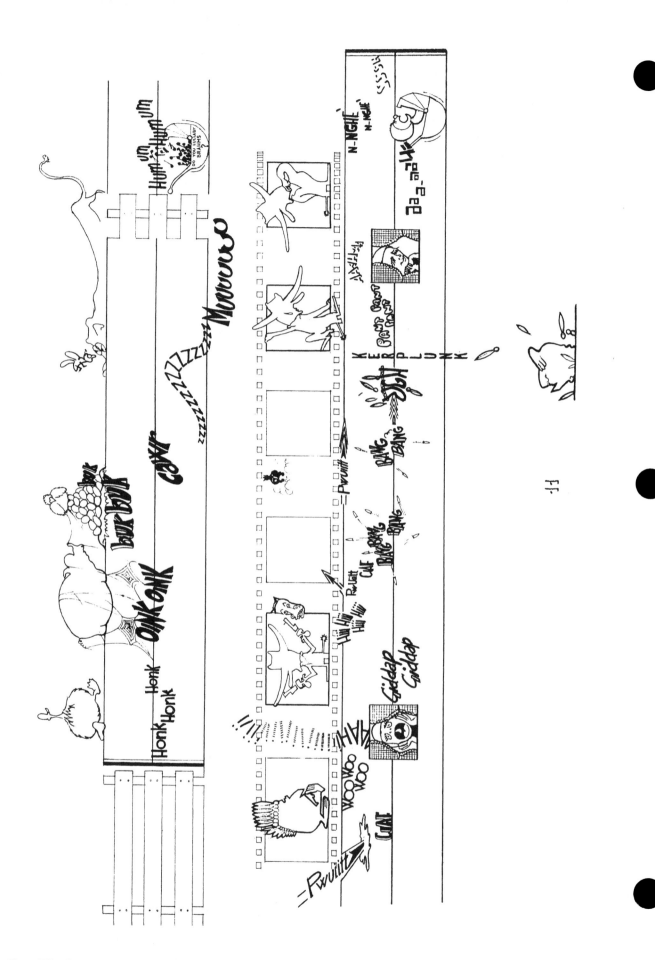

(1) Describe the rhythmic character of these pages. Is there a beat or meter? If so, where? How does the performer know when to make the sounds illustrated?

(2) Where is the most rhythmically active portion of this passage? Where is the least rhythmically active portion?

(3) Examine the sound content of each scene. How will the listener distinguish one scene from another?

Extra challenge: Try to perform this piece—it is much harder than it looks! Then write a "scene" of your own to perform in class.

CHAPTER 36

New Ways to Articulate Musical Form

Basic Elements

I. Defining "music"

On your own paper, write a short essay that answers the question: What is music? Make sure your definition includes any sounds or activities that you associate with music and excludes those that are not music. Refer to the pieces *In the Woods* in this chapter and Cage's *4'33"* from Chapter 35 in your discussion. Are they or are they not music according to your definition? Defend your answer. Mention at least one other composition in your answer. Be prepared to discuss your essay in class.

II. Defining form without tonality

Write an essay that answers the questions: Can composers write in traditional forms in the absence of tonality? How (or how not)? Argue pro or con, mentioning specific examples from pieces we have studied in the last few chapters. Take one of the following compositions as the focus of your discussion, or choose another: Schoenberg, *Klavierstück*, Op. 33a, as a sonata; Webern, Op. 5, No. 4, as ternary; or Webern, Variations for Piano, second movement, as binary.

Analysis

I. Brief analysis

A. Béla Bartók, *Mikrokosmos*, No. 141 ("Subject and Reflection"), mm. 1–6

Begin by playing through this excerpt at a keyboard. Make a pitch-time graph on the grid provided on page 458. Divide the pitch axis into semitones and label the Cs; divide the time axis into eighth notes.

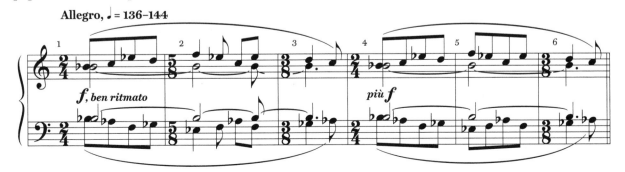

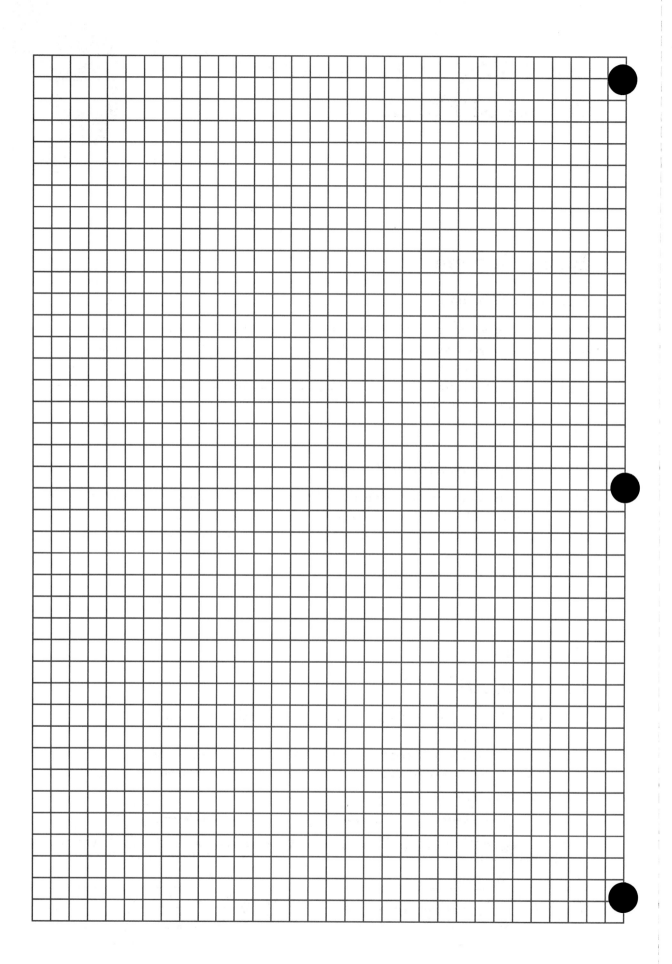

(1) What is the center of the pitch symmetry? Does that pitch seem to be an important one in this segment?

(2) What pitch class is most emphasized in this passage? How is it emphasized?

(3) Write out the pitch classes in each hand part. What is the relationship between these pcsets? To what set class(es) do they belong?

(4) Which of the metrical or rhythmic procedures that we studied in Chapter 35 are demonstrated in this example? Explain.

B. Anton Webern, "Dies ist ein Lied," Op. 3, No. 1, mm. 1–5a (p. 240)   **3.53** 🎧
Listen to this song while following the score in your anthology.

(1) Play through the vocal line of measures 1–5a several times. Try playing the vocal line along with the upper line of the accompaniment. What type of counterpoint is used between the vocal line in measures 1–2 and the upper line of the piano part in measures 1–3? Comment on the exact or inexact nature of this counterpoint, as well as the rhythmic relationship between the two voices.

(2) How are the vocal subphrases in measures 3 and 4 related? What traditional tonal language might we use to describe this relationship? Is there any motivic relationship between these vocal statements and the melody line of the accompaniment?

C. Alan Hovhaness, "Sicut locutus est," from *Magnificat*, mm. 44–45

Perform this passage with your class.

Translation: As he promised to our forefathers.

On your own paper, write a paragraph that addresses the following questions. How is sectional form created in this example? Which musical elements take the lead in shaping the passage?

II. Extended analysis

A. Bartok, *Bagatelle*, Op. 6, No. 2 (p. 21)   **1.26**

(1) Using the score in your anthology and your own graph paper, make a pitch/time graph for measures 17–30 of this piece, like that of Example 36.1b in the text. What additional observations can you make about range and register in this piece, based on your graph?

(2) Consider the cadence at the end of the work. It sounds definitive—why? What elements come into play?

(3) What do you think motivates the changing meter in the middle section? How could this section have been notated differently?

B. LaMonte Young, *Composition 1960, No. 2*

Read the score given below, then write an essay discussing the form of this piece. Like many text pieces, this one may vary in the details from performance to performance, but it will have consistent elements, too, if the score is followed precisely. In your essay, consider which elements are variable and which will be the same in every performance.

> *Build a fire in front of the audience. Preferably, use wood, although other combustibles may be used as necessary for starting the fire or controlling the smoke. The fire may be of any size, but it should not be the kind which is associated with another object, such as a candle or a cigarette lighter. The lights may be turned out.*
>
> *After the fire is burning, the builder(s) may sit by and watch it for the duration of the composition; however, he (they) should not sit between the fire and the audience in order that its members will be able to see and enjoy the fire.*
>
> *The composition may be of any duration.*
>
> *In the event that the performance is broadcast, the microphone may be brought up close to the fire.*

C. Igor Stravinsky, "Bransle Gay," from *Agon* (p. 230)   **3.46** 🎧

Listen through this piece while following the score in your anthology. In Chapter 35, we considered some of the piece's rhythmic elements, including polymeter, changing meter, and asymmetrical meters; now we focus on its form.

(1) For each segment below, identify the pitch classes, and write them in ascending order with pc integers.

(a) Measures 2–5: _____

(b) Measures 7–10: _____

(c) Measures 12–20 (watch out for the clarinet in B♭): _____

(d) Measures 21–22: _____

(e) Measures 23–25: _____

(2) Now consider the rhythmic and metrical aspects of each segment. What are the rhythmic patterns associated with each? Which segments feature changing meter?

(3) What musical aspects partition these particular measures off from the other parts of the piece?

(4) What is the formal design of this movement? Which aspects of the music contribute to the perception of form?

D. Steve Reich, *Piano Phase* (p. 187)   **3.11** 🎧

(1) Analytical graphing

Listen to this work while following the score in your anthology.
 In the alignment graphs below, the squares along the horizontal axis represent sixteenth-note durations; the squares up the vertical axis represent semitones. The pattern played by piano 1 is marked with Xs. Begin your study of the piece by graphing the pattern shifts played by piano 2, using Os. For alignment 1, piano 2 is tacet (silent); for alignment 2, it is playing in unison with piano 1. In each of the other alignments, piano 2's part shifts forward one sixteenth note (represented here by one square). In alignments 3 and 4 (completed for you), piano 2's part is shown with an O. (When pianos 1 and 2 play the same note simultaneously, circle the X within the O.)
 Complete the graphs for each alignment, then listen carefully to the piece. When you hear the parts "click" into each alignment, circle (on the graphs) the rhythmic patterns that emerge—sometimes the lower pitches stand out, sometimes the upper ones. When you hear the piano parts beginning to shift, listen for the next alignment. When you have finished circling the emerging rhythmic patterns, below each graph write out in rhythmic notation (with the sixteenth note as the basic unit) the rhythmic pattern you heard.

Alignments 1, 2, and 14

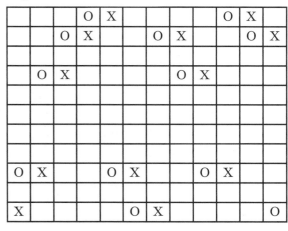

Alignment 3

Alignment 4

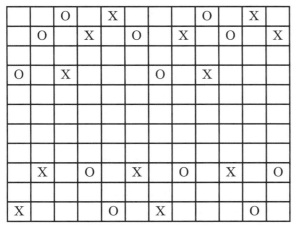

Alignment 5

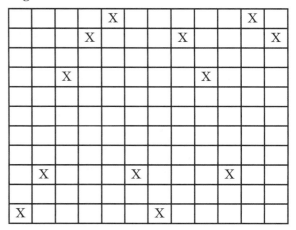

Alignment 6

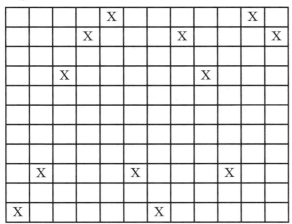

Alignment 7

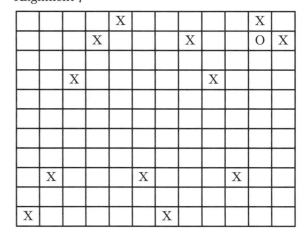

Alignment 8

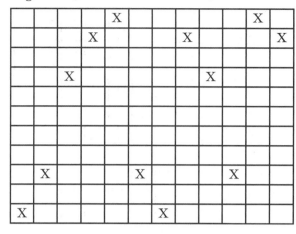

Alignment 9

Alignment 10

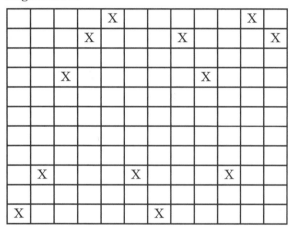

Alignment 11

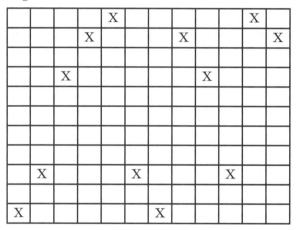

Alignment 12

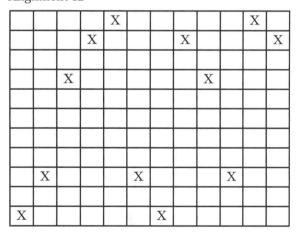

Alignment 13

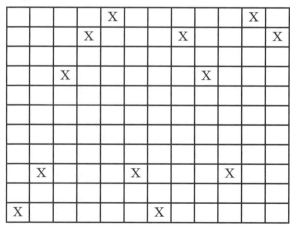

(2) What scale is implied by the pitch content of this section of *Piano Phase*? Does it sound major or minor? Which melodic and harmonic intervals are formed as the patterns realign?

(3) The close to this section sounds like a cadence, but there are no traditional cadential elements—harmonic or intervallic resolution, longer note values, falling melodic shape, and so on. How is the close created?

E. Webern, "Dies ist ein Lied," Op. 3, No. 1 (p. 240)   **3.53**

Listen to the entire song while following the score in your anthology and thinking about its large-scale form; then answer the following questions.

(1) This song falls into a ternary (**A B A′**) form. Where are the divisions? To what extent does the poetic text generate the musical form?

(2) Discuss the musical features that link the **A** and **A**′ sections. What elements are contrasting in the **B** section? What other musical cues separate one section from the next?

(3) We identified a type of counterpoint in this song in "Brief Analysis"/B. Find other instances of this type of writing elsewhere in the song.

The Composer's
Materials Today

CHAPTER 37

Writing Exercises

Exploring contemporary counterpoint

A. Write a modal melody on your own staff paper. Keep it simple, with no more than three different durations and a range an octave or less. Now set your melody against itself to make counterpoint, like that of Steve Reich's "Proverb" (Example 37.1 in the text). Begin by trying several temporal alignments, then select the one you like best. Label the intervals between the voices. Prepare a performance with a friend for class.

B. Carefully inspect the first four measures to Arvo Pärt's *Magnificat* in "Extended analysis"/A. Using the D-Dorian scale, set the text "Gloria in excelsis Deo, et in terra pax hominibus bonae voluntatis" (Glory to God in the highest, and on earth peace to men of good will) or a brief text of your choosing (mottos work well) syllabically (one pitch to each syllable) after the style of Pärt. Choose longer rhythmic values for important words of the text. Then write a counterpoint above the melody with the closest chord members of the D-minor triad. Perform your composition in class.

C. Many of the melodic motives from Reich's *City Life* were drawn from spoken phrases. With a tape, CD, or MP3 recorder or sequencer, record several brief snips of spoken language that you think have musical characteristics. Then make melodic motives that mimic your recorded samples. Copy both the contour or pitch content and the rhythm of speech. Combine the motives you have composed and, if desired, the recorded snips to make a short passage of counterpoint. You may incorporate transposition, imitation, inversion, canon, other traditional contrapuntal techniques, or phasing (as in *Piano Phase*, from Chapter 36). Arrange for a performance of your work in class.

Analysis

I. Brief analysis

A. John Corigliano, "Come now, my darling," from *The Ghosts of Versailles*, mm. 1–61 (p. 81)   **1.82**

Listen to this passage while following the score in your anthology.

(1) On your own paper, list as many characteristics of the music as you can that are Mozart-like. For each characteristic, cite the measure number and explain your reasoning.

(2) Now list as many characteristics of the music as you can that indicate that the music was not composed in the eighteenth century. As before, cite measure numbers and explain your reasoning.

B. György Ligeti, "Désordre," from *Piano Etudes*, Book I, mm. 1–8

Examine Example 37.5 in the chapter more closely, then answer the following questions.

(1) Collections: Which collection appears in the right-hand part? Write the pcs here:

Which collection appears in the left-hand part? Write the pcs here:

When combined, the two hand parts make which collection?

(2) Composite rhythm: In the grid below, consider the top row as the right-hand part and the bottom row as the left-hand part; one box equals an eighth note. Shade in the box for each accented eighth note, to show the placement of the accents in the composite rhythm. The first measure has been completed for you.

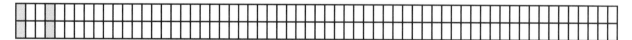

What does the grid illustrate about the rhythmic character of this excerpt?

II. Extended analysis

A. Pärt, *Magnificat*, first four phrases

Perform this passage with your class (use a keyboard to accompany, if necessary).

Translation: My soul magnifies the Lord, and my spirit rejoices in God my Savior. For he has regarded the lowliness of his servant. Behold, from henceforth all generations shall call me blessed.

(1) List the pitches (e.g., C5) in each vocal part below, and consider which voice carries the primary melody and which are accompaniment in each phrase. Circle the primary melodic line.

Phrase 1:   Soprano 1 _____   Soprano 2 _____

Phrase 2:   Tenors _____   Basses _____

Phrase 3:   Soprano solo _____   Tenors _____

Phrase 4:   Sopranos 1 and 2 _____   Tenors _____

              Basses _____

(2) How does Pärt use register to distinguish between phrases and delineate form?

(3) What aspects of the excerpt evoke the musical traditions of church music?

B. Toru Takemitsu, "Rain Tree Sketch," mm. 1–13

(1) Begin by labeling the pitch intervals and exact pitches in the opening measure. Then compare measures 1 and 3, and 2 and 4. Which motives and intervals reappear? How are they changed?

(2) Which measure(s) do 8 and 10 resemble? What is similar in all these measures? What has changed in 8 and 10?

(3) Measure 13 seems to be the close of a section. What elements in 12–13 indicate a close here?

C. Corigliano, "Come now, my darling," from *The Ghosts of Versailles*, mm. 1–61 (p. 81)   **1.82** 🎧

Listen to this passage while following the score. Write in a harmonic analysis of the entire passage in your anthology, and examine the melodic lines. Then answer the following questions.

(1) Which key areas are implied in measures 1–38? (Give measure numbers.) How do they relate to the emotional state of each character and the story line of a gradual seduction?

(2) Now consider measures 38–61. When Rosina joins Cherubino in measure 51, how are their melodic lines related? How does his line change from the previous presentation in measures 38–50? What does this change indicate about their relationship at this point.

Index of Music Examples